BLACKETT

BLACKETT

Physics, War, and Politics in the Twentieth Century

Mary Jo Nye

HARVARD UNIVERSITY PRESS

Cambridge, Massachusetts

London, England

2004

Library of Congress Cataloging-in-Publication Data

Nye, Mary Jo.
  Blackett : physics, war, and politics in the twentieth century / Mary Jo Nye.
    p.   cm.
  Includes bibliographical references and index.
  ISBN 0-674-01548-7 (hardcover : alk. paper)
  1. Blackett, P. M. S. (Patrick Maynard Stuart), Baron Blackett,
1897–1974—Contributions in nuclear physics.   2. Blackett, P.M.S. (Patrick
Maynard Stuart), Baron Blackett, 1897–1974—Political and social views.
3. Nuclear physicists—Great Britain—Biography.   4. World War, 1939–1945—
Science.   I. Title.

QC16.B59N94   2004
539.7′092—dc22
[B]   2004047369

To Bob

CONTENTS

ILLUSTRATIONS

Following page 64

New cadets waiting for the ferry to the Royal Naval College, September 1910

Blackett with Costanza (Pat) Bayon around the time of their marriage, 1924

The ejection of protons from nitrogen nuclei by fast alpha-particles

Blackett on holiday, 1929

Blackett, 1932

Pencil drawing of Giuseppe Occhialini and Blackett as polar explorers

Schematic design of astatic magnetometer

Blackett's magnetometer at Jodrell Bank

Giovanna Blackett, Blackett, and Costanza Blackett, November 1948

Blackett and Homi Bhabha, British Association Meeting, Dublin, 1957

Her Majesty Queen Elizabeth II and Blackett at the official opening of the Royal Society's new residence at Carlton House Terrace, 1968

Blackett, 1963

ACKNOWLEDGMENTS

For permission to consult the correspondence and papers of Patrick Maynard Stuart Blackett at the Royal Society, I thank his daughter, Giovanna Blackett Bloor, and his son, Nicolas Maynard Blackett, who passed away in April 2002. Giovanna Bloor has been generous and kind in corresponding with me and in welcoming me for a visit with her and her cousin John Milner in London in September 2003. I am grateful to her for these conversations and for arranging access to papers held privately by the family with permission to quote from them. Her insights and her suggestions about her father have been invaluable.

For their cordial help on my several visits to the Royal Society, I thank especially Sandra Cumming and Mary Sampson. I also appreciate assistance at the American Institute of Physics (especially Caroline Moseley), the Regenstein Library of the University of Chicago (for the Michael Polanyi Papers), and the Churchill College Archives (for the Edward Crisp Bullard Papers and the Lise Meitner Papers). Many thanks to Tore Frängsmyr, Karl Grandin, Anne Wiktorsson, and Maria Asp for their help and hospitality at the Nobel Archive of the Royal Swedish Academy of Sciences, Stockholm.

I am grateful to Churchill College, where I was a By-Fellow during the Easter term of 1995 and a visitor during the summers of 1996 and 1998, the National Science Foundation (grant no. SBR-9321305), the Dibner Institute for the History of Science and Technology (for a Senior Fellowship during 2000–2001), and the Thomas Hart and Mary Jones Horning Endowment at Oregon State University for enabling me to do research for this study. I thank C. W. F. (Francis) Everitt for impressions of Blackett at Imperial College during the late 1950s, for solid advice and comments on technical matters, and for reading and criticizing the entire original manuscript of this book. Both Francis Everitt and Robert A. Nye insisted that I think analytically about masculinity in studying Blackett's character.

I am grateful to S. S. Schweber for helping with particle physics and "charisma"; Jonathan Rosenhead for comments on operational research; Henry Frankel for permission to cite his unpublished book manuscript; and especially Edward (Ted) Irving for invaluable assistance on geophysics and continental drift, and for his observations on Blackett. Elisabeth Crawford gave good advice and critical insights on the system of the Nobel awards; an inspiration as a scholar and a friend, she passed away just as this book was coming to publication.

I also appreciate comments on different parts of this study by Robert Anderson, Barton Bernstein, G. Brent Dalrymple, Ronald E. Doel, Peter Galison, C. Stewart Gillmor, Peter Hore, David Kaiser, David M. Knight, Rachel Laudan, Naomi Oreskes, anonymous readers, and the OSU Lunch Bunch, especially Paul Farber. I am grateful to Erwin N. Hiebert for photocopies of some materials in the Blackett Papers that he turned over to me from his personal library. Ann Downer-Hazell guided me to Michael Fisher at Harvard University Press, who has been a supportive and insightful editor, just as Richard Audet has been a skillful copy-editor. As always, Robert A. Nye has been my most valuable critic, my intrepid traveling companion, and my personal chef, while Lesley Nye and Dominic Barth have given cheerful support.

Photographs are reproduced courtesy of the Royal Society, the Blackett family, Jane Ramsey Burch, and the University of Dundee Archive Services. Chapter 3 is a revision, with substantially more discussion on operational research, of my article "A Physicist in the Corridors of Power: P. M. S. Blackett's Opposition to Atomic Weapons following the War," *Physics in Perspective,* 1 (1999), 136–156, reprinted in Peter Hore, ed., *P. M. S. Blackett: Sailor, Scientist, Socialist* (London: Frank Cass, 2003), pp. 269–293. Chapter 4 is largely identical to my article "Temptations of Theory, Strategies of Evidence: P. M. S. Blackett and the Earth's Magnetism, 1947–1952," *British Journal for the History of Science,* 32 (1999), 69–92.

Introduction: A Life of Controversy

Among British physicists of the twentieth century, Patrick Maynard Stuart Blackett was one of the most distinguished and best known. His life and career spanned almost three-quarters of the century, from 1897 to 1974. He was wide-ranging in talent and expertise. The geophysicist Edward Crisp Bullard admired Blackett as a man who had made his reputation in experimental nuclear physics, but who also provided crucial evidence for the geophysical theory of continental drift. Bullard judged Blackett "the most versatile and the best loved physicist of his generation."[1] Outside physics, Blackett was well known for his role in developing the scientific field of operational research. Although he had been a youthful naval officer in the First World War, he became a hero in the Second World War, credited with determining operational strategies for the antisubmarine campaign that turned the tide of the European war by late 1943.[2] When Blackett received the Nobel Prize in Physics in 1948, mention was made at the ceremonies in Stockholm of his war work as well as his physics.[3]

Not everyone, however, agreed with Bullard that Blackett was the best-loved physicist of his generation. Though Blackett was a great physicist and a member of the Cambridge physics elite of the 1920s and 1930s, he was a controversial figure. The controversies sometimes had to do with physics, but most prominently they had to do with politics. From the 1920s on, Blackett's political views were on the Left, "moderately red" to one observer.[4] Friends who visited Patrick Blackett and his wife Costanza were entertained with biscuits and lemonade and Sunday films depicting the wonders of the Soviet Union.[5] In 1934 Blackett gave a

1

BBC radio lecture that some people regarded as the "reddest" talk ever transmitted from the Broadcasting House.[6]

Blackett allied himself with the scientists for social responsibility movement known in Great Britain as "Bernalism," whose members argued that the cures to economic and political troubles lay in science and socialism.[7] Named for John Desmond Bernal, a Cambridge-educated physicist and pioneer in x-ray crystallography who was Marxist and communist in his political views, the Bernalists were sympathetic to the Soviet Union, even in the face of increasing numbers of reports in the 1930s of arrests and purges. Blackett parted company, however, with socialists who used pacifism as an argument against the need for preparation for war, and he was an early member of the group of British scientists who began planning in 1935 for radar defense in a war with Germany that they thought most probable. Some of the private stands that Blackett took during wartime against bombing strategies favored by Winston Churchill's science advisor Frederick Lindemann tarred Blackett in government circles with the label "defeatist," and his initially secret postwar opposition to British development of nuclear weapons brought him into disagreement in the late 1940s with the new Labour leader and Prime Minister, Clement Attlee.[8]

In 1948 Blackett's book *The Atomic and Military Consequences of Atomic Energy* launched a storm of protest and invective against him, which only became more heated when his revised version, *Fear, War, and the Bomb,* appeared in the United States in 1949. Furious critics, including Lindemann, disputed Blackett's analysis of Allied wartime civilian bombing strategy and Blackett's arguments against excluding the Soviet Union from postwar development of atomic energy. Newspapers and magazines carried story after story and review after review about this physicist Blackett and his anti-American, pro-Soviet views. "Who is Blackett?" was a front-page headline in the left-wing *Tribune des Nations,* where editors featured articles about Blackett and Blackett's essay "The Scientist as Citizen."[9] A New York City news periodical reported that the US War Department had bought up all copies of Blackett's book in Washington, D.C., bookstores in order to read and counter his arguments.[10]

President Harry S. Truman signed the citation for Blackett's Medal for Merit in the United States in October 1946, recognizing Blackett's pioneering role in the field of operational research that had played a decisive role in the past World War.[11] By the late 1940s, however, Blackett's name was a kindling point in arguments over American and British military and foreign policy. In 1949 he narrowly won approval in Parliament for membership on the National Research Development Corporation and found himself excluded from important government committees at Whitehall, despite his many responsibilities as a leader in physics research and university administration. He became a target for American Federal Bureau of Investigation intelligence, and although he did not know it, his name appeared on a list of thirty-eight journalists, writers, and actors whom George Orwell identified in May 1949 as "crypto-communists, fellow-travellers or inclined that way," according to the list Orwell gave his friend Celia Kirwan in the Information Research Department of the British Foreign Office. Identified by Orwell as a "scientific popularizer" in physics, Blackett, as Orwell put it, was one of those who should "not be trusted as propagandists."[12]

Blackett's increasing commitment in the 1940s and 1950s to the development of science and technology in India and the Third World also proved controversial. In 1957 he delivered the most criticized Presidential speech in the history of the British Association for the Advancement of Science (BAAS). His plea for setting up a special foreign-aid fund for former colonies in the Third World evoked anger or ridicule from many of his scientific colleagues. No one was more vitriolic than the anticommunist tabloid journalist Chapman Pincher—a *Daily Express* headline read "Chapman Pincher Tells What Happens When a Scientist Strays into Politics. I Say the Professor Should Have Stayed Home." Pincher deplored Blackett's having used his broadcast speech as President of the BAAS "to advance his Left-wing politics and denigrate the civilising influence of the Empire . . . so the world's most overtaxed families . . . should stump up to help Nasser's Egyptians, Nehru's Indians, and Sukarno's swarming Indonesians."[13]

By 1964 the British political climate had changed, and Blackett, who had been meeting with a scientific group advising the Labour Party's leadership, became scientific advisor in Harold Wilson's Ministry of Technology. Many of Blackett's radically outspoken views on military policy had become more widely accepted, in particular his questioning the efficiency and morality of the British wartime strategy of bombing German civilians. His postwar judgment was proving correct that nuclear weapons would fail to render conventional weapons unnecessary.

His scientific and political career would conclude with the members of the Royal Society extending to him its greatest responsibility as the official representative of the British scientific community in the office of President of the Royal Society from 1965 to 1970.

Blackett took political stands that threatened to undermine his reputation in experimental physics. It might be suggested that he had a naturally combative constitution. In his physics, however, he was more cautious and patient than in his politics, although by no means determined to avoid strife. One of the great controversies over the awarding of Nobel Prizes in Physics centered on Blackett's work, not in 1948, when he received the Prize, but in 1936 when he did not. The issue was that Carl Anderson alone received recognition in 1936 for discovery of the positron or positively charged electron, and British physicists continued to discuss the failure to recognize Blackett even after Blackett singly received the 1948 Prize.

Newspapers had announced in February 1933 that Blackett and Giuseppe Occhialini (who never received a Nobel award) had made a revolutionary discovery in yet another triumph at the Cavendish Laboratory. Newspapers gave the new subnuclear particle a specifically British name, the "googlie" electron, because, like a cricket ball, it "breaks the wrong way." It was a British particle. The physicist E. N. da C. Andrade called it "probably the most important completely new development in physics within the last twenty years."[14] From the beginning, however, Blackett emphasized that Anderson at Pasadena had previously found tracks that seemed to indicate the existence of a positive electron. Only in one interview did Blackett add that his and Occhialini's work had been in progress for some months before they published their results from the Cavendish Laboratory in early 1933.[15] A *New York Times* headline announced that Blackett credited Anderson and "Says American Should Not Be Robbed of Leads in Discovery."[16] Nor was Anderson robbed. What everyone acknowledged and admired in this matter was that Blackett behaved impeccably and did not himself engage in disputes about recognition for the positron.

Controversy surrounded some of Blackett's work on cosmic rays in the late 1930s, as he debated with Anderson and other physicists the identity of another peculiar particle found in cosmic radiation, which was tentatively called a meson. However, this debate was nothing out of the ordinary for the physics community. By the 1940s Blackett was becoming somewhat more assertive about matters of discovery and priority, encouraging his coworkers Clifford Butler and George Rochester to publish an announcement in 1947 of a new "strange particle" after photographing only two V-shaped tracks revealing the particle. Blackett showed up unexpectedly at the Birmingham meeting of the BAAS in August 1950, five minutes before the close of the physics session, with a stack of cosmic-ray photographs that he had just received from the observation hut on the Pic-du-Midi in the Pyrenees. It was a thrilling moment as Blackett announced the further confirmation of Butler and Rochester's earlier work, again in competition with Carl Anderson's group at Caltech.[17]

In the spring of 1947 Blackett staged a well-publicized announcement at the Royal Society of what he suggested might be a new fundamental law of physics unifying electromagnetic and gravitational theory. The announcement got international coverage in newspapers and newsmagazines. It was some years before the law was proven wrong, but Blackett recouped his losses by constructing a new instrument and establishing a program for studying magnetism in rocks, which helped establish empirical evidence for the controversial theory of continental drift. The Princeton physicist Freeman Dyson recalled his youthful disappointment when he went to hear Blackett lecture in London after the war, expecting to hear about new nuclear particles:

> I was disgusted to find he had lost interest and only talked about some dull stuff that he had done for the Navy, measuring the magnetisation of mud and rocks on the seabed. For some inscrutable reason he seemed to think the patterns of magnetisation on the seabed were scientifically exciting. I decided that too many years of working for the Navy had addled his brains. . . . Just seventeen years after his lecture, a systematic programme of measurements of magnetisation on both side of the mid-Atlantic ridge provided the crucial evidence that established the reality of continental drift and gave birth to the new science of plate tectonics.[18]

As a scientist Blackett made choices that again and again placed him in scientific debate or put him in the public eye. Yet he was a quiet man, not given to wasting time or words. No chitchat from him, according to family and friends.[19] If he was not garrulous, he was nonetheless fully in charge of what was going on under his supervision and ready to give direction and explain how to do things. Politics never came into his laboratory, where physics reigned supreme. In the laboratory he was a virtuoso, a much-admired master craftsman, who emphasized to junior researchers and students the do-it-yourself approach, optimizing experimental design, and getting the most from the data.[20] In Blackett's lectures he never used a single note as he delivered clear and authoritative accounts that dazzled his students.[21] Once, having attended a lecture delivered by a young man who had mumbled throughout, his head buried in a mass of notes, Blackett was overheard by Bernard Lovell, then a junior physicist, to say "no lecturer should require more notes than could be got on a postcard." Lovell wondered whether Blackett meant one side or two.[22]

What drove Blackett was a passionate belief in the power of science and scientists to learn about the world and to do good in the world. This conviction kept him very busy. His friend Solly Zuckerman, an expert on primates and a frequent scientific advisor to the government, described Blackett as a one-man army fighting for reason.[23] For Blackett, his belief required a socialist politics that campaigned for expanding scientific education, providing increased government support for fundamental and applied scientific research, targeting research areas for high priority, and creating more efficient links between scientific laboratories and industrial production. Achieving these aims required cultivating popular interest in science and taking on the role of public scientist, no matter how uncomfortable or inconvenient this role might become.

The role required some boosterism, no matter how one might like a little peace and quiet. When he moved from Cambridge to Birkbeck College, Blackett encouraged popular accounts of his big project for housing a giant magnet, built by Metropolitan-Vickers at great expense, in an abandoned part of the London underground. The *Morning Post* announced that the googlie electron was leaving Cambridge for London, and *The Evening News* touted the headline "They Have Their Other Side, These London Geniuses Who Lead the World," parading a lineup of photographs of the geneticist J. B. S. Haldane, the physiologist A. V. Hill, the astronomer James Jeans, the physicist E. V. Appleton, the zoologist Peter Chalmers Mitchell, and Blackett. "These men are brilliant . . . the peers of Einstein or anyone else—all British, all Londoners."[24]

Like all scientists, Blackett made choices every day about how he would spend his time and how he would live his life—what problems he would study, how he would organize his laboratory, who would be part of his research group, what administrative responsibilities he would take on, how many committees he would serve, what radio broadcasts he would make, what popular articles he would write, not to mention what he would do with his weekends, and how much time he would spend with his family and friends outside his professional life.

Blackett read widely and had strong interests in fields well outside the physical sciences, including philosophy, history, anthropology, and psychology. He took in art museums, theater, and music as time allowed.[25] He was a good photographer outside as well as in his laboratory, where he made his reputation with photographs of particles leaving vapor trails in the cloud chamber. His lively and sociable wife Costanza, known as Pat, traveled with him on some professional trips and hosted parties and evenings at home. She was fluent in Italian and French, continuing to learn languages as she got older, including German and Russian in her sixties and Welsh in her seventies.[26] Following an exhibition of Picasso's *Guernica* in Manchester, it was Costanza who packed it up for an exhibition in New York City, where Blackett saw the painting in September 1946.[27]

Since they were at boarding schools during the school year, the Blacketts' children Giovanna and Nicolas saw little of their father and mother outside vacation holidays. Nor did the sister and brother see much of each other since Giovanna's school was in the south of England and Nicolas's in the north. Both followed up their father's professional interests in some measure. Giovanna became a photographer before marrying and raising a family of four children. Nicolas became a medical physicist doing research on the effects of radiation on cells, which had applications in chemotherapy and in bone-marrow and organ transplantation.[28]

They were not a wealthy family, and the £12,500 in Nobel Prize money was a considerable sum. On Giovanna's suggestion, some of the money bought a motorized wheelchair for a disabled friend of Giovanna's.[29] But the money also gave Blackett the opportunity to realize his dream of having a boat of his own, the descriptively named "Red Witch," twenty-six feet long with red sails. Blackett was sailing it by the summer of 1949, later taking month-long trips to France and Ireland with friends as crew. On one of the first trips with two family friends, Giovanna, and Nicolas, Blackett wrote Costanza how happy he was to be on his new boat. He thought the children (who were now in their early twenties) liked it, that it was a wonderful holiday, and that he felt better than he had for years.[30]

Beginning in the late 1930s the family often took summer vacations in the north of Wales, near the sea, renting a cottage up the slope from the architect Bertram Clough Williams-Ellis's estate Plas Brondanw, near the hamlet of Croesor, the village of Portmeirion, and the larger towns of Penrhyndeudraeth and Porthmadog. Over the decades the area became a small conclave of leftist intellectuals, described by one of its later residents, the historian Eric Hobsbawm, as not quite a Welsh Bloomsbury. Bertrand Russell and the Cambridge biologist Joseph Needham were in Portmeirion. Like the Blacketts, John Maddox, for many years editor of *Nature,* rented one of Clough's cottages. Clough's wife Amabel was a Strachey. Her brother John Strachey had published the widely read *Theory and Practice of Socialism* in 1936 and was a minister in the Labour party after 1945. He visited the valley regularly, as did the Labour politician Anthony Greenwood. On the more conservative side, Arthur Koestler rented one of the cottages. The Left historians E. P. Thompson and Dorothy Thompson, like Hobsbawm, arrived in the 1960s.[31]

Hobsbawm wrote that it was not comfort that brought them to the Welsh mountains. "In our Welsh cottages we voluntarily lived under the sort of conditions we condemned capitalism for imposing on its exploited toilers."[32] The natural beauty of the place and the escape from urban life were restful and intoxicating, although these intellectuals hardly left their politics behind. Nor did they abandon friends and colleagues: the Blacketts entertained regularly in their rural retreat. Costanza Blackett settled there after her husband's death, living near her daughter's sixteenth-century cottage.

Among Blackett's Welsh friends was Michael Burn, a writer and poet who spent three years in the German high-security prison Colditz during the war. Blackett and Burn sailed together often, once nearly going astray as Burn was daydreaming at the helm until Blackett gently reminded him that he really should watch the compass while steering. Burn said of Blackett that what he admired about him was his total honesty.[33] For most people, whether or not they agreed with him, what was striking in Blackett was precisely this trait: what friends and admirers called his honesty, integrity, or moral force. Some found his manner overbearing and intimidating, despite what friends, colleagues, and journalists alike called his tall and film-star-quality good looks. "Un jeune premier de cinéma," said the French daily *France Soir*.[34] His sympathetic views to the Soviet Union were idealistic and often seemingly blind to the ugly realities of Russian economic failures and political oppression. One colleague remarked, "There was a political barrier between us. I could not attune myself to what seemed to me to be an oversimplified left-wing outlook and when I argued he always replied 'We can't put the clock back.'" This was a phrase that Blackett repeated at the Nobel banquet in Stockholm.[35]

Many critics, among them friends, regarded Blackett as a courageous man, suggesting that he sacrificed advantages and promotions in his early career because of the public stands that he took. A journalist wrote in 1948, when Blackett was head of the Physics Laboratory at Manchester, "One cannot help feeling that something went wrong somewhere in his career. His present appointment does not match up to his great talents. Had he been less emphatic in expressing his political views, he might now perhaps fill with distinction the positions that his teacher [Ernest] Rutherford occupied."[36]

Regardless of whether his political views interfered with his professional advancement, Blackett did not step back from the public role he had assumed for himself. The problem for Blackett was not simply that he embraced the politics of the Left, but that he embraced active politics at all. The mainstream of members of the scientific community generally argued that the objectivity and autonomy of scientific work required separation of science and politics. The kind of politics that was suitable for scientists only lay in acting to preserve the circumstances and freedoms that enabled scientists to do their work.

To be sure, Blackett was not alone among scientists in taking stands on political matters that affected far broader questions than scientists and scientific communities. In the postwar period, the French physicist Frédéric Joliot and the American chemist Linus Pauling are examples on the left side of the political spectrum and the Hungarian-born physicist Edward Teller on the right. The American physicist Robert Oppenheimer's exclusion on political grounds from decision-making in the Atomic Energy Commission is well known. Werner Heisenberg also found himself excluded from government circles in the early 1950s when he ran afoul of Chancellor Konrad Adenauer on the issue of equipping the German army with tactical nuclear weapons.[37]

Within the British physics community, Blackett's leadership abilities often were compared to those of Ernest Rutherford and W. Lawrence Bragg. Bragg succeeded Rutherford at Manchester in 1919, where Blackett replaced Bragg in 1937. After Rutherford's death in 1937, physicists predicted that Blackett, James Chadwick, or Edward Appleton would be selected for Rutherford's position at Cambridge, but it was Bragg who was chosen.[38] Rutherford's politics were squarely Liberal, including a strong belief in the necessary independence of science from political systems. He deplored public controversy, both in science and in politics, although he signed a manifesto in 1935 supporting the national government, composed of a coalition of Conservatives, Liberals, and some Labour parliamentary members that came into power in 1931.[39] As President of the Royal Society from 1926 to 1931, Rutherford had to involve himself in quasi-governmental organizations and affairs, and beginning in 1933 he served as President of the Academic Assistance Council that helped find posts for scientists expelled from Central Europe.[40] Rutherford was skeptical about left-wing causes and placed himself on the middle Liberal side of the political spectrum.

While Bragg's politics were perhaps more conservative than Rutherford's, Bragg agreed with Rutherford in most things, including the independence of science and politics. Thus, in an exchange in 1969 with David Edge, a sociologist of science, Bragg's remarks were typical of scientists who strived to maintain the tradition of separation of science and politics. When Edge asked about Bragg's political views and those of his father, William Henry Bragg, with whom Sir Lawrence shared the 1915 Nobel Prize in Physics, Bragg replied that both he and his father were apolitical. When asked whether they voted, he replied that they generally voted conservative. Responding to Edge's explicit question whether Sir Lawrence saw any relationship between scientific work and scientific values and political matters, Bragg denied that this was the case.[41]

While Rutherford and Bragg took the mainstream, P. M. S. Blackett made a different choice and lived a different kind of life. This biography follows the choices and struggles of that life. The format runs on roughly chronological lines, with some overlap due to the thematic organization of the book. Chapter 1 begins with Blackett's boyhood and naval education, his experiences in naval combat, and the development of his political outlook. The connection between his naval education and his scientific work is an important one, and historians of science might do well to examine more thoroughly the impact of military education on the approaches taken by some scientists in their later work. Blackett's mastery of the experimental craft of particle physics and cosmic-ray physics, using the cloud chamber, Geiger counters, and magnetic fields, is the focus of Chapter 2, which examines his personal work and his directorship of research groups at Cambridge, Birkbeck College in London, and Manchester from 1921 to 1947. It was in this period that his international reputation was made for his achievements with the cloud chamber in the study of nuclear transformations, cosmic-ray particle showers and electron pairs, the heavy electron (or mesotron), and the "strange" particles with their V-tracks.

Chapter 3 focuses on Blackett's increasing involvement as scientific advisor on military matters in the 1930s, including his support of the development of radar. He spent the war years mainly in London in the halls of Whitehall and the Admiralty. While in these corridors of power, he opposed wartime British development of an atomic bomb and favored cooperation with the United States and Canada on the North American continent. Privately, as a member of the British atomic advisory committee, and publicly after the United Kingdom embarked on a postwar nuclear weapons program, Blackett spoke out against Cold War nuclear strategy from 1946 through the early 1960s. His experiences were often unpleasant ones, and some of his views proved shortsighted, but he never relented in his warnings against faith in the hegemony of air power.

As narrated in Chapter 4, after returning to the Manchester physics department following the war, and long fascinated by astronomy and cosmology, Blackett noticed a mathematical coincidence in equations relating angular momentum to magnetic momentum for the earth and the sun. Exploring the possible meaning of this coincidence turned him to the development of a simple law and an experimental test for the theory that the earth's rotation is responsible for its magnetic field. As he followed ongoing work in astrophysics and began investigations in geophysics in his Manchester department, Blackett developed a network of evidence that, along with his magnetometer data for the magnetism of a rotating body, led to his own theory's demise. Chapter 5 examines Blackett's move from the failed magnetic theory into the newly developing field of paleomagnetism and studies of continental mobilism, or continental drift. He began a program of research, first at Manchester and then at Imperial College, to marshal evidence for continental drift and, in particular, latitude effects as evidence for the phenomenon. That some of the evidence could be found in rocks in India provided Blackett yet one more reason to visit a country to which he became deeply politically committed in his later years.

Chapter 6 begins with a discussion of the attribution of scientific eminence through the process of the awarding of the Nobel Prize, continuing with a detailed analysis of the circumstances that brought the Physics Prize to Blackett in 1948. Blackett's role as an increasingly busy and powerful leader in the British scientific community loomed larger and larger in the 1950s and 1960s. By deciding not to let his name go forward for director of the Cavendish Laboratory and choosing Imperial College as his permanent home in 1953, Blackett committed himself to building science outside the Oxbridge axis and to living an urban and cosmopolitan life in London. His role in advising the government of India on science and technology policy, as well as the British government, brought him considerable criticism as well as appreciation. The book concludes with an examination of some idealized traits of scientific leadership, both in research schools and the larger scientific community, and with an assessment of Blackett's personal qualities and struggles that helped define his place in British scientific life.

The still controversial character of Blackett's historical role as public citizen brings into sharp focus the tension between the scientific ethos of value-free objectivity, on the one hand, and the scientific imperative for social and civic improvement, on the other. Scientists have long been expected to remain nonpartisan in their service to the state: Blackett's scientific life provoked controversy about the public roles that he assumed, but unanimity about his contributions to physics. This biography engages with the choices he made in physics, war, and politics.

The Shaping of a Scientific Politics: From the Royal Navy to the British Left, 1914–1945

On 5 November 1948, two different notices about P. M. S. Blackett appeared on facing pages of the *Manchester Guardian*. One short news item reported the announcement from Stockholm that the Nobel Prize in Literature was to be awarded to T. S. Eliot and the Prize in Physics to P. M. S. Blackett "for his work on cosmic radiation and his development of the Wilson method." In sharp contrast, a second article, a brief review essay of Blackett's newly published book *The Military and Political Consequences of Atomic Energy*, denounced Blackett as a Stalinist apologist who was opposing American and British development of atomic weapons. As the reviewer, Edward A. Shils, put it, Blackett's "great analytical powers put in the service of his strong political prejudices and aided by his over-rationalistic conception of human motives produce a picture which frequently bears little resemblance to reality."[1]

The acid tone of Shils's remarks correctly conveys the polarization of views in Britain at the mid-twentieth century about a distinguished physicist's public political role. Shils could not have known, of course, that Blackett's Nobel Prize would be announced on the same day that Shils's review was to appear, thereby bringing into clear focus, on facing pages of the *Guardian*, their difference of opinion about the role of the Soviet Union in the world and the place of scientists in national politics. Following Blackett's death in July 1974, *The Times* noted the long controversy about Blackett's politics, with the obituary headline "Lord Blackett: Radical Nobel-Prize Winning Physicist." According to *The Times*, a Nobel laureate in physics, leader of operational research during the Second World War, scientific advisor to the British government,

President of the Royal Society, and member of the House of Lords was thought in the 1940s and 1950s to have been "committed too far to the left for [even] a Labour Government to employ with ease."[2]

Unlike J. D. Bernal, Joseph Needham, Hyman Levy, J. B. S. Haldane, and some other scientists in the social relations of science movement of the 1930s, Blackett never was a member of the Communist party nor was he a Marxist, although he became tagged by security forces and political foes as a communist sympathizer. He was a socialist, a member of the Labour party, an antifascist, a trade unionist. In all this, it is accurate to say that his convictions were to the left. He was the grandson of a vicar, son of a stockbroker, a graduate of naval schools, and an officer in the Royal Navy during the First World War. His socialist politics began to emerge about the time Blackett entered Cambridge University and the Cavendish Laboratory of Physics following naval service that had included action in the Battle of the Falklands and the Battle of Jutland. Blackett's full-fledged commitment to an integrated life of science and politics took place in the 1930s in the face of worldwide economic collapse, the rise of fascism, and the events of the Civil War in Spain.

Blackett was a member of the British generation that Noel Annan characterized as "our age": the intellectuals who came of age and went to university in the thirty years between 1919, the end of the Great War, and 1949–1951, the beginning of the Cold War. It was a generation whose greatest intellectual triumphs, in Annan's view, "were won by the scientists and the mathematicians," some of whom became statesmen of science on all sides of the political spectrum, including Blackett, John Cockcroft, and Alexander Todd. Whenever one talked to these university scientists, wrote Annan in *Our Age: Portrait of a Generation* (1990), "you could sense the excitement and pride they took in their calling."[3]

Some of the scientists who turned to the left took their cues from the varieties of British socialism associated with G. Bernard Shaw, Sidney and Beatrice Webb, and H. G. Wells more than from Marx or the Soviet Union. Fabian socialism, with which Blackett explicitly came to identify his views, aimed to influence by rational argument the "2000 who really mattered" rather than the proletariat.[4] Both Marxist and Fabian-inclined scientists—Blackett, Bernal, Cockcroft, C. P. Snow, C. F. Powell, Eric Burhop, and others—staked out the claim that social and economic decisions should be conducted on scientific principles. This was not a new idea. Comte had given it wide expression in his positive philosophy of the 1830s, to the great dismay of John Stuart Mill, who saw dangers to individual liberty and parliamentary discussion in scientific decision-making.[5] A newer form of positivism received expression in H. G. Wells's novels and political writings of the 1920s and 1930s, which had enormous impact on the scientists of Blackett's generation. In Wells's view, the wars made possible by science and technology would force the world into a technocratic world dictatorship (the Air Dictatorship, he once called it) if scientists and intellectuals did not take the lead in helping to shape a benevolent and responsible world organization of government.[6]

Among his generation of scientists and science advisors, Blackett was unusual in his professional and political itinerary. He was one of the few physicists of his generation to have served during the First World War before he began university studies. His service as an officer in the Royal Navy not only gave Blackett experience and confidence unusual for a young man entering Rutherford's Cavendish Laboratory in the 1920s, but his naval experience prepared him to want to take a scientific advisory role on military matters in the British government by the mid-1930s. Blackett's life and work reflect the optimistic and progressivist Victorian and Edwardian milieu of his childhood and early education, as well as the Enlightenment and positivist tradition of science. His life and work also reflect the political radicalization that occurred among many scientists and intellectuals of his generation in the face of the economic and political hardships and turmoils of the 1930s. The evolution of Blackett's scientific politics poses the question of how well the scientific life fits with a political life and what price a scientist must be willing to pay, in scientific reputation and personal life, for an active role in politics, both among peers and public.

An Edwardian Childhood and Naval Education

Patrick Maynard Stuart Blackett was born in Kensington, London, on 18 November 1897. His father, Arthur Stuart Blackett (1865–1922), who worked as a stock jobber at the Stock Exchange, was the son of an Anglican clergyman who had been vicar of the church in Woburn Square and vicar of St. Andrew's Croydon. Two of Arthur's brothers were clergymen, and one was a missionary in India.[7] Patrick's mother, Caroline Frances Maynard (1868–1960), was the daughter of an officer in India who served during the Indian Mutiny. Her uncle had lived in India as a tea planter. In an earlier generation of the Maynard family, Patrick's great-great-grandfather William Whitmore had served in the Royal Navy and interested himself in inventions after retirement. The inventor of the calculating machine, Charles Babbage, married Whitmore's daughter, the sister of Patrick's great-grandmother.[8]

One of three children, Patrick was the only son. His elder sister, Winifred, became an architect who practiced professionally in the 1920s until she married. His younger sister, Marion, or Molly (later Marion Milner), became a well-known industrial psychologist and psychoanalyst. She published *A Life of One's Own* in 1937, modeling the title on Virginia Woolf's *A Room of One's Own* (1929), using the pseudonym Joanna Field, laying out the discovery of what she called the bisexuality of the personality and understanding. She used the pseudonym because she was doing research for the Girls' Public Day School Trust, working with so-called problem children, and she thought the teachers might be alarmed by her book.[9]

Marion's next book, *On Not Being Able to Paint,* written just after declaration of war in 1939, became a milestone in the use of drawings in psychological therapy.[10] Patrick had given her a copy of Freud's newly translated *Introductory Lectures* in the early 1920s. By then Blackett was in Cambridge, where Freud was much in vogue.[11] Years earlier, at home in London, Marion had helped her older brother develop a lifelong interest in bird-watching. The first lecture he ever gave, to a University Physics Undergraduate Society, was on the migration of birds.[12]

Blackett remembered being "brought up in the kindly security of an Edwardian middle-class home."[13] It was a home in which overt affection was not shown and children were not praised, "lest they became conceited."[14] Blackett remembered his father as a man who had been Liberal but became Conservative.[15] Arthur Blackett sang in the Stock Exchange choir and collected butterflies, loved the sea and fishing. When he inherited some money from an aunt in 1911, he retired from the Stock Exchange and worked as a village postman in Hindhead during the war, reading their sons' postcards from the trenches to the illiterate gypsies living in the Devil's Punchbowl, a hollow in the middle of Hindhead. The Blackett family already had moved several times, from Kensington to Kenley, then to Woking in 1904 and Guildford in 1907, where, at the age of nine, Blackett attended the Allen House preparatory school.[16] He cycled regularly from Guildford to Brooklands, where an airfield was adjacent to the Brooklands motor racetrack.[17]

Caroline Blackett was tall and elegant. The family did not have a great deal of money, but they did have a cook and maid. When these servants left to do war work in 1914, Marion climbed the stairs to the attic bedroom where they had slept and was stunned at the bareness of the room. Winifred and her mother attended a cooking course and took over the household meals, and Winifred began cooking in the wartime kitchen at Great Ormond Street Hospital.[18] In 1917 Marion left her schooling after only one term in the sixth form because of too little money for school fees. She briefly took a job in the country as a tutor before being able to go to university with a grant provided by an organization concerned with women's postwar training.[19]

In a later article in *Punch,* titled "The Education of an Agnostic," Blackett irreverently recalled of his childhood that he was "baptised into the Church of England, then vaccinated and finally confirmed" as was the usual order in those stately days. "With me confirmation did not take."

> I regularly attended Sunday morning service and no doubt it did me a power of good by extracting me for a restful hour from the wooden shed in our garden where I spent every hour out of school making wireless sets and model aeroplanes. I found that I could turn this Sunday ritual to good effect when I discovered that the enforced repose of a sermon was excellently conducive to bright ideas as to how to mount a galena crystal or to carve the propellor of a model aeroplane.[20]

Thinking about airplanes served him well once it was decided that twelve-year-old Patrick should apply to become a cadet at the Royal Naval College at Osborne. When he arrived for an interview with a board of four Admirals, he was asked what he knew about Charles Rolls's flying machine, which had made the first double crossing of the Channel the previous day. Blackett had no trouble answering the question. Thus, just before his thirteenth birthday, in September 1910, Blackett entered the Naval College in the Isle of Wight with about sixty-five or so other cadets, joining an elite group that included the future King George VI.[21] As Blackett recalled later, "For the next few years I received, at government expense, an excellent modern and scientific education, with a background of naval history, and the confident expectation that the naval arms race with Germany then in full swing would inevitably lead to war."[22]

Blackett's future was mapped out. After two years at Osborne, he would be ready to enter Britannia Royal Naval College at Dartmouth, then go to sea in September 1914. After service in a training cruiser, a ship in the Fleet, examinations, further months at sea, more examinations and courses at the Gunnery School and the Torpedo (Electrical) School, he likely would be Sub-Lieutenant about February 1918. If he ranked high in his classes, he could expect to be a Captain about 1935 and, perhaps, Admiral before 1948, especially since demand for officers with technical skills in electrical engineering was rising.[23]

At the time Blackett entered Osborne, fees normally were paid by parents, and his parents did so. Admission to the school was ranked at the prestige of a Winchester scholarship.[24] The cadets wore naval officers' uniforms with cadet badges; the young men believed that they were in the Navy, although this was not the case.[25] The naval schools probably provided the best education available in any secondary school in Britain.[26] This education had only recently been reformed under the 1902 Selborne Scheme led by Lord Selborne, the First Lord of the Admiralty, and Jacky Fisher (Admiral of the Fleet John Arbuthnot, Lord Fisher of Kilverstone), the Navy's most energetic leader of the century. Fisher was responsible for the creation of the all-big-gun battleships such as HMS *Dreadnought,* launched in 1906, and he would oversee British victory at the Battle of the Falkland Islands in December 1914.

Selborne and Fisher's aim in modernizing naval schools was to increase engineering education in the basic officer training scheme and make officers interchangeable. All officers were to be trained and educated in common to the rank of Sub-Lieutenant, with officers' career paths diverging at Lieutenant level, when an officer could specialize as seaman, gunner, torpedo officer, instructor or engineer, or Royal Marine. Then at some later stage officers could come back together on a general list.[27]

By the time Blackett entered Osborne, a revised scheme gave one-third of the cadets' time to engineering, a high proportion in comparison to the curricula of English public schools. The Naval Colleges were supplied with workshops and laboratories; and at Dartmouth about nine hours per week were spent in workshops (out of 43¾ hours). As a consequence Blackett received what was probably the most intensive physical science and engineering education available at secondary-school level in England.[28] In a publication explaining the four-year course followed at Osborne and Dartmouth, the Admiralty informed parents and guardians that

The aim of the course as a whole is to provide as far as possible a liberal education, together with the groundwork in mathematics and science, engineering, and navigation, which the professional requirements of the officers make it necessary to desire that they should possess before they go to sea. The claims of the technical subjects are so strong that the curriculum inevitably leans towards the side of mathematics and science, and their applications. . . . But the claims of the humane studies are not forgotten: English, history and modern languages take an important place.[29]

In addition to exercises in science laboratories, all cadets were expected to learn the rudiments of using tools in pattern-making, fitting, and turning and forging. They operated lathes and engaged in metal filing, as well as in carpentry. When later interviewed, many officers remembered the time spent in workshops and the smithy more vividly than that spent in classrooms.[30] Among purely academic subjects, naval history stood out as a favorite course, especially as taught by Geoffrey Callender. Mathematics and modern languages were well-enough taught that, when Naval Intelligence needed translations of German cipher telegrams at the outbreak of war in August 1914, Sir Alfred Ewing turned to the mathematics and modern languages departments at Osborne and Dartmouth for a first wave of recruits for "Room 40" at the Admiralty. One of the recruits, A. G. Dennistron, became Head of Bletchley Park, working on the breaking of the German Enigma ciphers, from 1939 to 1942.[31]

Blackett and other cadets equally received an education in elite leadership. To be sure, there was an expectation that leadership was a natural attribute of character among cadets whom interview boards selected from the upper and middle classes. Admission boards were explicit about the qualities that were sought:

What is the right sort of boy? . . . that boy has the best chance that is resourceful, resolute, quick to decide, and ready to act on his decision. He must be no slacker, but keen to work and play. He should be sound alike in wind and limb and in the big and little principles of conduct . . . cheerful, unselfish, and considerate. . . . He should give promise of being responsive and observant, closely in touch with his surroundings, but master of himself. The boy of sensitive, poetic spirit, the ruminating young philosopher, the scholar whose whole heart [is] in his books are types that have a real use in the world, but their proper place is not the Navy. . . . If he is fond of an outdoor life, excels in sports, has a turn for practical mechanics, and does well in his studies, especially in mathematics, so much the better.[32]

If the naval officers' education was aimed at cultivating the habits of "command," "self-reliance," "fertility of resource," and "fearlessness of responsibility," an important means of furthering these qualities was games and sportsmanship, just as in the public schools.[33] All cadets were expected to spend from one and a half to two hours each week on gymnastics and physical training. Except when excused on medical grounds, cadets also were required to play games. Boxing was compulsory. Tennis was left to the afternoons when cricket or other organized games were not played.[34]

In some of these sporting activities Blackett was not as successful as other boys. Captain Lord Alastair Graham later read to Blackett from notes that he had made on Blackett as a cadet: "Games: does not shine. Remarks on character: Clever, quiet and nice."[35] Still, Blackett was reported to have been kicking off at a students' football match when he was informed of winning the Nobel Prize.[36] As a cadet Blackett enjoyed sailing, and he continued bird-watching, taking photographs, remarkable for their quality and clarity, with a camera that he built himself.[37] He chafed a bit at required church services, as at gunnery drills.[38]

In church services the chaplain routinely exhorted cadets to the exercise of self-discipline and self-control, as well as love of God and country. It was imperative to maintain "the tone of the college," and character was the key to success: "Not only does your own future depend upon it, but the future of Osborne depends upon it, the future of the Navy depends upon it, and England depends on the Navy. . . . [I]f your character gets corrupt and low, decline will surely set in and be our ruin. In the long run everything depends on CHARACTER [emphasis in the original]. . . . You must keep England's honour 'pure and high' . . . keep this place 'clean and healthy and good.'"[39] Among the dangers that Reverend Horan especially addressed, over and over, was the danger of unclean and immoral language, which was judged "hateful, low and ungentlemanly." "Get out of your head, once and for all the falsehood that bad language is manly." Given the repetition of this injunction, it seems not to have been dependably obeyed by the cadets.[40] For Blackett, if the sermons didn't take, academic work did. He was a great success academically, second in his class at Osborne and top cadet at Dartmouth.[41]

Blackett in Action

On 1 August 1914, when war broke out, Blackett had taken the first of his passing-out exams.[42] That day, the 400 cadets at Dartmouth were told to pack their chests: "There were large crowds at Dartmouth but not cheering," Blackett wrote in the diary that he kept from 1 August 1914 until 24 April 1918.[43] The cadets went to Devonport, where they stayed at Keyham College, taking the exams in navigation and electricity on 3 August. They played cricket all the next day "whether we liked it or not which was a great bore," and twelve of the sixteen-year old cadets were told the same day that they immediately would join HMS *Monmouth* to take passage to HMS *Carnarvon*. From the *Monmouth*, the Dartmouth cadets sighted Madeira on 10 August and arrived in the sweltering heat of St. Vincent on 13 August, where they boarded *Carnarvon*. They had feared that *Monmouth* would be too late for the rendezvous because of earlier delays in dock. Had Blackett stayed on board *Monmouth,* he would have been killed, with all the ship's crew, at Coronel on 1 November 1914. This near-miss is said by Blackett's family to have moved him profoundly.[44]

HMS *Carnarvon* spent two months patrolling off the Cape Verde Islands, hunting for German raiders and escorting convoys. In October the ship set off for Brazil, continuing to Montevideo and then sailing south for Falklands on 28 November, arriving 8 December. At the Battle of Falklands, in early December 1914, the German battleships *Scharnhorst* and *Gneisenau,* which had sunk *Monmouth,* were themselves sunk, together with the cruisers *Leipzig* and *Nuremberg.* Since the *Carnarvon* was the slowest ship of the British squadron and only lightly armored, she was mostly on the edge of the battle, although she joined in the firing that sank the *Gneisenau* and took survivors on board.[45]

Onboard ship, when the men were not engaged in action, dinners were good and lectures often interesting, focusing on naval history and the conduct of the present war. Sometimes there was a concert after dinner. Blackett's observations of animal life and southern hemisphere terrain, like Charles Darwin's and other naturalists over the last hundred years, were enthusiastic for all the new forms that he could see. For Blackett, the birds were captivating: curious little swallows, a magnificent albatross, small white "ice birds," penguins near Port Stanley, turkey buzzards. He continued to make photographs. Port calls included cricket and tennis. While in Montreal in June 1915 mixed teams of officers and men joined in a football match. Games were played on shipboard too, with a hockey game on quarterdeck losing all twenty balls.[46] Church services occurred regularly. "It struck me," Blackett later wrote, that "the Germans were praying to God to similarly help them."[47] Mail shipments brought Blackett his issues of the magazine *Flight,* as well as letters and foodstuffs.[48]

After three months looking for the German ship *Dresden* off the southeastern and southern seaboards of Argentina and Chile, *Carnarvon* turned north in mid-January, but hit a rock and had to have repairs. The crew reached Montreal in late May 1915, where Blackett left the ship and returned to England to join the new HMS *Barham* on 19 August 1915. *Barham* was the third of the five Queen Elizabeth-class battleships that were probably the Royal Navy's most important and successful battleship design of the First World War period. They were the first British battleships to exceed twenty-one knots service speed and the first battleships with fifteen-inch guns and oil-fired boilers, whereas *Carnarvon* was coal-fired and served by colliers.[49]

It was from the foremost twin fifteen-inch turret of *Barham* that Blackett witnessed the Battle of Jutland, sixty miles from the Danish coast, the only major encounter between the British and German fleets during World War I and the most re-fought of the Royal Navy's twentieth-century battles. Only the Armada of 1588 and Trafalgar can possibly compete for the volume of their literature, writes one naval historian. The Royal Navy did not win as expected. At best, the battle was, tactically, a draw with the balance of casualties in the German favor, although Britain retained control of the North Sea.[50]

Blackett mostly could see only flashes of German guns from his post on *Barham.* In battle on 31 May 1916, he saw an oily patch on the water that the crew later learned was the *Queen Mary,* which had sunk, and the bow, lurching out of the water, of one of the Royal Navy's M-class destroyers. As the *Barham* began to take fire, the crew received the news that the Grand Fleet was coming up.

> It was horrible seeing the flashes, then waiting for the salvoes to fall. . . . We were silhouetted against the bright western sky and they were merged in a great haze. . . . [I]t is estimated that some 500 12-inch bricks were fired at us and the rest of the squadron. . . . Many people

did not know . . . that we had been hit. . . . There was an extraordinary reek of TNT fumes, which, mixed with the smell of disinfectants and blood, was awful. Nearly all the killed, some twenty-four in number, were lying, laid out on the deck, and many were terribly wounded, limbs completely blown off and nearly all burnt.[51]

By June 5 *Barham* was in port for battle repairs at Devonport, from where Blackett's diary entries show scorn for a senior admiral who addressed the ship's company. It may be that at this point Blackett became seriously disillusioned with the Navy.[52] Blackett later vividly recalled the Battle of Jutland, and his gazing through the periscope at the patch of oily water in which a dozen survivors, from a crew of twelve hundred men, were clinging to pieces of wreckage from the battle cruiser *Queen Mary*. Jutland taught him, he repeated on several occasions, the danger of assuming superiority over the enemy in military technique and the folly of failing to design defensive measures against the offensive weapons in which one claims superiority.[53] At the Battle of Jutland, in Blackett's opinion, "The new Germany navy . . . had proved itself superior in gunnery and in ship construction."[54]

At Devonport, Blackett and his peers prepared again for oral and written examinations, in which he placed at the top.[55] Blackett thought of applying to the Admiralty to be transferred to the Royal Naval Air Service, but he was told that no transfer was likely since it took six years to train a naval officer and only six weeks to train a flying officer.[56] In October 1916 Blackett was promoted to Second Lieutentant (Sub-Lieutenant) and appointed to P17, a patrol boat in the Dover patrol. His first brush with a submarine occurred 25 May 1917 in the eastern Channel, and he attacked but did not think he sank a U-boat.[57] He joined the destroyer HMS *Sturgeon*, based at Scapa Flow on the east coast of Scotland with the Grand Fleet, in July 1917. His destroyer was transferred to the Harwich force, where on 11 March 1918 *Sturgeon,* with the destroyers *Thruster* and *Retriever,* attacked and sank a U-boat.[58]

Blackett's last action was a classic destroyer battle off Terschelling on 20 April 1918, much overshadowed in the history of the war by the British raid on Zeebrugge during 22–23 April. Blackett's ship, along with light cruisers and four destroyers, discovered that what had been taken to be German minesweepers were powerful German destroyers closing in range at high speed. As the *Sturgeon* turned, a shell hit near starboard, blowing a large hole in the side of the engine room. "This was superb gunnery," Blackett later wrote in his diary, "and far beyond the competence of the British destroyers: I knew because I was controlling our fire."[59] With the engine room flooded, the turbines worked for the next thirty minutes, even though underwater, before they were stopped as seawater began to get into the boilers; *Sturgeon* finally was towed to Harwich. As First Lieutenant, it was Blackett's responsibility to control the damage and pass a tow while under enemy fire. He managed to get off some rounds of shots as well.[60]

On 15 May 1918 Blackett was promoted to Lieutenant, but he had become doubtful, as he put it later in autobiographical notes, that he would relish peacetime in the Navy. Shooting targets was less appealing to him than shooting ships. By the time the war was over in November 1918, Blackett had decided to resign from the Navy and was making inquiries about admission to the University of London and about employment at the instrument firm Barr and Stroud. He had been constructing wireless sets and optical spectroscopes from his boyhood, and he had enjoyed excellent training in machine shops at Osborne and Dartmouth. In 1916, while on *Barham,* Blackett and Lieutenant Edward Bellars had obtained a secret Admiralty patent by designing a more accurate instrument for measuring the rate of change of bearing, essential if ships were to be able to compute a firing solution for guns. Although the instrument was never brought into service, it was a forerunner of the Mark XIV bombsight that Blackett later helped design, so that aircraft could drop bombs accurately without the need to fly level.[61]

Cambridge Years, 1919–1933

To Blackett's great joy, the Admiralty publicly announced on 18 January 1919 a plan to send some 400 junior officers to a six-month course of general studies at Cambridge University, taking over blocks of accommodation in colleges. On 24 January the *Cambridge Review* printed a college guide to naval ranks and terminology that was meant to help readers unfamiliar with military customs.[62] Still in uniform, Blackett dined for the first time at Magdalene College on 25 January 1919, where he met Geoffrey Webb, just back from the Merchant Marine and a future art historian, and Kingsley Martin, a conscientious objector who had been a stretcher bearer in France during the war and would later become editor of the *New Statesman*. This socialist and radical Liberal magazine, founded in 1913 by Sidney and Beatrice Webb, George Bernard Shaw, and a small group of Fabians, became one of the most widely read weeklies among the British Left's intellectual and political elite under Martin's editorship from 1931 to 1960.[63]

A few days after settling into his College rooms, Blackett wandered into the Cavendish Laboratory to look at a scientific laboratory. Three weeks later he resigned from the Navy, unpersuaded by the disappointment of his commanding officer, Commander H. E. Piggott. In the Magdalene photograph for the term, Blackett appeared in the front row, but it seems that he did not go to the Cambridge naval ball. In May he completed Part I of the Mathematics Tripos, with a Second Class. In October he enrolled as a physics student, completing Part II of the Physics Tripos with a First in May 1921 and receiving his degree, with two terms allowed for war service.[64]

Ivor Richards recalled first meeting Blackett in 1920 when Richards was a young philosophy don living in a garret in Free School Lane a door or so from the Cavendish Laboratory. In a striking image, Richards described Blackett as a "young Oedipus": "tall, slim, beautifully balanced and looking always better dressed than anyone." (He was 6 feet, 2 inches in height.) The intense face, the "haunted visage," was mobile and alive with intelligence, modesty, and friendliness.[65] Mark Oliphant similarly recalled the charming smile of the handsome and impressive young man.[66] Blackett struck his new friends as possessing a combination of versatility of imagination and tough skepticism. Richards introduced him to members of the Heretics Club, finding Blackett "not easily convinced even by his own ideas."[67] Blackett was doing physics, but writing a paper on the migration of birds. His interests ranged over anthropology, psychology, economics, and world politics.[68] A Cambridge don who most impressed him was William H. R. Rivers, who had been a psychologist in the Cambridge anthropological expedition to the Torres Straits in 1898 and spent the war years as a medical psychologist specializing in war neuroses.[69]

Blackett's political views were changing. He had voted Conservative in the Khaki election of 1918: he was in the wardroom, the Naval Officers' Mess, at the time, he later said, and that was the natural thing to do.[70] By 1922 he was a supporter of the Labour party and a campaigner in the 1924 general election for Hugh Dalton, who later taught at the London

School of Economics and became Chancellor of the Exchequer under the Labour Prime Minister, Clement Attlee, in 1945. In 1926 Blackett favored the General Strike, which began with the miners' strike on May Day. He drove a Ford motor car from Cambridge to London to fetch copies of the *British Worker* for the Cambridge community.[71]

There was a good deal of politics from which to choose at Cambridge. The Heretics Club discussed religion, philosophy, and art, with speakers including the English post-Impressionist painter Roger Fry, the philosopher and pacifist Bertrand Russell, the feminist and educator Dora Russell, and the astronomer (and pacifist) Arthur S. Eddington. The Club was described by one of its members, the physicist John Cockcroft, as "non-religious but highly respectable; of the Ten Commandments, it held that only six need be attempted."[72] The Cambridge University Socialist Society met weekly in 1920, and the Labour Club first convened in March 1920. Sidney Webb lectured in Cambridge on the Fabian approach to socialism in 1921, and G. D. H. Cole laid out counterarguments for guild socialism the following month. The new National Union of Scientific Workers first met in Cambridge on 26 May 1920, where Professor Frederick Soddy of Oxford spoke on socialism. Soddy would receive the Nobel Prize in Chemistry the following year for his pioneering work, much of it with Rutherford, on radioactivity and chemical isotopes. While some Cambridge men and women joined both the Communist and Labour parties in the early 1920s, the Labour party voted in autumn 1925 to expel communists from party membership.[73]

Elected to a two year Bye-Fellowship at Magdalene College, Blackett entered the Cavendish Laboratory in autumn 1921 as a research student under Ernest Rutherford. A campaign to institute the Ph.D. degree at Cambridge had begun in 1920. During the next fifteen years, 1922–1937, 104 research students would submit doctoral dissertations in experimental physics at the Cavendish, but Blackett would be unusual in never taking the Ph.D.[74] Just as Blackett started at the Cavendish, Peter Kapitza arrived from Leningrad, where he had done research in A. F. Ioffe's laboratory with N. N. Semenov on the magnetic moment of an atom in an inhomogenous magnetic field. Rutherford's attitude toward politics, especially left-wing politics, was stated clearly when he declared to Kapitza that there would be no communist propaganda in the Laboratory. It was well known that Rutherford could not abide J. D. Bernal, partly because of Bernal's open communism and allegiance to left-wing causes. The young Bernal left Cambridge in 1923 for a position with William Henry Bragg at the Royal Institution, but returned to Cambridge and taught structural cyrstallography there from 1927 to 1937.[75]

Personal and scientific differences provoked some tensions between Kapitza and Blackett. Writing to his mother from Cambridge in June 1922, Kapitza found Blackett difficult and said, somewhat surprisingly, that Blackett "has the reputation of being not very likeable." Kapitza complained that he could not undertake work by himself for improving the cloud chamber because Blackett had already started it. Differences in approach led them to part ways on the project in the autumn of 1922, when Rutherford gave Kapitza a large space of his own and funds for equipment.[76] Kapitza, three years older than Blackett, quickly became the most colorful figure in the Laboratory and Rutherford's favorite son; to many observers Kapitza was outrageous in his successful efforts at flattering and charming Rutherford.[77] Kapitza organized a physics group that met in his rooms, eventually in Trinity College, and became known as the Kapitza Club.[78] Blackett was a member of the Kapitza Club, as well as the Δ-Squared Club, a group of experimental and theoretical physicists who met in Paul Dirac's room at St. John's College.[79] In 1934 Kapitza's time at Cambridge ended abruptly to general outrage, when Kapitza was refused permission to return to England after making a trip to Russia for his annual summer vacation.

By the summer of 1923 Blackett decided to marry. He had met Costanza Bayon, a beautiful dark-eyed woman who was studying modern languages at Newnham College. Fluent in Italian and French, she had an English mother and Italian father, but had been raised by an English couple in Florence, where she was known as Dora Higgs. As a child Costanza nicknamed herself "Pat" while the Higgs's niece Teddy was staying with them for a year. Costanza, *aka* Dora, arrived in England to attend St. Albans School for Girls and then matriculated at Newnham, where she took back the name Costanza Bayon.[80] Blackett and Costanza married in March 1924 and, to intimate friends, they were the two Pats. They spent the summer in Italy, and went to Germany during the second year of his two-year Royal Society Moseley Research Fellowship, so that Blackett could spend the academic year with James Franck.[81]

Returning to Cambridge from Berlin, the two Pats settled into a house at 59 Bateman Street, about a mile from the Cavendish Laboratory and off Trumpington Road, where they kept open house at least once a week.

Theirs was a tall, four-story house with a long garden in the back, and it was here that their daughter Giovanna (Gio or Jo) was born in 1926 and their son Nicolas (Niki or Nick) in 1928. Reports were that guests tended to be semi-bohemian and left-wing, but nothing like as far left as Bernal's friends. Since extra money was scarce, open house was simple—lemonade and biscuits. Since they could not afford carpeting, they placed rush mats on the floor, and Costanza painted the treads of the stairs in alternate black and white. Witty, amusing, and good company, Blackett and Costanza were said to be the "handsomest, gayest, happiest pair in Cambridge."[82]

Busy in his new married life and his fast-paced laboratory life, Blackett was not very active in political matters for the next decade, until the awful years of the worldwide economic depression, the rise of Hitler and fascism, and the events of the Spanish Civil War.[83]

> Like many other scientists, I gradually became drawn to more active concern with the outside world. The Crash, the Slump, Hitler, the Spanish war all had this effect. Looking back on this tragic period it seems likely without the Great Crash and its consequences Hitler might not have gained power and perhaps 30 million Europeans might not have died. What went wrong? Could the final tragedy have been avoided? . . . [T]he climateric [sic] period 1930 to 1940 is indelibly stained on the memory of my generation.[84]

Blackett and Costanza worked to raise money to bring children to England from Spain.[85] He later copied out a verse that appeared in the magazine *Country Life*.[86]

> In a quiet, wide
> green countryside–
> To have no sense of trouble brewing
> Never to ask "What's Hitler doing?"

He dated his entry into active political engagement, which would characterize the rest of his scientific and military life, to his appearance in 1934 on the BBC radio series "Whither Britain."[87]

London Politics in the 1930s

As discussed in the next chapter, Blackett's experimental work, strongly infused with theoretical curiosity and commitment, was wildly successful in the period from 1923 to 1933, when he left Cambridge for London. Blackett's classic paper, published in the *Proceedings of the Royal Society* in 1925, included photographs that have been widely reprinted ever since of the transformation of a nucleus with expulsion of protons in a cloud chamber. In February 1933 Blackett and Giuseppe Occhialini communicated the results of their Cavendish Laboratory data for 700 automatic expansions resulting in 500 tracks of cosmic-ray particles, of which fourteen tracks were evidence for a positive electron, which had just been announced as a possibly new particle in the fall by Carl Anderson at Caltech. In contrast to Anderson's 1932 paper, Blackett and Occhialini explicitly associated the new particle with Dirac's recent formulation of quantum mechanics predicting pair production of an electron and an antielectron.

In the autumn of 1933, the year that Blackett was elected Fellow of the Royal Society (FRS), he moved to Birkbeck College in London in order to direct his own research laboratory outside Rutherford's bailiwick. The opening in 1933 of Kapitza's Mond Laboratory at Cambridge probably also contributed to Blackett's decision to leave. Other reasons, as he characterized them, were a conservative milieu at Cambridge University, his great liking for the London metropolis, and his sympathy with Fabian aims of education for the kinds of urban students who attended Birkbeck College, originally founded in 1823 as the London Mechanics' Institute. Sidney Webb, one of the founders of the London School of Economics in 1895 and a former Birkbeck student, had secured Birkbeck's integration into the University of London as a "School of the University in the Faculties of Arts and Science for evening and part-time students" in 1920, with a royal charter in 1926. According to A. J. Caraffi, later Clerk to the College, the coming of Blackett "made" the college.[88]

Blackett's move to Birkbeck was greeted with fanfare. As he set up equipment for detection of cosmic rays 100 feet below ground at an unused platform in the Holborn Tube Station, science journalists wrote stories calling him the new Sherlock Holmes of Baker Street.[89] The problem for the new Holmes was the poor funding of the college and its effects on his physics laboratory, as discussed in the next chapter. However, living in London, Blackett found himself at the national center of political discussions, and he felt more at liberty to involve himself in matters of politics than in Cambridge, which he viewed as a "still feudal-Victorian environment."[90] He and his family settled in a flat in Gordon Square, just a few blocks from his laboratory, the College, and Russell Square, in the heart of Bloomsbury.

Like many scientists who visited or heard reports of research institutes and scientific conferences in the Soviet Union in the early 1930s, Blackett was impressed that the new Marxist state appeared strongly committed to building science and technology in order to transform the feudalist system of czarist Russia. Nowhere in Europe, nor in the United States, was a higher proportion of national income being spent on research and development than in the USSR.[91] Blackett also liked what he heard from lectures given in London in 1931 by members of the Soviet delegation to the Second International Congress of the History of Science. Boris Hessen's argument in his widely publicized paper on the "Social and Economic Roots of Newton's *Principia*" made sense to Blackett. Practical economic needs had driven Newton's revolutionary science just as they drive modern science. Blackett had always been bored by standard histories of science and the way these histories treated scientists as if they were "living so to speak in a social vacuum."[92] The social and economic interpretation was considerably more interesting to him.

Blackett himself visited Moscow for conferences in September 1935 and again in September 1937. On the first visit, he called on Peter Kapitza, chatting with him in the early hours after midnight, just a year after Kapitza had been refused permission to return to England. Despite Kapitza's ordeal, Kapitza himself still felt some tension between the two of them, writing to his wife Anna, who was in Cambridge at the time, that "I always have the feeling that he doesn't care for me and his wife even less."[93]

Bernal and Julian Huxley had visited the USSR in 1931, and Huxley published an account, *A Scientist among the Soviets,* in 1932.[94] While Blackett still was in Cambridge, he occasionally saw Bernal after Bernal's return from his USSR trip. Bernal was among the Cambridge scientists who helped revive the Association of Scientific Workers (ASW), which had been languishing in the last several years. Bernal also published an article in *Cambridge Left* in 1933, arguing that intellectuals must be engaged politically, an argument frowned upon by those scientists who agreed with the perspective of A. V. Hill, the 1922 Nobel laureate, physiologist, and Secretary of the Royal Society from 1935 to 1945. Hill warned that "the Society frowns on inducting members who meddle in politics."[95]

With the appointment of Adolf Hitler to the German Chancellorship in January 1933 and the expulsion of Jewish and politically suspect intellectuals from government and university jobs in April 1933, it was becoming evident that politics was intervening decisively in the conduct of scientific work, however independent of politics scientists might want to be. In France leftist scientists, including Paul Langevin, Jean Perrin, Emile Borel, Jacques Hadamard, and Frédéric Joliot, had been involved in the organization of antifascist groups and meetings in Paris since the late 1920s. Following antiparliamentary riots by veterans' groups and paramilitary leagues in Paris in 1934, these scientists were among those who founded the Comité d'Action Antifasciste et de Vigilance, popularly dubbed in the press the "intellectuels antifascistes." Explaining French scientists' abandonment of the laboratory workbench for marches in the street, Langevin said, "The scientific work that I do can be done by others, possibly soon, possibly not for some years; but unless the political work is done there will be no science at all." Perrin's similar reasoning was that "you can scarcely cultivate the garden while the house is burning."[96]

About the time that Blackett moved from Cambridge to London, some Cambridge scientists formed the Cambridge Scientists' Anti-War Group (CSAWG), an antifascist, but fundamentally pacifist, group that took part in local demonstrations when the RAF had air displays at neighboring airfields at Mildenhall or Duxford.[97] Many of the CSAWG scientists were working in the laboratories of Rutherford and of biochemist Frederick Gowland Hopkins. C. P. Snow estimated that by 1936 three-quarters of the 200 "brightest" young physicists in Britain considered themselves left of political center.[98]

Nevill F. Mott, who left the Cavendish Laboratory for Bristol in 1933, joined the left-wing Society for Cultural Relations with the Soviet Union. "Most of us were politically committed in the Nazi period," he later wrote, "and were friendly to the Soviet Union because they were against the Nazis." Mott recalled a chemistry conference in the USSR in 1934 in celebration of the 100th anniversary of the birth of Mendeleev. There was a park "where you could gain a prize by throwing balls at Hitler, Austen Chamberlain, Mussolini, and Ramsay McDonald."[99] However, in their attitude toward McDonald's government, "Some of my friends believed that the National Government of the 1930s (Conservative in essence) should be opposed in all that it did, and since it was proposing some limited rearmament should be opposed. This seemed to me neither in the interests of our potential ally Russia or our own. I became suspicious of the Left."[100]

In London, Blackett was asked to join a group of scientists who were participating in a series of BBC radio-broadcast programs on science and society, which began to be aired in 1931. First established as a private corporation in 1922, the British Broadcasting Corporation had become a public corporation in 1927 upon the recommendation of a parliamentary committee. Its mission very specifically was to bring into British homes the best in every "department of knowledge, endeavour and achievement" and "to give the public what we think they need—and not what they want," as bluntly put by John Reith (later Lord Reith), who was BBC general manager, then director-general, from 1922 to 1938.[101]

In 1931 a series of programs on science was organized by the Marxist mathematician Hyman Levy, who was friends with Mary Adams, a producer with the BBC. Blackett appeared in the 1934 series "Scientific Research and Social Needs," which was edited as a book by Julian Huxley, with a foreword by Levy, who justified the need for the series by noting that science was being regarded with suspicion as a possible cause of the social dislocations of the Great Depression. Huxley, in turn, reminded listeners and readers that science is a social activity and that this is a lesson for scientists to learn as well as statesmen and the public.[102]

Blackett's radio talk on "Pure Science" was moderated by Huxley, and Blackett agreed in the broadcast with Huxley's argument that science is a social activity. Blackett also agreed that scientists should not delude themselves into thinking that they could be aloof from politics. Scientists' interests were dependent on material and moral support from government and industry. In Blackett's view, scientists needed to step up and make clear to the public the virtues and advantages of science at a time when one could see so clearly in Germany the development of anti-scientific and anti-intellectual movements.[103] However, the notion that there could be scientific consensus in matters of politics was pie-in-the-sky, as far as Blackett was concerned: "No, there I disagree. As a matter of scientific observation, I find that my scientific colleagues, between them, represent all the possible outlooks you have mentioned. . . . Don't be too optimistic. I am afraid that if society thinks that the scientist is going to be its saviour, it will find him a broken reed."[104]

On the matter of what was being called "planned capitalism" in British economic and political circles in the 1930s, Blackett was skeptical, as he expressed his view in another BBC program, which would gain him renown as a committed "red." The National government, composed of a coalition of Conservatives, Liberals, and some Labour MPs, had been in power in the House of Commons since 1931.[105] "You are being told there is a third way," Blackett warned, a planned capitalism or planned economy:

> I believe that there are only two ways to go, and the way we now seem to be starting leads to Fascism; with it comes restriction of output, a lowering of the standard of life of the working classes, and a renunciation of scientific progress. I believe that the only other way is complete Socialism. Socialism will want all the science it can get to produce the greatest possible wealth. Scientists have not perhaps very long to make up their minds on which side they stand.[106]

The conviction that scientists could not avoid taking a political stand was becoming increasingly prominent, and noncommunist members of the Left increasingly looked to Blackett for leadership.[107] This was true of Fabians such as Beatrice Webb, who contacted him in May 1935 to ask his opinion on the Webbs's chapter on science in the USSR and on their interpretation of the Marxist dialectic in the forthcoming book *Soviet Communism: A New Civilization?*[108] Some Labour party activists looked to Blackett, too, including Alex Wood, who asked Blackett in early 1935 to let himself be nominated as Labour candidate to Parliament for Cambridge University. Blackett declined.[109]

Blackett was among British intellectuals who in 1935 organized the group For Intellectual Liberty (FIL), a parallel organization to the French Intellectuels Antifascistes. The FIL's organizers included Bernal, Snow, Aldous Huxley, whose *Brave New World* had appeared in 1932, and Leonard Woolf, a central figure with his wife Virginia Woolf in the Bloomsbury group and the editor from 1923 to 1930 of *The New Statesman*'s friendly rival, *The Nation*.[110] The FIL executive committee on which Blackett and his colleagues served met twenty-nine times from 1936 to 1939, promoting meetings and seminars, sending delegates abroad, and arranging asylum and employment for Central European refugees, in concert with activities of the first Academic Assistance Council, established in May 1933 with Rutherford as President and with offices in the Royal Society.[111] Among the refugees to England whom

Blackett knew well or who worked in his laboratories at Birkbeck College, or, after 1937, Manchester, were Hans Bethe, Rudolf Peierls, Léon Rosenfeld, Otto Robert Frisch, Walther Heitler, and Lajos Jánossy. On the other hand, by early 1935 Blackett was parting company politically with friends who took strongly pacifist positions, among them Kingsley Martin, who in 1939, after the invasion of Poland, still argued that the British should make a diplomatic approach to Hitler.[112]

Like Mott, Blackett was unsympathetic with radical pacifism among the Left. In late 1934 Harry E. Wimperis, Director of Scientific Research in the Air Ministry, along with meteorologist Albert Percival Rowe, convinced Air Ministry officials to establish a Committee for the Scientific Survey of Air Defence. By late January 1935 Wimperis and Rowe had enlisted Hill and Blackett on the committee, along with Sir Henry T. Tizard, a chemist and rector of Imperial College, with long service in the government and Air Ministry.[113] Tizard asked Robert Watson-Watt, superintendent of the National Physical Laboratory's Radio Research Department, to explore the potential of using radio waves as an antiaircraft weapon. Instead, his staff suggested that radio waves might be used to detect and locate enemy aircraft. Thus began a series of unofficial air defense trials of prototype radar instruments at sites like Biggin Hill, just outside London, under major air routes connecting the metropolitan area to central European cities. These experiments were well underway by mid-1936, as discussed in Chapter 3.[114]

By then the military forces of Italy and Germany were wreaking terror well beyond their national borders. During 1935–1936 Italian forces used aircraft to bomb and spray Ethiopian civilians with mustard gas. In March 1936 German forces occupied the Rhineland. The Spanish Civil War was underway, and the rest of the world soon learned of the German bombing of the Republican and Basque city of Guernica on 26 April 1937, a destruction that was immortalized by Pablo Picasso in his famous painting. The CSAWG now became actively concerned with British defense, testing claims made by the Home Office for its gas protection measures in the event of air raids and demonstrating civilian gas masks to be ineffective.[115] The group included the biochemists and biologists Joseph Needham, Norman Pirie, C. H. Waddington, and R. L. M. Synge, along with volunteers in Manchester. In 1937 the publisher Victor Gollancz, who started the Left Book Club with Labour MP John Strachey and the London School of Economics professor of political science, Harold Laski, published *The Protection of the Public from Aerial Attack*. In May 1938, Blackett and Hyman Levy opened an exhibition in London, sponsored by the Scientists' Group of the Left Book Club.[116]

In 1938, with considerable contention, a new division was established within the British Association for the Advancement of Science (BAAS) for the Social and International Relations of Science. The division, which existed until 1945, was the result of determined effort by Haldane, Levy, Needham, Bernal, and others, including Richard Gregory, the influential editor of *Nature* and an old friend of Ramsay MacDonald's.[117] Blackett served on the new division's subcommittee, which concerned itself with the influence of scientific and technological development on different industries and the volume of employment.[118]

Following discussion with Solly Zuckerman, whose scientific work was then focused on investigating primate evolution and behavior at the London Zoo, Bernal prepared a memorandum in late 1938 on "Science and National Defence," which was sent to the Secretary of War and to Liddell Hart, the military correspondent for *The Times*. It was a call for scientific workers to be placed in national service.[119] Following the Munich agreement of September 1938, the British ASW, which previously had condemned the use of science in warfare, called for the full use of science to defeat fascism.[120] Under the presidency of Sir William Henry Bragg, the Royal Society also prepared a memorandum in 1938 on organizing scientific workers for a national emergency, which, as it passed from the Prime Minister to the Ministry of Labour, led to the setting up of a central register of scientific and technical personnel. The register, among other things, reveals that by 1940 there were 1,175 physicists in Britain.[121]

Similar concerns about mobilization of scientists were voiced in the London men's group Tots and Quots (from the Latin "Quot homines, tot sententiae": "As many opinions as there are men"). Started in 1931 by Zuckerman, the group revived in autumn 1939, after Germany's invasion of Poland, and Britain and France's declaration of war. The club's membership came to include Bernal, Huxley, Needham, Blackett, Waddington, the geneticist C. D. Darlington, the geneticist and popular science writer Lancelot Hogben, and science correspondents J. G. Crowther of the *Manchester Guardian* and Peter Ritchie Calder of the *Daily Herald*.[122] They hosted French scientific colleagues, including Langevin, Pierre Auger, and Lieutenant Jacques Aller, a technical intelligence officer in the French Navy, with whom Crowther flew to Paris on 8 April to see French scientists Joliot, Francis Perrin, Jean Perrin, and Louis de Broglie. Crowther later recalled that during their meeting Joliot told the story that he had suggested Blackett as successor to Rutherford at the Cavendish but had been asked: "Isn't he rather left?"[123]

On 12 June 1940, a week after the invasion of France and evacuation of British troops from Dunkirk, Allen Lane, the publisher of the *Penguin* and *Pelican* sixpenny paperbacks, was a guest at a Tots and Quots dinner, and it was agreed that Zuckerman would anonymously edit a Penguin book on *Science in War*. It was a cooperative effort "written by twenty-five scientists," arguing to the public that full use must be made of science in the war. Thousands of copies were sold.[124] As discussions in Parliament demanded what use was being made of scientists, a Scientific Advisory Committee was set up in October 1940 after Churchill became Prime Minister. Chaired by Lord Hankey, its membership included Secretaries of the Royal Society, Department of Scientific and Industrial Research (DSIR), and Medical Research Council (MRC). The Oxford physicist Frederick Lindemann, who had been a guest at a Tots and Quots dinner in March 1940, became Churchill's personal scientific advisor. The Committee advised the Government on scientific problems referred to it. Following forceful lobbying by Tizard and by Hill, who was a member of Parliament (as an Independent Conservative, representing Cambridge University), the House of Commons voted in 1942 for a full-time Central Scientific and Technical Board to coordinate research and development for the war, directly advising the Ministry of Supply.[125] This provided scientists with a still greater voice in the war's conduct. By then Blackett was fully engaged as a civilian head of operational research in the British Admiralty.

Friends at Odds: Political Differences among Scientists

When Blackett spoke of the failure of agreement in matters of politics among scientists, he spoke as a scientist who had experienced such disagreements firsthand. Perhaps ironically, one of the most outspoken antagonists to the Tots and Quots group and its politics, certainly to the Soviet sympathies of left-wing scientists, was Blackett's good friend Michael Polanyi, who joined the Manchester Department of Physical Chemistry in 1933 as a refugee from Berlin where he had headed the division for reaction kinetics at the Kaiser Wilhelm Institute for Physical Chemistry. Polanyi and Blackett had first met in Berlin in 1930, and Costanza and Patrick Blackett saw Magda and Michael Polanyi regularly after the Blacketts moved to Manchester in 1937. Blackett addressed Polanyi by the familiar "Mischi," and Polanyi signed his letters to Blackett "Misi."[126] The Blacketts arranged for the Polanyis to visit them while on vacation in Wales.[127] During the war, when the Blacketts lived in London, the two Pats stayed with the Polanyis when they visited Manchester.[128]

Yet all through these years, certainly from the 1930s to the 1950s, Polanyi and Blackett argued. In a letter in October 1941 Polanyi expressed chagrin at what he thought was a hostile tone in their conversation earlier in the day, noting "we have always disagreed, yet maintained an entirely genuine link of sympathy."[129] Blackett responded by denying any personal hostility, but admitted he was hostile to "some of your views, and as you are to mine."[130]

Polanyi, whose brother was the noted economist and economic historian Karl Polanyi, had thought long and hard about capitalism, Marxism, and socialism since the late 1920s. By 1935 Polanyi had visited Russia four times. His reaction was different than Blackett's. Polanyi later recalled

> a conversation I had with Bukharin in Moscow in 1935. Though he was heading towards his fall and execution three years later, he was still a leading theoretician of the Communist Party. When I asked him about the pursuit of pure science in Soviet Russia, he said that pure science was a morbid symptom of a class society; under socialism the conception of science pursued for its own sake would disappear, for interests would spontaneously turn to problems of the current Five Year Plan.[131]

Polanyi began to put together a long paper critical of Soviet economics in which he closely examined claims and data from the Soviet Five-Year Plans.[132] He also began putting together what he called an economic film on "The Working of Money." It was a soundless film of diagrams illustrating economic processes with accompanying text, and Polanyi got financial support from the Rockefeller Foundation.[133] Once it was finished, selected viewers included members of the Manchester Statistical Society, the Hope Street Church Social Study Group in Liverpool, Walter

Lippmann's colloquium in Paris, and Friedrich von Hayek's seminar in London.[134] Bernal even arranged a viewing for the left-wing ASW in London, which seems to have been unpersuaded.[135]

Announcement of the German-Soviet nonaggression pact came in August of 1939. Blackett wrote Polanyi from Wales that he would not be surprised if Polanyi felt some "Schadenfreude" over the Russians' behavior, adding that he himself was completely surprised, as well as dismayed, as Polanyi would expect.[136] At the outbreak of the war in fall 1939, Blackett joined the instrument section of the Royal Aircraft Establishment at Farnborough, where he worked on the design of the Mark XIV bombsight. He was a member of the MAUD Committee to advise the British government on the feasibility of Britain's developing a fission bomb. In August 1940 he became scientific advisor to the Anti-Aircraft Command, organizing a scientific operational research group to coordinate the use of radar sets, guns, and mechanical calculators. He joined the Coastal Command in March 1941, heading a group that recalculated the depth settings for antisubmarine explosives and vastly improved the use of airborne radar for finding German submarines.

In the meantime Polanyi asked Blackett to help him get some defense work, but this proved impossible even though Polanyi had become a naturalized British citizen in September 1939.[137] Polanyi instead joined the Oxford zoologist John Baker in founding a scientific association that they called the Society for Freedom in Science, which first met in March 1941 under the chairmanship of Oxford's retired Professor of Botany Arthur George Tansley. The group aimed to fight any postwar attempt to allocate funds by central planning in service of social goals on a Soviet-style model.[138] In July 1941, in response to a circular soliciting members, the German refugee physicist Max Born, who now had a professorship in Edinburgh, wrote Blackett that he would not join this society since its freedom of science was coupled to an attack on planning and on socialist scientists, whom Baker had called "gangsters" in an essay review attacking Bernal's recent book *The Social Function of Science*.[139]

Polanyi collected a series of essays he had written about planning, the Soviet Union, and Bernalism into a book titled *The Contempt of Freedom: The Russian Experiment and After* (1940), which he sent to Blackett in October 1941.[140] Blackett found in the work a hostile attitude not toward the Soviet Union alone, but, as Blackett put it, "to all that is generally called progressive politics—'progressive obsessions,' in your words."

Following the German army's attack on the Soviet Union in June 1941, the Russians again were allies of the United Kingdom, and Blackett wrote Polanyi that he admired what he thought was a remarkable military feat in the Soviet Union's standing up to Germany during the past four months.

During the war Polanyi, Baker, Tansley, Hayek, the chemist Sherwood Taylor, and others argued against government planning for the future of science, linking their objections to a rejection of economic interpretations of the history of science.[141] As news began to leak out of the arrest in 1940 and disappearance of the geneticist Nikolai Vavilov, the virtues of Soviet science and the Soviet system became harder to defend in the United Kingdom, and anti-Soviet and anti-planning rhetoric became increasingly strident.[142] A. V. Hill, who had some sympathy with the Freedom group, nonetheless cautioned Tansley in June 1941 to moderate the group's adversarial language, saying, "Remember, that Haldane and Blackett, for all their queer political notions, are useful and cooperative members of the [Royal Society] Council: I am sure that Bernal and Hogben will be the same when their turn comes to serve. . . . We can keep them in order better by cooperating with them in scientific affairs than by formally setting up to oppose their political ideas in the name of science."[143]

By 1945, when the war was over, British scientists throughout the political spectrum, whether writing in *Nature* or in the circulars of the Freedom society, all emphasized the necessity for truth and freedom in science. There really was no argument on this issue. Polanyi was asked to address the Manchester section of the ASW in May 1945, and his talk was well received. As for scientists' right to be able to follow research paths of no obvious social utility, Blackett wrote a colleague that progressive thinking could go too far in reacting against the science-for-science's-sake attitude. A socialist society should devote an appreciable fraction of its resources to pure science, as well as to music and art.[144] In fact, this had always been his view.

There was some effort at planning for British universities right after the war. The Royal Society was enlisted to furnish a report on "The Balanced Development of Science in the United Kingdom," and Blackett was one of the committee's members. Polanyi submitted a document arguing that universities should be left to fill professorships with the most eminent candidates available, and the needs of industry, medicine, and defense should be considered only as subsidiary factors in the "relative endowment of various branches of pure science."[145]

In the end the committee report supported the "natural" development of science by "the most distinguished leaders."[146] Under Blackett's presidency the ASW, as well as other groups, recommended against the centralization of governmental scientific offices into a single Ministry of Science. The 1950s organization of science in the United Kingdom, then, turned out to be not much different than in the prewar period.[147]

Increasingly thoughtful by the late 1930s about spirituality and religion, Polanyi joined a group called the Moot in 1943. This small circle was convened by J. H. Oldham, an ecumenical Christian leader, and it met in a rural setting near Horsham. Its members included the Hungarian-born sociologist Karl Mannheim and the American-born poet T. S. Eliot.[148] Polanyi also became a member in the early 1950s of the international Congress for Cultural Freedom, an anti-Soviet organization of intellectuals and artists founded by Melvin Lasky and revealed in the mid-1960s to be funded by the CIA.[149] Polanyi was a close friend and political ally of Edward A. Shils, who made every effort to get him a permanent appointment at the University of Chicago in social science. Polanyi's classic article "The Republic of Science" appeared in the first issue of Shils's journal *Minerva,* founded in 1962.[150]

The appearance, then, of Shils's review of Blackett's book in 1948, facing an announcement of the award of Nobel Prizes in 1948 to the two British citizens, Blackett and Eliot, demonstrates in sharp relief the close-knit society of elites that dominated British intellectual life in the mid-twentieth century. There were those like Polanyi, Baker, and Tansley who argued for the freedom of science from social and economic influences or responsibilities, while Bernal, Huxley, Haldane, and Blackett insisted on scientists' responsibilities of stewardship to the public that supported them, whether in wartime or peacetime. Blackett, for all the charges that he was a radical figure in British science and politics, was the consummate insider in an elite of military, academic, and governmental experience and identity. The shaping of Blackett's scientific politics in Osborne and Dartmouth, the Royal Navy, Cambridge colleges, and the Cavendish Laboratory undeniably gave him status, whatever his political identity, as one of "our age" in Annan's memorable designation of status and place.

Blackett and Polanyi remained close friends, as did their wives, despite their differences in politics. After Blackett's death in 1974, two years before his own father's death, the theoretical chemist and disarmament activist John Polanyi wrote Costanza Blackett of his fond memories of the long friendship of his parents with the two Pats, a friendship that had endured political debates of the last forty years.[151]

2

Laboratory Life and the Craft of Nuclear Physics, 1921–1947

The year that Patrick Blackett was born, 1897, was the year that J. J. Thomson announced that cathode rays are negatively charged corpuscles and Marie Curie began investigating uranium radiations. In 1897 Ernest Rutherford, a postgraduate student working under Thomson at the Cavendish Laboratory, was just beginning his long career of research on radioactivity. At the time that Rutherford was directing experiments at Manchester to get experimental evidence for the structure of the atom, Blackett was entering the Royal Naval College, Osborne, only to have his naval education abruptly cut short by the war, plunging the seventeen-year-old Blackett into active duty. At war's end, after matriculating at Cambridge University for a six-month course of general studies, Blackett resigned from the Navy and entered a new world.

When Blackett began his studies of mathematics and physics in Cambridge in 1919, investigations of radioactivity were the focus of Cavendish laboratory life. Blackett quickly became one of the Cavendish physicists who engineered some of the great experimental triumphs of radioactivity physics and its metamorphosis into the fields of nuclear physics and cosmic-ray physics.[1] Blackett's work placed him in the forefront of the British scientific community by the 1930s as one of the leading experimentalists of his generation, with a special gift for instrument design and implementation. Blackett's approach was rooted in workshop methods, drawing upon techniques of mechanical engineering that he had first learned at the Naval Colleges at Osborne and Dartmouth.[2] Yet Blackett also cared deeply about *a priori* theories based in fundamental principles, his imagination kindled, as with so many physicists of his generation, by relativity theory and quantum electrodynamics. Blackett's combination of experimental skill and theoretical knowledge, coupled with intellectual courage, helped make him not only a versatile physicist but an outstanding one.

In what follows, we see Blackett's accomplishments as a nuclear physicist in the Cavendish tradition, his departure from the Cavendish Laboratory in 1933, and his development as an independent laboratory director and research leader in London and Manchester as part of the emerging field of nuclear physics. Blackett's work bridged the worlds of instrumental practice and high theory. It required skills of organization and leadership. Reflecting on the character of the physicist's life, Blackett later composed a poem playing upon the famous lines of Rudyard Kipling's poem "If," which had appeared in 1910. Blackett wrote:

> If you can organize your lab
> nor lose the power to think
> and deal with academic chores
> nor drive yourself to drink.
> If you can make a test of all your findings
> and risk it on one test of yes or no
> and lose, then
> you'll stay a prof my son.[3]

Cloud Chambers and Cosmic Rays at the Cavendish, 1921–1933

Blackett completed Part I of the Mathematics Tripos in May 1919 and Part II of the Natural Sciences Tripos (physics) in 1921, earning his undergraduate degree. In autumn 1921 he became a research postgraduate student under Rutherford, initially following James Chadwick's six-week "nursery" course of laboratory measurement and manipulation.[4] Blackett quickly demonstrated skill with laboratory apparatus, some of this skill dating back to his boyhood tinkering with crystal radio sets. This skill also was rooted in his education at Osborne and Dartmouth at a time when the scientific and, especially, engineering components of naval education had been much augmented.[5]

Among those who expressed envy of Blackett's feel for the experimental craft was J. Robert Oppenheimer, who came to Cambridge following graduation from Harvard University. In early 1926 Oppenheimer expressed despair to his friend Francis Fergusson about his own inept performance in the laboratory. In the spring of 1926, Oppenheimer told a startled John Edsall and Jeffries Wyman, while on vacation with them in Corsica, that he had left a poisoned apple on Blackett's desk and must return to Cambridge immediately to make sure that Blackett was all right. Oppenheimer's return to Cambridge proved uneventful, but his friends and family became concerned about his psychological state. Oppenheimer had some discussions with psychiatrists in Cambridge and London and soon left the Cavendish for Göttingen, at Max Born's invitation, to study theoretical physics instead of experimental physics. Oppenheimer and Blackett remained lifelong friends, if not intimate ones, but it appears that Blackett's experimental gifts had undermined the young Oppenheimer's confidence in his own. [6]

One of the experiments on which Blackett was first set to work in 1921, in collaboration with Charles Ellis, was the then-standard observation through a low-power microscope of scintillations produced by protons on a zinc sulfide screen as fast alpha particles bombarded nitrogen nuclei. This was a project on which Rutherford had been working since 1919, when he first thought he had observed charged hydrogen nuclei (called protons by 1921) as products of the nuclear disintegration of nitrogen. Blackett collaborated occasionally with Rutherford on these observations, although it was Chadwick who was Rutherford's primary coworker.

Rutherford soon asked Blackett to modify the automatic cloud chamber that Takeo Schimizu had begun designing before he returned to Japan. Rutherford wanted a visual record of nitrogen disintegration to complement the scintillation-counter data. To this end Blackett replaced Schimizu's reciprocating mechanism with a simple spring action for initiating very sudden expansions linked mechanically to a camera shutter so that a photograph was taken just as the expansion was completed. Blackett's first description of the improved cloud chamber and photographs of deflected alpha particles appeared in 1922,[7] but without confirmation of Rutherford's hypothesis that a nitrogen nucleus could be disintegrated by an alpha particle, expelling a proton and leaving behind a carbon atom as a residual nucleus.[8] On the basis of scintillation results from Rutherford and Chadwick, Blackett estimated that a million alpha particles fired into nitrogen should yield about twenty disintegration protons. It was one of these tracks that he was supposed to find.

Rutherford assigned Peter Kapitza, who earlier had been assisting Schimizu, to work with Blackett on developing a high-powered magnetic field around the cloud chamber. They collaborated off and on until late November 1922, disagreeing about the best method to follow. Kapitza published a paper from the collaboration with Blackett, H. W. B. Skinner, and E. Ya. Laurmann, but then turned exclusively to his own preoccupation with developing apparatus for a very large impulsive magnetic field. To assist Kapitza, Rutherford allocated to him almost the entire floor in the attic of the Cavendish as well as equipment costs.[9] Prodded by Rutherford in the summer of 1923 to apply for the three-year Clerk Maxwell Scholarship, to be presented to the best research worker in the laboratory, Kapitza learned that Blackett had applied for the award, but that Rutherford was determined that Kapitza should have the scholarship. Kapitza did get it, and felt somewhat badly about this outcome, writing his mother that he had told Rutherford that Blackett should have the fellowship, especially since he shortly was to be married.[10]

From 1922 on, Blackett improved the cloud chamber. Personal triumph came in the summer of 1924 when he obtained 23,000 photographs (at the rate of 270 photographs per hour) showing 415,000 tracks of ionized particles, of which eight tracks were of a strikingly different type. The photographs showed the paths of an incident alpha particle (which was captured by a nitrogen nucleus), an ejected proton, and the recoiling oxygen nucleus. Chadwick wrote Rutherford, who was in Toronto for a British Association meeting, that Blackett's photographs showed "the track of the H particle, the track of the recoil atom but no track for the α" following collision with nitrogen.[11] A nitrogen nucleus had been transformed into an isotope of oxygen, not carbon. Thus the photographs did not show the disintegration of the nucleus that Rutherford expected, but rather "integrations" or incorporations of the alpha particle into the nucleus before expulsion of a proton. Blackett had disproved Rutherford's working hypothesis, although Rutherford and Chadwick themselves had some evidence from early 1924 that there might be an attractive field between incident alpha particles and the inner core of an aluminum nucleus.[12] Blackett's classic paper, published in the *Proceedings of the Royal Society* in 1925, included photographs that have been widely reprinted ever since.[13]

At the same time that Blackett followed up on Rutherford's focus on the nucleus, Blackett also interested himself in the electrons outside the nucleus, which little concerned Rutherford. Blackett was meeting regularly with both Paul Dirac's Δ-squared Club and with the Kapitza Club. The Dirac group in the mid-1920s included Arthur S. Eddington, Harold Jeffreys, Edward Arthur Milne, Douglas Hartree, Ralph H. Fowler, Edmund Clifton Stoner, Chadwick, Kapitza, Dirac, and Blackett.[14] The Kapitza Club, which first began meeting on Tuesdays in October 1922, included Kapitza, Blackett, Stoner, Hartree, Herbert W. B. Skinner, and John Edward Lennard-Jones.[15] Kapitza invited foreign, as well as local speakers, to give talks, one of whom in 1924 was James Franck. Blackett was especially interested in this session, since he had recently presented a paper to the Cambridge Philosophical Society on the theoretical consequences of Franck's assumption in experimental work that there is exact conservation of energy and momentum during collision of an electron with an atom.[16] It was at the Kapitza Club that Blackett first heard a (skeptical) report on Louis de Broglie's wave theory of the electron. In 1925 Werner Heisenberg and Dirac spoke to club members on quantum mechanics.[17] It was also at the Kapitza Club that Oppenheimer first met Max Born in 1926, as well as Niels Bohr and Paul Ehrenfest. They won him over from experimental physics to theoretical physics: "I was fully aware that it was an unusual time, that great things were afoot."[18]

Against Rutherford's wishes Blackett decided to use the second year of a two-year Royal Society Moseley Research Fellowship to work with Franck in Göttingen during the academic year 1924–1925. Blackett flourished in the lively and cosmopolitan environment. It was here that he first met Heisenberg, who frequently visited Blackett and Costanza at their flat in Göttingen; the Blacketts also entertained Pascual Jordan, Friedrich Hund, and occasionally Enrico Fermi.[19] After writing a paper with Franck on the spectrum of hydrogen, Blackett returned to Cambridge "brimful of talk and enthusiasm about de Broglie and wave mechanics."[20] By his own account in a later conversation with historian John Heilbron, Blackett on his return to the Cavendish attempted to produce the electron diffraction effects predicted by the wave theory of the electron, but he gave up after a few months.[21]

In 1927 Blackett contributed a second theoretical paper to the Cambridge Philosophical Society on the limits of classical scattering theory.[22] At this time he was continuing to refine his cloud chamber, publishing a description in the *Journal of Scientific Instruments,* and carrying out experiments on both slow and fast alpha particles in gases.[23] Collaborating with Frank Champion in 1931, Blackett confirmed Nevill Mott's prediction from quantum mechanics, distinct from classical mechanics, of the collision tracks of alpha particles scattered by helium gas.[24] This, Blackett later said, was a rare experiment to confirm a very precise theoretical prediction at a theoretician's request.[25]

In the meantime the topic of cosmic rays began to attract Blackett's attention after Dmitry Skobelzyn published a paper in 1929 reporting cloud-chamber tracks of charged particles from cosmic radiation.[26] In the same year, Walther Bothe and Werner Kohlhörster in Berlin used data from two Geiger-Müller counters, placed in coincidence, to argue that cosmic radiation consisted of charged particles, not gamma rays as argued by Robert Millikan.[27] Electronic counters were just beginning to replace scintillation counters, and Bothe earlier had used the double-counter arrangement to investigate whether protons are emitted from beryllium, carbon, aluminum, or iron when bombarded with alpha particles, obtaining an uncharged penetrating radiation.[28]

In 1929 Skobelzyn was working at the Curie Radium Institute and at the private Parisian laboratory of Louis de Broglie's older brother Maurice, who was moving steadily toward cosmic-ray research and away from experiments requiring radioactive sources.[29] Skobeltzyn and Pierre Auger collaborated in de Broglie's laboratory with Louis Leprince-Ringuet during the years 1929–1931 to study variation in intensity of cosmic radiation under the influence of magnetic fields.[30] Bruno Rossi joined them in Paris briefly in 1932.[31]

Blackett first met Rossi when he returned with his family to Germany in 1930 to spend the summer in Berlin. At the time Rossi was there visiting Bothe's laboratory to study the coincidence-counters apparatus, which Rossi had been independently constructing at Arcetri, outside Florence.[32] Blackett was of a mind to learn all the theoretical physics he could in Berlin, taking in Lise Meitner's laboratory after writing her in the spring that he wanted to learn some "modern physics."[33] He met Hans Bethe for the first time in Berlin, and Bethe returned a visit to Blackett in Cambridge the following autumn, praising the cordiality of his British hosts Blackett and Fowler.[34] Blackett was the first experimentalist with whom Bethe interacted strongly, and Blackett was strongly interested in Bethe's work on the energy loss of charged particles in their passage through matter.[35]

Blackett and Rossi saw each other again in the autumn of 1931 at an international conference on nuclear physics in Rome. On that occasion Rossi argued that experiments he was doing with Giuseppe Occhialini, using an improved Bothe-Kohlhörster counter, favored a particle interpretation over Millikan's gamma-ray interpretation of cosmic radiation. Rossi sent Occhialini to Cambridge to learn the cloud-chamber technique from its master practitioner: Occhialini "had come for three weeks: he stayed for three years," Blackett said later.[36] The two became lifelong friends, as did their families.[37] Together Blackett and Occhialini integrated the cloud chamber with coincidence counters[38] at the Cavendish Laboratory, where adoption of Geiger counters had been slow under Rutherford's leadership.[39] The counter's usefulness had became harder to refute when valve amplifiers started to come in around 1930. Even so, the early Geiger counters were tricky devices. As Blackett later said in a conversation with Heilbron, "In order to make [the Geiger counter] work, you had to spit on the wire on some Friday in Lent."[40]

Blackett and Occhialini aimed at a radical improvement of Millikan and Carl Anderson's method of randomly photographing cosmic-ray tracks in a sporadic magnetic field. Using that method, tracks were found only in a small fraction of the total number of expansions of the cloud chamber. In contrast, in the Blackett-Occhialini arrangement the cloud-chamber expansion was triggered by the passage of a charged particle through the vertical plane, as registered by the coincident discharge of Geiger-Müller counters above and below the plane in a magnetic field at right angles.

The excitement of their work is conveyed by Occhialini's later account of the first photographs obtained with the counter-controlled cloud chamber. Speaking of Blackett, Occhialini recalled: "What not everyone had the chance to see was the passionate intensity with which he worked. I can still see him, that Saturday morning when we first ran the chamber, bursting out of the dark room with four dripping photographic plates held high, and shouting for all the Cavendish to hear 'one on each Beppe, one on each!'"[41]

During the fall of 1931 Blackett and Occhialini were accumulating hundreds of photographs, including pairs or showers of tracks.[42] In November Millikan paid a visit to Cambridge, giving a talk at the Kapitza Club on 23 November 1931. He had received photographs in the mail from Anderson, which he showed at the meeting. L. H. Gray wrote

Skobelzyn from Cambridge about the occasion: "On Monday we had a visit from Millikan. . . . [H]e showed eleven photographs of 'good' tracks . . . which from the sense of their curvature must have been positive particles. . . . In some cases a proton (?) [question mark in the original] and electron appeared on the same photograph and with the help of a vivid imagination one *might* conclude that they had a common origin."[43]

Gray was skeptical about Millikan's conviction that cosmic rays are gamma rays that trigger the disintegration of a nucleus into an electron and a proton. However, this was precisely the interpretation given one of the Caltech photographs in an article from the Science Service a few weeks later on 18 December 1931, entitled "Cosmic Rays Disrupt Atomic Heart."[44] Cosmic gamma rays, encountering the atomic nucleus, were reported to eject a proton and an electron from the nucleus.

By the summer of 1932 Blackett and Occhialini were getting a coincidence after an average wait of two minutes, with 0.01 second required for attainment of supersaturation, and a success rate of 75 percent on the photographs. Their method relied on the very assumption about which Millikan was skeptical: that the penetrating radiation that reached counters at sea level was electrically charged in the first place. However, the disadvantage of the Cavendish arrangement, in comparison to the Caltech apparatus, was that the magnetic field could not be as strong as a field that did not need to be maintained for several minutes.[45]

In reporting initial results in a paper submitted in late August 1932, Blackett and Occhialini noted that they had found both bent and straight tracks. Of those that were bent, they wrote, "Assuming them to be electrons, their energies lay between 2 and 20 million volts." The straight tracks were assumed to be either electrons or protons.[46] However, Blackett and Occhialini did not mention in their published article that some electron tracks appeared to bend in the magnetic field as though they were positively charged, an anomaly also noted by Millikan at the Kapitza Club meeting the previous autumn.

In September 1932 Cavendish Laboratory physicist Francis Aston visited Caltech, where he learned that Carl Anderson had photographed the previous month, on 2 August, what appeared to be a positively charged electron-like mass, not a proton, emerging through a lead plate in the cloud chamber. Anderson computed the particle's loss of energy, and hence its mass, from its track below the plate. During Aston's visit Anderson was sending off a short article to *Science,* published a week later, with three photographs.[47] In the article Anderson offered several different interpretations of the photographs, eliminating possibilities one by one in favor of the conclusion that "a positively charged particle comparable in mass and magnitude of charge with an electron" had been observed.[48] He and Millikan assumed the production of a positive electron to be a rare event, and they continued to interpret most high-energy positive tracks as protons.[49]

Blackett and Occhialini had come to think differently, and their approach derived largely from familiarity with the work of Paul Dirac. Dirac and Blackett had a long-standing acquaintance. Not only had they been seeing each other for years at the Δ-Squared and Kapitza Club meetings, but Dirac regularly came round to monthly meetings at the Cavendish Laboratory in the early 1930s, despite Rutherford's alleged caution "Don't talk about the universe here."[50] Dirac also came round to the Laboratory while Blackett and Occhialini worked feverishly to complete the work that finally appeared in early February 1933.[51]

Since 1928 Dirac had sought to meet objections to his relativistic theory of electrodynamics, published in that year, and he had come to the proposal in 1931 that there are states of negative energy that produce no detectable electromagnetic effect unless they become empty. If empty, these "holes" in the "Dirac sea" can appear in an electromagnetic field as particles with positive charge and the mass of an electron. After Blackett's death, Dirac gave an account of the relationship between his theoretical work and Blackett and Occhialini's experimental work:

> I was quite intimate with Blackett at the time and told him about my relativistic theory of the electron. . . . [W]e wondered whether the theory was correct and whether positrons really existed. A positron in a Wilson chamber would give a track like an electron, but it would be curved in the opposite direction under the influence of the magnetic field. If one examined a particular track one could not tell if it represented an electron or a positron, because one did not know in which way the particle that had produced it had been moving. In looking over many of Blackett's photographs and assuming a likely direction for the motion of the particle from the circumstances of the experiment, one seemed to have plenty of evidence for positrons. But one could not be sure, and Blackett would not publish such uncertain evidence. Then Blackett noticed that, if he had a radioactive source in the Wilson chamber, many of the particles coming out from it had tracks curved to

correspond to positrons. This seemed to me to be pretty conclusive evidence. But Blackett was not satisfied. He argued that there might be electrons from outside which, by chance, ran into the source. This was most unlikely, but not impossible. So Blackett would not publish his findings. In order to settle the question Blackett proceeded to work out the statistics of how many chance electrons would have to run back into the source to account for his observations, and see if it was at all reasonable. While Blackett was engaged in this work the news came that Anderson had discovered the positron.[52]

Blackett and Occhialini's February 1933 paper "Some Photographs of the Tracks of Penetrating Radiation" provides a stark contrast to Anderson's brief announcement of September 1932. In an article of twenty-seven pages, including fifteen photographs, Blackett and Occhialini described their novel method of "making particles of high energy take their own cloud photographs." They summarized features of some 500 photographs showing tracks of high-energy particles. Eighteen of these displayed tracks of more than eight particles, and four photographs showed more than twenty tracks in which a group appears to diverge from a single point, in a shower of particles. Blackett and Occhialini reported "confirmation of the view put forward by Anderson" that particles exist with a positive charge but with a mass comparable to that of an electron rather than a proton.

Drawing upon recent discussions of nuclear structure, they argued that, on the view that there are no free electrons in light nuclei, "the negative and positive electrons in the showers must be said to have been created during the process," "born in pairs" during the disintegration of light nuclei. In a remarkable passage that places the puzzling positive electron into a clear theoretical perspective, Blackett and Occhialini wrote the following of positive electrons:

> Why have they hitherto eluded observation? They can have only a limited life. Most likely they disappear by reacting with a negative electron to form two or more quanta. This latter mechanism is given immediately by Dirac's theory of electrons. In this theory all but a few of the quantum states of negative kinetic energy, which had previously defied physical interpretation, are taken to be filled with negative electrons. The few states which are unoccupied behave like ordinary particles with positive kinetic energy and with positive charge. Dirac originally wished to identify these holes with the proton, but this had to be aban-

doned. The positive electrons have only a short life, since it is easy for a
negative electron to jump down into an unoccupied state, so filling up
a hole and leading to simultaneous annihilation of a positive and negative electron, the energy being radiated as two quanta.

Blackett and Occhialini further went on to suggest that anomalous results in recent radioactivity studies might be explained by the existence
of positive electrons, for example, reports by Irène Curie and Frédéric
Joliot of a negative electron moving toward a neutron source.[53]

Anderson, just finishing a follow-up paper for *Physical Review,* saw
press reports of the Blackett-Occhialini paper before he published a ten-
page paper in which he used the new term "positron" for the first time.
Anderson did not invent the word, but followed the suggestion of Watson Davis of Science Service, who also suggested "negatron" for the negative electron, a term that never caught on.[54] However, neither Anderson
nor Millikan immediately accepted the Dirac interpretation of the positron. Indeed, in 1934 Millikan coauthored a paper with Anderson expressing doubts about the particle assumptions on which the coincidence-counter cloud chamber was based. The historian Peter Galison
has called the paper "Millikan's last stand."[55]

Anderson began distancing himself from Millikan's prejudices and
adopted the Blackett-Occhialini coincidence-counter technique.[56] He
later explained, at least in part, the change in his views. While he knew
of Dirac's theory around 1932, it had no effect on his own work,[57] Anderson said at a symposium at Fermilab in Batavia, Illinois, in 1980. "The
discovery of the positron was wholly accidental. . . . [I]t was not until several months later when Patrick M. S. Blackett and Giuseppe
P. S. Occhialini suggested the pair-creation hypothesis that this seemed
the obvious answer to the production of positrons in the cosmic radiation."[58]

In his philosophical book on *The Concept of the Positron* (1963), N.
Russell Hanson distinguished three related conceptual discoveries of
1932: the "Anderson particle," the "Dirac particle," and the "Blackett
particle." The "Blackett particle" was what Hanson called a metaphysical
discovery since Blackett was the one who realized that "the prior discoveries of Anderson and Dirac were the *same* discovery."[59] For his part
Blackett rejected Hanson's philosophical approach to this history. "He
seems to be trying to puff up the positron into something more com-

plicated than it was. I have never felt that it was anything but fairly straightforward," Blackett wrote Oppenheimer. Oppenheimer, who had been Anderson's colleague at Caltech, had the view that "we were all lucky that Paul Dirac existed."[60]

Still, in late 1932 Blackett and Occhialini had missed credit for making a major discovery, a fact made all the clearer by the award in 1936 of the Nobel Prize jointly to Viktor Hess, who had first established the existence and extraterrestrial origins of the radiations, and Carl Anderson, who had identified and defined a new particle as a positive electron. Other physicists were also on the positron's track. One was Julius Paul Kunze, Director of the Physics Institute at Rostock in 1936, whose early publications included work on cosmic rays and positively charged particles.[61] From records at the Swedish Academy of Sciences, we know that Maurice de Broglie and Jean Perrin each nominated Anderson and Blackett jointly for the 1936 Physics Prize. Louis de Broglie recommended that Anderson receive half the Prize, and Blackett and Occhialini the other half.[62] H. H. Dale much later wrote Blackett that he thought Blackett had been badly treated in 1936, but had consoled himself by reflecting that Blackett's future work eventually would earn him an unshared prize.[63] More will be said in Chapter 6 about the Nobel process and the attribution of discovery.

What solidified opinion in 1936 that cosmic rays deserved a prize was the earlier announcements in 1933 that Dirac would share the Physics Nobel Prize with Erwin Schrödinger and that Heisenberg would receive alone the 1932 award, all for having "created and developed the basic ideas of modern atomic physics." As noted by Henning Pleijel in the Physics Nobel presentation speech of 1933, the "difficulty which at first opposed [Dirac's] theory has now become a brilliant confirmation of its validity. For . . . positive electrons, the positrons, whose existence was stipulated in Dirac's theoretical investigation, have been found by experiment."[64]

New Particles, New Theories: Birkbeck and Manchester, 1933–1947

For Blackett, the year 1933 was not only the year of the positron, but the year that he resigned from Cambridge University and struck out on his own to establish a laboratory and research group at Birkbeck College in

London. There were several reasons for the move, including disgruntlement that Rutherford wanted Blackett to increase his teaching responsibilities and disappointment that Rutherford was reluctant to expand work in nuclear physics, a disappointment that James Chadwick shared with Blackett and that influenced Chadwick in his decision to move to Liverpool in 1935.[65] Frank Champion recalled an occasion when Blackett emerged from Rutherford's office white-faced with rage and said, "If physics laboratories have to be run dictatorially . . . I would rather be my own dictator."[66]

Blackett must have been chagrined too by Rutherford's initial response to Blackett's communication in February 1933 of his first positive-electron results to the Cambridge Philosophical Society. Rutherford was surprisingly cool, declaring that one could not yet feel certain about this as a discovery, and that he would prefer to see the particle produced by laboratory methods, that is, by radioactivity studies.[67] Nor did it help assuage Blackett's pride that in that same month, February 1933, Kapitza's new Royal Society Mond Laboratory officially opened at Cambridge, embellished with a carving of the crocodile that had become Kapitza's affectionate eponym for his patron Rutherford.[68]

When he arrived at Birkbeck in fall 1933, one of Blackett's first priorities was construction of an eleven-ton electromagnet that would amplify deviations in the tracks of charged particles. The project garnered front-page headlines in London newspapers, as the apparatus, christened "Josephine," eventually took its place 100 feet underground at an unused tube platform below the new "magnet hut" on Malet Street.[69] When Blackett moved from Birkbeck to Manchester in 1937, the electromagnet went with him, again with considerable publicity.[70] It would eventually be moved, piece by piece, up to an observatory on the Pic du Midi in the French Pyrenees, then to Durham University for further experiments on cosmic rays. In the late 1970s the electromagnet had sufficiently aged to become unsafe, and it was sold to be broken up, with the proceeds to finance future research. Thus the life of an electromagnet.[71]

In order to build the electromagnet, Blackett received a grant of £1,500 from the Royal Society's Mond Fund, a rather large sum of money at a time when his new Birkbeck Laboratory had a very stringent budget.[72] Otto Robert Frisch, who was in Blackett's laboratory from the fall of 1933 to the fall of 1934, recalled later to Charles Weiner just how stringent that budget could be:

[T]he lab had very little provision for instrumentation and none of the sort of rather pedantic tidiness that was the usual thing in Germany. I found after a while that my imagination to think up experiments was cramped when I felt that any experiment that required a rubber tube three feet long was impossible, because the only rubber tube we had in the lab was one foot and two inches. . . . I had to go to the lab steward who considered it an extravagance to buy an extra piece of rubber tube. If there were things one could buy at Woolworth's, I just bought them myself out of my own pocket. . . . Pencil caps for counters. . . . I made my geiger counters out of pencil caps.[73]

Blackett's mechanic Arthur Chapman was overworked as he tried to meet the needs of an international group that included Occhialini and coworkers from Switzerland, India, and Singapore. At this time there were no formal colloquia but instead discussions over lunch or tea or sometimes at a nearby Italian restaurant. Not everyone who wanted to work with Blackett could find a place at Birkbeck, however. Bernard Lovell arrived with a recommendation from A. M. Tyndall at Bristol and the hope that Blackett would select him as a research worker, but the post went instead to John G. Wilson. Lovell tried hard to impress Blackett on their first meeting by playing the Russian card known to be one of Blackett's preoccupations: Lovell tucked under his arm a copy of N. A. Berdyaev's *Revelation about Man in the Creativity of Dostoevsky*, but to no avail.[74]

While Blackett was mainly concerned with cosmic-ray research at Birkbeck, Frisch began to work on artificial radioactivity shortly after announcement of its discovery by Curie and Joliot in Paris in January 1934. Within a few weeks Frisch completed a paper on induced radioactivity in sodium and phosphorus, a paper that appeared in just nine days after Blackett personally telephoned the editor of *Nature* and instructed Frisch to hand-deliver the manuscript. Frisch concluded that Blackett wanted his new Birkbeck Laboratory to get priority for original work, but that he also wanted Frisch to have personal credit that would help him establish credentials as an emigré scientist.[75]

While working in the Birkbeck Laboratory to establish energy values for cosmic-ray particles, Blackett also was paying attention to worldwide projects for establishing a latitude effect for cosmic radiation.[76] As he said in his Halley Lecture of 1936, "An attractive feature of cosmic-ray work is the number of voyages, mountain ascents, descents into mines, and expeditions to the stratosphere which are necessary."[77] The latitude effect was the prediction that if primary cosmic radiation is made up of charged particles, then the intensity of radiation at different latitudes is affected by the earth's magnetic field at different latitudes. In global surveys organized by Arthur H. Compton and others, the radiation intensity was found in late 1933 to be greater at the poles than at the equator.[78] This result refuted Millikan's point of view that the primary cosmic radiations are gamma rays.

Physicists were beginning to recognize in the early 1930s that there are two components of cosmic radiation, a "soft" component that does not make it to the surface of the earth and a very "penetrating" component that is found at sea level. These components were first distinguished clearly by Rossi in 1933 and by Auger and Leprince-Ringuet in 1934.[79] In their paper of February 1933, as noted above, Blackett and Occhialini remarked on the cascade or shower effect, which produces particles that are easily absorbed by lead. These particles became known as the "soft" component of cosmic radiation. In contrast, Anderson and his collaborator Seth Neddermeyer reported that cosmic-ray particles can penetrate several centimeters of lead. These were the "hard" component.

However, the hard, or penetrating, component of cosmic radiation posed a serious problem for quantum electrodynamical theory. Making use of both Blackett's and Anderson's results, Bethe and Walther Heitler calculated in February 1934 that high-energy electrons should radiate away most of their energy before reaching sea level and should be absorbed by a few centimeters of water.[80] Thus they concluded "the [relativistic quantum electrodynamical] theory does not agree with Anderson's measurements of the stopping of electrons of 300 million volts energy." So quantum theory appeared to be wrong for electrons of high energy, presumably for $E_0 > 137mc^2$, where $(1/137)^n$ was the probability, according to Dirac, of n particles being produced in pair production.[81] J. C. Street, at Harvard, reported sea-level particles could pass through forty-five centimeters of lead.[82]

In October 1934 at an international conference on cosmic rays held in London and Cambridge, Anderson and Neddermeyer announced their view that relativistic quantum electrodynamics breaks down in the energy range above 100 Mev, a step in what Galison called a "failed revolution against quantum electrodynamics."[83] E. J. Williams had already suggested that it was possible that the lead-penetrating cosmic particles might be protons rather than electrons. Shortly after the London meeting, Compton and Bethe published a paper supporting this hypothesis.[84] In contrast, Anderson and Neddermeyer distinguished what they playfully began to call red electrons (which are easily absorbable) and green electrons (which are not). In a paper of June 1936, they claimed that "if one assumes that these penetrating particles are not electrons and that the theory of absorption of photons and electrons remains approximately valid up to very high energies, some well-known cosmic ray phenomena find explanation."[85] Thus they were proposing a new particle, a green electron.

At Birkbeck, Blackett worked with R. B. Brode who had come from Berkeley on a Guggenheim Fellowhip. Together they studied the energy spectrum of electrons and positrons, establishing energies up to 2×10^{10} eV, about ten times higher than Anderson's values. Blackett arrived at comparisons of energy values with absorption values, and by December 1936 he further established that no more than 15 percent of the hard component at sea level could be protons.[86] Brode, working with collaborators at Berkeley, concluded that about 1 percent of sea-level ionization is due to heavy particles.[87]

Very shortly, Homi J. Bhabha and Heitler, and independently J. F. Carlson and Oppenheimer, developed theoretical formulations for cascade showers showing experimental data to be consistent with the 1934 quantum electrodynamical approach in the Bethe-Heitler paper. In late 1936 their cascade theory explained that hundreds of low-energy positrons and electrons could be produced by a high-energy electron, which could only travel a short distance before its energy was divided among a few quanta, each of which created an electron pair, which created further quanta in collision with nuclei, in a continuing cascade process.[88]

Thus in a given medium the average distance traversed by an electron before it is deflected in the electric field of a nucleus, with emission of a photon, is about the same as the average distance traveled by a photon before producing an electron-positron pair. This distance is the "radiation length": it is about 300 meters in air but only half a centimeter in lead. Thus an electron will travel on average one radiation length before producing a photon, which will typically have one-half the electron's energy. The photon will travel on average a radiation length before producing an electron-positron pair. Meanwhile the original electron will have produced another photon. After two radiation lengths, there are two electrons, one positron, and one photon, a total of four particles (counting photons as particles). After t radiation lengths, there are 2^t particles, and the process continues until ionization losses deplete the electron component, and photon energies become too small for pair production.[89]

Also in late 1936, following a colloquium at Caltech where Anderson and Neddermeyer again suggested that the highly penetrating sea-level particle is not a proton, Oppenheimer and Carlson concluded "either that the theoretical estimates of the probability of these processes are inapplicable in the domain of cosmic-ray energies, or that the actual penetration of these rays has to be ascribed to the presence of a component other than electrons and photons. The second alternative is necessarily radical."[90] Toward the conclusion of his Nobel Lecture in December 1936 Anderson alluded to evidence of new particles (the green electrons).[91]

Shortly afterwards, Blackett and Wilson published data on the absorption of cosmic particles by metal plates inside the cloud chamber. Their results agreed with the estimates of Anderson and Neddermeyer and with those of Street and E. C. Stevenson at Harvard.[92] Street and Stevenson were becoming convinced that evidence against identifying protons with the penetrating radiation was conclusive, although it was not until fall 1937 that they published photographs showing a track with an ionization and curvature consistent with a charged particle of 130 electron masses, considerably smaller than a proton.[93]

Having himself rejected the proton as the lead-plate penetrator by early 1937, Blackett had two options: either Anderson was correct in proposing that the green particle is not an electron; or the green particle is an electron, but it is an electron that does not behave according to the rules used by Bethe, Heitler, Carlson, Oppenheimer, and other theorists.

Blackett then nearly took a very bold step. Sometime in late 1937 or early 1938 he drafted a paper entitled "On the Nature of the Heavy Component of Cosmic Rays" in which he stated that Anderson and Neddermeyer's conclusion was unwarranted. In contrast, Blackett, wrote that such "sub-protons, if they exist, must be so exceedingly rare that they can play no important part in normal cosmic ray phenomena." A penciled annotation at the top of the draft typescript reads "Never published luckily."[94]

It may be that Blackett's move from Birkbeck to Manchester in late 1937 interfered with his decision about what to do with this draft paper. He puzzled over the significance of the heavy-particle track and he puzzled over how an electron could behave. In his work with J. G. Wilson, Blackett employed without enthusiasm L. W. Nordheim's device of a critical maximum value at which an electron's radiation might cut off.[95] Blackett then offered an alternate interpretation that very energetic electrons (greater than 2×10^8 eV) are heavier than less energetic ones, and that they change their mass as their energy drops below a critical value, or they give rise to the light ordinary electrons. "Some new mechanism, not contained in the present structure of quantum mechanics," he wrote, "is certainly necessary to explain all the facts."[96]

Convening a conference on cosmic rays at his new laboratory in Manchester in March of 1938, Blackett found considerable skepticism about his bias against the hypothesis of a new particle, now often called a mesotron. The meeting took place during a horrendous time for one of its participants, Werner Heisenberg. He was under scrutiny in Germany from both the Reich Education Ministry and the Berlin Gestapo office of the SS, and he would finally receive a positive letter about his future prospects in Germany in the summer from SS director Heinrich Himmler. Friends and colleagues of Heisenberg's rushed to hear him speak in Cambridge and in Manchester in March 1938. Nonetheless, Heisenberg was in good form. "I hardly ever get to bed before 12:30," he wrote his wife, "get up around 8; and talk the entire day through with physicists without a break. It is important to me now to lose myself entirely in physics."[97]

A novel theory completely independent from cosmic-ray experiments, namely Hideki Yukawa's 1935 conjecture of a heavy particle in a theory of nuclear forces, now provided a convenient rationale for accepting the green electron as a subproton. Oppenheimer and Robert Serber had first made this connection in 1937. The penetrating particle's mass was estimated at 130 to 170 electron masses, lower than Yukawa's predicted 200 electron masses, but close enough to provisionally settle the matter.[98] Heisenberg argued that the particle was in fact a new particle. Blackett found himself under siege as well by Bhabha, who was backed up in broader discussions by Rossi and Lajos Jánossy.[99]

For Heisenberg, the discussions at Manchester led to his altering a concept that he had worked out for a fundamental constant defined by analogy to the classical electron radius using Fermi's electron-neutrino field theory. Returning to Leipzig from England, Heisenberg replaced the critical length of Fermi's theory with the critical length of mesotron theory, where

$$l_o = h/mc$$

with m the mesotron mass. For Heisenberg, the fundamental length marked the lower length boundary and the upper energy boundary for the application of m.[100]

For Blackett, discussions at the March conference led to his giving in and concluding that "one of the outstanding problems of cosmic ray research" was the determination of the mesotron's time of decay into an electron or positron, and its mass.[101] His earlier proposal that a heavy electron might give rise in some way to light electrons became the postulate that the Anderson-Neddermeyer "mesotron" or "meson" was unstable and radioactive. This hypothesis had occurred to Oppenheimer in 1937 but he had allowed himself to be persuaded by Millikan not to publish it.[102] Drawing upon a theoretical paper by Heisenberg and H. Euler, in December 1938 Blackett and Rossi each calculated decay times for the mesotron.[103]

The mesotron, later renamed the mu-meson or muon, was not Yukawa's predicted particle. The mesotron's mass is lower, and it does not interact with nuclei. This began to be realized in the later 1940s, after the conclusion of the war, when once again Anderson's and Blackett's research groups were in competition with each other.

The war over, one new project in the Manchester Physics Department was the use of war-surplus radar equipment for the study of cosmic-ray events in the upper atmosphere. This became Bernard Lovell's radio-astronomy unit at Jodrell Bank twenty miles south of Manchester.[104] Another project was a continuation of work that George Rochester and Jánossy had carried out at Manchester during the war. Clifford Butler replaced Jánossy, who had moved to Dublin, in these ongoing cloud-chamber cosmic-ray studies. Rochester and Butler were assisted by a new recruit to the physics laboratory, Keith Runcorn. Wilson returned to the prewar work on the meson energy spectrum.[105]

In autumn 1946 Rochester and Butler noted a cloud-chamber V-shaped track that Blackett became convinced showed a new decay process. By Butler's own account, Blackett cautioned against immediate publication of the discovery, delaying an announcement until a second event was observed in May 1947. While Butler emphasized Blackett's caution following the first photograph, others characterized Blackett's work as bold in drawing a radical conclusion on the basis of only two photographs.[106] Blackett took a leading role in writing a paper for *Nature,* which appeared under Butler's and Rochester's names alone, interpreting the V-shaped event as the result of decay of a heavy neutral particle, of mass approximately $1000m_e$.[107]

It is instructive to pause over Butler's recollections of Blackett's style as research director and as research author. Butler reports that, while Blackett clearly was in charge of research projects, he left day-to-day work to Butler and Rochester, calling in at the laboratory to discuss results or advise on technique. Pragmatic and flexible in his suggestions on instrument design and in his reaction to experimental results, Blackett became a perfectionist in the writing of a paper.

In the case of the strange tracks, Blackett offered every conceivable explanation of the V-track photographs until all but one had to be rejected. Numerous drafts of the papers were prepared and revised with attention to logical order of presentation. Blackett's preference was to compose the paper by beginning with first principles, but he accepted a more direct calculational approach preferred by Rochester and Butler.[108]

Like other classic experimental papers in the field of nuclear physics, the 1947 Rochester-Butler paper begins with a brief, but not exhaustive, description of apparatus and method. (Blackett often followed up his experimental papers with instrumental papers describing the theory and construction of the apparatus.) There is a strong statement of hard-won data:

> Among some fifty counter-controlled cloud-chamber photographs of penetrating showers which we have obtained during the past year . . . [t]here are two photographs containing forked tracks of a very striking character. These photographs have been selected from five thousand photographs taken in an effective time of operation of 1,500 hours.[109]

There follows a statement of conviction—"We believe, on the basis of the analysis below . . ."—followed by a laying out of possible alternative explanations, which are eliminated one by one. In short, this is a classic experimental paper, but one not bereft of theory—in this case the hypothesis of new elementary particles and their possible transformations.

As in Blackett's 1933 paper with Occhialini, the role of a theoretical physicist is acknowledged by the experimentalists. In 1933 it had been Dirac. In 1947 it was their colleague at Manchester, Léon Rosenfeld.

Following up on the paper on V-events, Blackett's group realized that a multiplication of V-events could be obtained at high-altitude observation. Since the large electromagnet in use at Manchester could not be transported uphill, a new magnet had to be built that could be broken down into loads suitable for lifting to the Jungfraujoch laboratory in Switzerland. All this was not completed until early 1951.

In the meantime, to his research group's dismay, Blackett received a letter from Carl Anderson reporting that the Caltech group had confirmed some thirty V-particle decays in a small mountain-top chamber. Just as with Anderson's work on the positron in the early 1930s, the Caltech photographs suffered from distortions that compromised the quality of the photographs in comparison to the ones that Blackett's groups achieved at the Pic du Midi and the Jungfraujoch in the early 1950s.[110] By 1953 the V-events were interpreted as four kinds of particles, comprising the neutral and charged kaons. Their study devolved increasingly away from high altitudes and cloud chambers to big accelerators and bubble chambers.[111]

One of the last great discoveries of the 1940s was the recognition at Bristol in 1947 by Cecil Powell of another component of cosmic radiations, a charged particle with mass approximately 270 times the mass of an electron. This work was accomplished using photographic emulsions rather than the cloud chamber. The emulsions were thicker and made with far more silver than ordinary film. They were stacked together and after exposure, usually at high altitude, individual films were mounted on glass plates. With this technique, nuclear interactions and the particles produced could be followed through several plates. The new particle discovered by Powell's group fit Yukawa's theory better than the mesotron, and it soon was confirmed to decay into a mesotron, or mu meson, and a neutrino.[112]

Craftsmanship, Phenomenology, and Fundamental Theory

As noted above, Keith Runcorn assisted Rochester and Butler in the investigations that discovered the V-track particles. Runcorn's name is synonymous in Britain with geophysics, however, not nuclear physics. A transition was beginning to occur in 1947 in Blackett's personal research program, a transition that the physicist Robert Marshak recalled in 1980 at a conference at Fermilab, although with the error of hindsight.

Marshak visited Blackett's Manchester physics laboratory in November 1947 where, Marshak said, he was briefed by Rochester and Butler on the V-particles. "By that time," Marshak continued, Blackett "had transferred his interests to the creation of the new field of paleomagnetism."[113] Marshak's statement is a little misleading since Blackett had no interest in 1947 in paleomagnetism. But that interest would come shortly as a result of Blackett's turn from nuclear physics and cosmic-ray physics to the physics of the earth's magnetism.

In Blackett's laboratory work in nuclear physics, from the 1920s through the 1940s, he consistently attributed the strength of experimental practice to the creative tension between theory and craft. In a 1933 essay, he characterized the experimentalist as a "Jack-of-all Trades"—a glass-blower, a mechanic, a carpenter, a photographer, an engineer, a mathematician. Blackett added that, as a physicist, the experimentalist "must be enough of a theorist to know what experiments are worth doing and enough of a craftsman to be able to do them."[114]

By the 1950s Blackett and other experimentalists freely employed the word "phenomenological" to describe the kind of physics that they did. The plethora of new particles identified from the 1930s to the 1950s eventually led to patterns that allowed particle physicists "to find order in the complex phenomena, and so be in a position to formulate phenomenological theories from which to make predictions about the detailed behaviour of some of the particles or, in some cases, to predict the existence of new ones."[115]

Extending the term "phenomenological" to an earlier period of physics, Blackett used the word to characterize Rutherford and Frederick Soddy's interpretation in the early 1900s of the observed exponential decay over time of radioactivity as the result of the spontaneous disintegration of atoms. "A quarter of a century elapsed," said Blackett in the Rutherford Memorial Lecture at McGill University in 1958, "before this brilliant phenomenological interpretation by Rutherford and Soddy was to receive a theoretical explanation in terms of wave mechanics," that is, a mathematically formulated explanation based in first principles.[116]

As Blackett saw it by the late 1950s, the methodology of radioactivity, nuclear physics, and particle physics had been one of increasing the precision of measurements of individual events and increasing the number of events studied, paying attention all the while to unexpected effects and anything that might turn up. His account of the history of nuclear physics at the Rutherford Memorial Lecture was an account of one unexpected discovery after another, a narrative account punctuated by warnings to his audience and his readers that attractive experiments should not be ruled out because theories predict their failure. Nor, Blackett suggested, should the apparent outlandishness of a theory's conclusions force the theorist to alter an attractive theory if plausible tests seem possible.[117] These were norms that Blackett applied in his own work in nuclear physics and, as we shall see in the next chapters, in other fields of physics as well.

What is striking in Blackett's approach to nuclear physics is the tension between his commitment to experimental craft, based in exploratory theories and precision engineering, and his commitment to the deep meaning of fundamentalist principles and "talking about the universe." Phenomenology put him in the camp of Anderson; fundamentalism compelled him to contend with the work of Heisenberg, Dirac, and Rosenfeld. In short, Blackett's phenomenology in nuclear physics by no means defined his vision of all that was possible in physics.

New cadets waiting for the ferry to the Isle of Wight and the Royal Naval College, Osborne. Twelve-year-old Blackett, center right, facing camera, September 1910. Blackett Family Papers. Courtesy of Giovanna Blackett Bloor.

Blackett with Costanza (Pat) Bayon around the time of their marriage, 1924. Blackett Family Papers. Courtesy of Giovanna Blackett Bloor.

The ejection of protons from nitrogen nuclei by fast alpha-particles. The short, somewhat bent, arms are the tracks of the oxygen nucleus of mass 17 and atomic number 8. This famous set of photographs first appeared in Blackett's article in *Proceedings of the Royal Society of London* (1925).

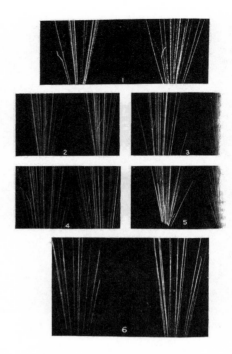

Blackett on holiday, 1929. Blackett Family Papers. Courtesy of Giovanna Blackett Bloor.

Blackett, 1932. Photograph by Lettice Ramsey, Cambridge. Courtesy of The Royal Society. Used by permission of Jane Ramsey Burch and Giovanna Blackett Bloor.

Pencil drawing of Giuseppe Occhialini (left) and Blackett as polar explorers, with Ernest Rutherford as walrus. Blackett Family Papers. Courtesy of Giovanna Blackett Bloor.

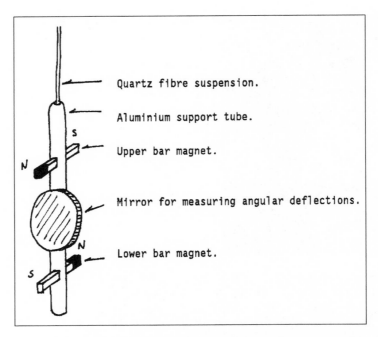

Schematic design of the astatic magnetometer, made by M. Genevey, Danish Meteorological Institute. From Fritz Primdahl, "A Pedestrian's Approach to Magnetic Cleanliness," DRI 2-90, Danish Space Research Institute, 1990.

Blackett's magnetometer at Jodrell Bank, for measuring the magnetic field of a static body. This photograph appeared in *Philosophical Transactions of the Royal Society* (1952). Blackett Papers, Royal Society Library. © The Royal Society.

Giovanna Blackett (left), Blackett, and Costanza Blackett, in November 1948, after learning of the Nobel Prize award. Blackett Family Papers. Courtesy of Giovanna Blackett Bloor.

Blackett and Homi Bhabha, British Association Meeting, Dublin, 1957, where Blackett delivered his controversial Presidential Address on aiding Third World development of science and technology. Blackett Family Papers. Courtesy of Giovanna Blackett Bloor.

Her Majesty Queen
Elizabeth II and
Blackett at the
official opening of
the Royal Society
by the Queen, 22
January 1968,
when the Society
moved from
Burlington House
to Carlton House
Terrace. Blackett
Family Papers.
Courtesy of
Giovanna Blackett
Bloor.

Blackett, 1963. Photograph by Michael Peto, courtesy of University of
Dundee Archive Services. Blackett Family Papers. Courtesy of
Giovanna Blackett Bloor.

3

Corridors of Power: Operational Research and Atomic Weapons, 1936–1962

In his novel *Corridors of Power* (1964), one of C. P. Snow's main characters is the physicist "Francis Getliffe" who, as Snow described him,

> had thought more effectively about military-scientific strategy than anyone had. . . . [H]e had not long before screwed himself up to write a pamphlet. In it he had said that there was no military rationale behind the nuclear policy. This analysis got him into trouble, mostly in America, but also in England. In some Right-thinking circles, it had seemed not only preposterous, but also heretical, and something like wicked.[1]

The Getliffe character is largely modeled on Blackett.[2] Lord Snow knew Blackett well. During the late 1920s and early 1930s their paths frequently crossed in Cambridge where Blackett was working in Ernest Rutherford's Cavendish Laboratory and Snow was engaged in molecular spectroscopy while a Fellow at Christ's College.[3] In the war years and afterwards, they met in government ministries in London, where Snow was chief of scientific personnel for the Ministry of Labour. In the 1950s they were part of the dinner group of scientists and politicians who met to advise Hugh Gaitskell and Harold Wilson on science policy for the Labour party. Thus Snow knew precisely Blackett's position on nuclear policy, as well as the outrage it provoked in the United States and the United Kingdom. Snow further understood the roots of Blackett's views in his personal experiences in operational research during World War II.[4]

Historians have analyzed the attitudes of American scientists toward the first military use of the atomic bomb in the war against Japan, as well as the efforts of American scientists during 1945 to 1947 to ensure civilian control over an atomic energy commission and to set up international control of atomic energy research and development. Few American scientists spoke out publicly against the expansion of the American nuclear arsenal immediately after the war. Indeed, opposition became legally risky after President Truman issued the "Loyalty Order" for federal employees in March 1947, an order soon copied by state legislatures.[5]

There was little opposition, too, among British scientists to the development of an atomic arsenal in the United Kingdom. Exceptions were Kathleen Lonsdale and Lionel Penrose, both Quakers, Nevill Mott, and left-wing scientists, including J. D. Bernal, E. H. S. Burhop, Cecil F. Powell, and Blackett, all officers of the allegedly communist-infiltrated Association of Scientific Workers.[6] Among these, Blackett was the most outspoken and the most vilified of British scientists who opposed American and British nuclear policies from the mid-1940s to around 1960. One of the few comparable cases is that of the chemist Linus Pauling in the United States who campaigned publicly in the 1950s and 1960s against testing of nuclear weapons and against war. Similarly, Werner Heisenberg and seventeen other German scientists who signed the "Göttingen Manifesto" in 1958 suffered rebukes from Chancellor Konrad Adenauer and other political leaders for opposing the government's decision to cooperate with NATO in equipping the West German army with tactical nuclear weapons.[7]

Neither communist nor pacifist, Blackett had no argument with war. Why did Blackett the real physicist, like Getliffe the fictional physicist, take an outspoken and unpopular political position on matters of nuclear policy immediately following the Second World War? The answer lies largely in his founding role in the science of operational research (OR) within branches of the military services during the Second World War and his experiences in Whitehall in studying and predicting outcomes of military strategy during that period. The OR work is the subject of the first sections of this chapter, including Blackett's role in the development of radar defense of British coastlines and sea-lanes and his pioneering work in laying out principles of operational research. Indeed, OR was to become a methodological pillar in what historians have called "a revolution in management science, risk assessment and military planning" in the twentieth century.[8]

Blackett's postwar opposition to Cold War policy on nuclear weapons and total war is examined in the later sections of this chapter. The opposition was based partly in his OR work, partly in his Navy background, and partly in his political and moral points of view. The experiences of Blackett in his public campaign against atomic weapons illustrate the risks to a physicist of writing about a subject other than physics, as well as the circumstances that might compel one to do so. Many twentieth-century scientists faced the choices of whether to do scientific work in support of war and whether to enter the forum of public debate. Blackett chose both these paths.

Radar and Uranium: The Tizard and MAUD Committees

Just over a year after Blackett moved in late 1933 from the Cavendish Laboratory to Birkbeck College in London, Henry T. Tizard enlisted Blackett to advise the Air Ministry on priorities for national defense. In late 1934 the engineer Harry E. Wimperis, who was the Air Ministry's Director of Scientific Research, and meteorologist Albert Percival Rowe were authorized to establish a Committee for the Scientific Survey of Air Defence. In general, British military thinking after the war of 1914–1918 abhorred any prospect of ground or trench warfare in the future. Instead, Sir Hugh Trenchard, Chief of Air Staff, and Charles Portal, who would be Chief of Air Staff during World War II, embraced an offensive bombing doctrine. Thus, by inverse reasoning, they recognized that defense against enemy bombers had to be a matter of priority.[9]

What became known as the Tizard Committee, initially five members, first met in January 1935. In addition to Tizard, Wimperis, Rowe, and Blackett, the Committee included Archibald Vivian Hill, a physiologist and Nobel laureate who had studied air defense problems during the previous war. Tizard, whose scientific education had included a stint with the physical chemist Walther Nernst in Berlin, was the son of a Navy captain who had been navigator to the Challenger expedition. A lecturer in natural sciences at Oxford when the war broke out in August 1914, Tizard became a pilot in the Royal Flying Corps and took charge of test flying after the war for the Air Ministry.[10] In 1935 he was Rector of Imperial College of London University.

Following his Committee's initial discussions, Tizard asked Robert Watson-Watt, who was superintendent of the National Physical Laboratory's Radio Research Department, about the feasibility of using radio waves as a kind of "death-ray" to damage enemy aircraft. Instead, Watson-Watt's staff, led by A. F. Wilkins, proposed that radio waves could be used to detect and locate aircraft. In Great Britain this technology took the name RDF (radio-direction finding), although the name eventually gave way to the American term radar (*radio detection and ranging*), which was under study in the Naval Research Laboratory and the Army's Signal Corps.[11] British development of radar began first at Orfordness in spring 1935 and then at Bawdsey Manor a few miles away on the English coast, near the River Deben. Tizard directed a series of trials at a fighter station at Biggin Hill, located outside London under air routes connecting the London area to European destinations. Prototype radar instruments tracked mock attack bombers, and information systems were set up to coordinate radar and observer stations, filtering of information, and plotting of results on large table maps. The young engineer Eric C. Williams worked with a team to identify information bottlenecks in the system, and Rowe began referring to this group as the "operational research section."[12]

In the summer of 1939, following a discussion between Tizard and Cavendish Laboratory physicist John Cockcroft in the club rooms of the Athenaeum in London, it was agreed that Cockcroft would approach physicists, who would be sworn to secrecy, to spend a week or two that summer on the south coast of England in order to see how the radar systems worked. The Australian-born Cavendish physicist Mark Oliphant was among those who visited the coast to become familiar with the installations. When war was declared in September 1939, the Royal Air Force (RAF) took over the radar chains along the east and southeast coasts.[13] When war broke out, the Germans had a radar system of great accuracy but shorter range than that of the British. What the Germans did not have was a method of operational use as efficient as the British one.[14]

Meanwhile the original Tizard Committee briefly fell apart, with Blackett and Hill resigning in August 1936, but returning in a few weeks. Following the first successful demonstration of radar at Orfordness, Winston Churchill had pressured the Air Ministry to add his scientific consultant and personal friend Frederick A. Lindemann to the Committee in July 1935. At this time Churchill was a member of Prime Minister Stanley Baldwin's Committee of Imperial Defence on Air-Defence Research, the so-called Swinton Committee, to which the Tizard

Committee was a subcommittee.[15] Lindemann, professor of physics at Oxford University, was Churchill's trusted advisor, and he would remain so after Prime Minister Neville Chamberlain appointed Churchill to his former post in charge of the Admiralty when Britain declared war on Germany on 3 September 1939. Churchill took for himself the leadership of the Ministry of Defence when he became Prime Minister in May 1940, and engineered a formal position for Lindemann in the government as Paymaster-General in late 1942.[16]

Twelve years younger than Churchill, Lindemann had made his reputation in low-temperature physics. Born in Baden-Baden, where his American-born mother was taking a cure, he was educated initially in Britain, where his family lived, and then went to Germany to complete his education at the high school and university levels. He took his Ph.D. in Berlin with Nernst. Lindemann's father was an Alsatian-born, naturalized British subject, but Lindemann was assumed by many who did not know him to be German. Some also assumed him to be Jewish. During the war of 1914–1918 he was one of a small group of scientists, George P. Thomson among them, who undertook aircraft research, including experimental flying, at the Royal Aircraft Factory (Establishment) at Farnborough. In 1919 Lindemann became Professor of Experimental Philosophy and Director of the Clarendon Laboratory at Oxford. Although he did little work in physics after 1924, the Clarendon became an increasingly important laboratory, with great strength in low-temperature physics after the arrival of German emigrés in the 1930s, including Francis Simon. Despite Churchill's considerable confidence in him, Lindemann viewed himself as a man with few friends. Even those friends he had characterized him as cynical, caustic, and arrogant, politically identified with a wealthy, snobbish, and illiberal right. Nor was he regarded highly as a physicist by his colleagues, and Rutherford was said to loathe him.[17]

Meeting with the Tizard Committee during 1935–1936, Lindemann argued that the Committee's highest priority should be given to the detection of night aircraft by infrared radiation, a project on which Reginald Victor Jones, who took his doctorate at Oxford in 1934, began working at the Clarendon in January 1936. Lindemann also argued for the dropping of parachute-carrying bombs in front of enemy night bombers and, in comparison, gave lower priority to radar. Disputes between Lindemann and other Committee members became so rancorous that on one occasion the secretaries were asked to leave the room. Resentment also was high in the Committee against Lindemann for lining up Watson-Watt to criticize their pace of deliberations to Churchill.[18] Following Blackett's and Hill's resignations, Lord Swinton dissolved the group and then reappointed the original Committee in autumn 1936, without Lindemann, adding the physicist Edward V. Appleton and, later, Thomas Ralph Merton. The Tizard Committee amalgamated with a new Committee for the Scientific Survey of Air Offence, which Tizard headed, becoming the Committee for the Scientific Survey of Air Warfare in October 1939.[19]

During 1937 and 1938 members of the Tizard Committee assessed a large number of projects, discussing defense problems with air marshals, pilot officers, and laboratory scientists. Another source of contention with Lindemann, which lasted into the war years, emerged from a suggestion that Jones made to Lindemann in 1937 for development of thin metal foil strips (the "Window") as a device to confuse enemy radar. By early 1942 the weapon was ready to be deployed when D. A. Jackson, a radar officer at Fighter Command, prevailed on Lindemann ("the Prof") to hold up implementation because there was evidence that the Germans might in turn use it to devastate British radar defense. British bomber crews received authorization to release the aluminum strips in their attack on Hamburg in July 1943, successfully confusing German searchlights and radar while destroying the city.[20] By then Blackett, Tizard, and Lindemann were again at loggerheads, this time over air force bombing strategy, as discussed in the next section of this chapter.

At the outbreak of war in September 1939, it became a concern that facilities for radar research and development were vulnerable to German air attack on the Suffolk coast. Most scientists and engineers working on ground radar were moved from Bawdsey to Dundee, while those designing airborne radar were sent to South Wales.[21] In May 1940 the war in western Europe began, with the Germans invading Norway and Denmark, followed by the Netherlands, Belgium, and Luxembourg. Between 26 May and 3 June 1940, over 224,000 British troops, out of a total of 400,000 when the campaign began, were evacuated from France, along with 142,000 French troops. Paris fell on 14 June 1940. The first attacks against Britain by the German Luftwaffe began in July, with the main attack coming in August 1940, mostly in southeast England. Hitler's "Operation Sealion" was suspended in mid-September, after unsustainable losses of German planes. The winter of 1940–1941 brought night attacks on British cities. The Germans also turned their attention to blockading Britain by submarine, with German sinkings of ships reaching a monthly average in April 1941 of 200,000 tons.[22]

The need for airborne radar was pressing. Early radar sets performed similarly to the old sound-ranging equipment they replaced, with precision limited by the low-frequency range (longer wavelengths) that were produced by existing vacuum tubes. The research group at St. Athan in South Wales, which soon moved to locations near Swanage, concentrated on airborne radar. Eddie Bowen headed it, with physicists Alan Hodgkin and Bernard Lovell among the scientists working in the group. The first airborne radar to achieve operational success was the 1½-meter ASV sets that enabled airplanes to detect ships, but Bowen concentrated on developing a radar that would operate at 5–10 centimeters. However, as German bombing of England began, worries increased that radar research facilities might not be able to operate effectively.[23]

In November 1939 Tizard sent Hill to Washington, D.C., to discuss getting scientific help on defense. Through the offices of Lord Lothian, the British ambassador to the United States, President Roosevelt became convinced of the importance of scientific interchanges. One factor likely in Roosevelt's thinking was the letter delivered to him by his friend Alexander Sachs and written by Albert Einstein, warning that German scientists could develop a new kind of bomb using uranium.

In the summer of 1940 a National Defense Research Committee (NDRC) was established in the United States under the leadership of Vannevar Bush, previously a professor of power transmission at MIT and President of the Carnegie Institution in Washington. The NDRC included James B. Conant, chemist and the president of Harvard University; Karl T. Compton, physicist and the President of MIT; Frank B. Jewett, Director of Bell Laboratories and President of the National Academy of Sciences; and Richard C. Tolman, a physical chemist from Caltech. The Committee's mandate was to "correlate and support scientific research on the mechanisms and devices of warfare, except those relating to problems of flight," by entering into contracts with individuals and institutions both private and public.[24]

In September 1940, with bombs raining down on London, Tizard arrived in Washington, accompanied by Cockcroft and Bowen among others, to meet with the NDRC. The British scientists brought with them a black box containing samples, blueprints, and reports on nearly all important new British war devices. As Blackett later summarized in his Tizard Memorial Lecture, the information covered "radar, fire control, underwater detection, aircraft turrets, Whittle's jet engine, and, above all, a sample 9.1 centimeter resonant cavity magnetron."[25] The device could produce microwave pulses of wavelength below 10 centimeters and peak powers of 10 kilowatts. Bush and the NDRC immediately set up the Radiation Laboratory for microwave research at MIT. On 13 November Cockroft wrote Hodgkin, "We have done our set job—to get the US moving. . . . [D]elivery of a large amount of gear for the first five experimental 10 centimetre airborne sets is expected by 23 November."[26] Following his reelection in November, Roosevelt announced that 50 percent of American armament production was being made available to Britain. Negotiations were completed for supplying four-engined "Flying Fortress" bombers, as well as cargo ships, to Britain.[27]

After wartime mobilization in Great Britain, the Tizard Committee ceased meeting, and its members were incorporated into other groups. In addition to his duties at the University of Manchester, Blackett was dividing his time among the new Ministry of Supply RDF (Radar) Applications Committee, the Royal Aircraft Establishment at Farnborough, and the MAUD Committee. The MAUD Committee was set up in the spring of 1940, in response to Tizard's receipt of calculations by Otto Robert Frisch and Rudolf Peierls on a "super-bomb." Chaired by the physicist George Thomson, the Committee's charge was to advise the British government on the feasibility of Britain's developing a fission bomb.[28] The origin of the name of the Committee was somewhat ambiguous. Some claimed it to be a contraction designating its role as the Ministry of Aircraft Production *U*ranium *D*evelopment Committee, while others said the name was a reference to a message from Niels and Margherita Bohr in April 1940 mentioning Cockcroft and "Maud Ray, Kent." Since Bohr sent the message at the time of the German invasion of Denmark, it was thought that "Maud Ray, Kent" might be a code word. In fact, Maud turned out to be the former governess of Bohr's children and living in Kent.[29]

Frisch, a nephew of Lise Meitner's, was a refugee, like Meitner, in 1938, with Meitner in Stockholm and Frisch in Copenhagen. Following Otto Hahn and Fritz Strassmann's observation in Berlin in December 1938 of the apparent splitting of the uranium nucleus by slow neutrons,

Meitner and Frisch worked out a physical theory of nuclear fission.[30] Carrying their results to the United States in early 1939, Niels Bohr figured out in collaboration with John A. Wheeler at Princeton that it is a rare isotope (0.7 percent) of uranium (uranium 235), and not the common uranium 238, that is fissionable by slow neutrons. Their calculation suggested a huge difficulty in using uranium to construct either an energy source or an explosive weapon. By the end of 1939, some 100 papers on fission had appeared in western Europe and the United States, 40 percent of them in the United States, 25 percent in France, 15 percent in Germany, and 10 percent in Great Britain. [31]

Frédéric Joliot's laboratory in Paris was the leading research center on uranium fission in late 1939. When the Germans advanced on Paris in 1940, Joliot arranged for Hans von Halban and Lew Kowarski to smuggle to England the Parisian stocks of heavy water used in controlling fission reactions. Frisch and Peierls, both now in England and classified as "enemy aliens," collaborated at the University of Birmingham, coming to the astonishing calculation that the minimum amount of the fissionable isotope of uranium (U-235) required for a self-sustaining chain reaction was only ten kilograms, considerably lower than the figure of thirteen tons calculated by Francis Perrin, or the figure of several tons first calculated by Peierls.

The MAUD Committee included James Chadwick (who had left Cambridge for a chair of physics at the University of Liverpool in 1935), Oliphant, Cockcroft, Blackett, and P. B. Moon, with a technical subcommittee of foreign emigrés including von Halban, Kowarski, Frisch, and Peierls. The British group gained confidence that gaseous diffusion could be used to separate U-235 from U-238 in natural uranium compounds. They also knew of the report by Berkeley physicists Edwin McMillan and Philip Abelson that accelerated neutrons can transform U-238 into fissionable plutonium. By July 1941 the majority of MAUD Committee members had reached the conclusion that there was a good chance that a uranium bomb, with an explosive capacity of 1,800 tons of TNT, could be produced before the war was over. Lindemann supported the MAUD Committee's conclusion in a minute to the Prime Minister, and at the end of August 1941 Churchill authorized manufacture of the new bomb, which was subsequently delegated to a Directorate of Tube Alloys in the Ministry of Supply, under the administration of Sir John Anderson, who had been Home Secretary from 1939 to 1940 and would become Chancellor of the Exchequer in 1943. A draft of the MAUD Committee report was transmitted to Bush and Conant at the NDRC.[32]

Blackett was the single member of the Maud Committee who dissented from the view that a British bomb could be produced by 1943 at a cost of £5 million. He did not believe that such a large project could be carried out in wartime in Britain, and he recommended that the project be discussed with the Americans.[33] In October 1941 Roosevelt offered Churchill joint American collaboration on atomic development, but received no response. The American Uranium Committee forged ahead, meeting on 6 December 1941 to organize a systematic plan in which Harold Urey would develop gaseous diffusion at Columbia University; Ernest Lawrence would undertake electromagnetic separation of uranium isotopes at Berkeley; Eger V. Murphree, the director of research for Standard Oil of New Jersey, would supervise centrifuge development; and Arthur Holly Compton would lead theoretical studies and design of both uranium and plutonium bombs at the University of Chicago. The next day, the Japanese attack of 7 December 1941 on the American naval installation at Pearl Harbor precipitated US entry into both the European and Asian wars.

In June 1942 Roosevelt and Churchill discussed Anglo-American cooperation on construction of the bomb in language of an "equal partnership." In August 1943 an agreement was signed between Britain, the United States, and Canada on the development of atomic energy, with Lindemann a representative on the British side. In fact, British and emigré scientists who embarked for America from Tube Alloys were excluded from access to information that they freely enjoyed in Britain, and the Quebec agreement simply legitimated the absorption of British physicists into American teams. This result would have repercussions in Blackett's and other British responses to US policies on atomic weapons both during and after the war.[34] By 1943 Blackett was arguing against the recruitment of scientists to work on the "Manhattan Project," and he increasingly voiced the opinion that the British government had become a puppet of the Americans.[35] The only physicist to walk out of the Manhattan Project, when it became clear in November 1944 that the Germans had not built a uranium bomb, was Joseph Rotblat, one of the Central European emigré physicists who had worked in Liverpool with Chadwick before they both departed for Los Alamos in 1943.[36]

Wartime Operational Research:
A New Tool for Military Strategy

At the outbreak of the war, Blackett joined the instrument section of the Royal Aircraft Establishment where he worked on the design of the Mark XIV bombsight, which eliminated the need for a level bombing run at the time of bomb release. Flight logs for 1940 list Blackett as flying in Wellingtons, Blenheims, Oxfords, Magisters, and Hampdens on experiments with bombsights, static vents, electrical pitch indicators, sextants, and compasses.[37] Blackett also studied magnetic mines, investigating with Evan J. Williams how to trigger magnetic depth charges to explode when passing under a U-boat. Radar continued to occupy him. When Hodgkin arrived at Farnborough in 1939 in a temporary unpaid post in aviation medicine (investigating oxygen supply to pilots at high altitude and nitrogen bubbles in pilots' blood), Blackett and Hill found Hodgkin a position in radar at Biggin Hill.[38]

It was Hill who suggested to Anti-Aircraft Command's top officer, Army General Sir Frederick Pile, that Blackett should be brought into the AAC as scientific counsel. Pile was concerned about failures in gun-laying radar sets, which appeared to be due to problems of linkage between incoming radar data and control of the guns. Blackett recruited a small team of scientists into his Anti-Aircraft Command Research Group, which the Army officers began referring to as "Blackett's Circus." Its members were diverse in background, including three physiologists (one of them Hill's son D. K. Hill), two mathematical physicists, one astrophysicist, one surveyor, one general physicist, two mathematicians, and an Army officer.[39] Blackett later remembered "fire-watching on the roof of a block of flats in Westminster in September 1940, on the evening of the day the 'blitz' began. We were watching the glow from the burning East London docks, and bombs were falling on central London. A young bomber pilot by me said: 'I can hardly bear to wait till we can do it back to them.'[40]

Thanks to research and implementation already carried out before the war, Britain had an operational early-warning radar system around its east and south coasts, as well as fighter squadrons and antiaircraft guns to intercept German bombers by using radar plots. Blackett's group worked out methods of plotting radar data and predicting future enemy positions on the basis of pencil and paper, range, and fuse tables. They improved design of plotting machines and the training methods for predictor crews.

By the spring of 1941 both the Germans and the British increasingly concentrated on shipping lanes in the Atlantic and along coastlines. In March 1941 Air Marshal Sir Philip Joubert de la Ferté engineered Blackett's transfer to Coastal Command in the RAF, breaking the news to Pile that Blackett had been lured away from "Ack-Ack." Blackett became Joubert's personal scientific advisor and assembled a small group at Coastal Command's headquarters at Northwood, Middlesex. Members included Evan J. Williams, C. H. Waddington, J. C. Kendrew, and J. Henry C. Whitehead. The group became known as the Operational Research Section. Oliphant succeeded Blackett as scientific counsel to Pile.[41] Air Marshal Sir John Slessor later said: "A few years ago it would never have occurred to me—or I think to any officer of any fighting service—that what the RAF soon came to call a 'Boffin,' a gentleman in grey flannel bags, whose occupation in life had previously been something markedly unmilitary such as biology or physiology, would be able to teach us a great deal about our business. Yet so it was."[42] In the Navy "boffin had been an unkind word for officers over forty."[43]

One of the first problems studied in Coastal Command was the setting of depth charges dropped by airplanes when a U-boat was spotted. After Evan Williams was recruited from Farnborough to work on data, he concluded that the existing method of attack failed to sink U-boats when they dived deeply because of low bombing accuracy, and the method failed to sink U-boats on the surface due to too-deep depth settings. After implementation of a change in the depth setting, Blackett learned that "captured German U-boat crews thought that we had introduced a new and much more powerful explosive. Actually we had only turned a depth-setting adjuster from the 100-foot to the 25-foot mark. There can be few cases where such a great operational gain had been obtained by such a small and simple change of tactics."[44] The kill rate rose from 2 or 3 percent in 1941 to 40 percent in 1944.[45]

Another relatively simple change was Blackett's persuading Coastal Command to paint antisubmarine aircraft white instead of black, after data suggested that, while bomber aircraft were painted black in order to reflect as little light as possible from searchlights, in Coastal Command operations the aircraft were easily spotted by submarines because they were dark objects against a light sky. Blackett's group proved the point by comparing photographs of crows and seagulls against different skies and correctly estimated an increase of 30 percent in sinkings as a result of the paint job.[46]

A less simple recommendation to Coastal Command was based in an application of probability theory to defense of shipping lanes west of Ireland, where Coastal Command had positioned ten fighters. The tactical question was whether to fly the fighters only when all ten were serviceable, so that they could "sweep clean" the German area of operation. What Blackett recognized as fallacious reasoning was the argument that when ten aircraft were flown, the whole area was swept clean so that the chance of sighting the enemy was 100 percent, or "certain," but that when any fewer number of fighters was flown, then the enemy might not be sighted at all. The probability that German aircraft would be in the area on the one day that all ten fighters were up, as well as the probability of success when fewer fighters fly every day, can be calculated by using the mathematics of a Poisson distribution. Eventually the argument for success by summing small probabilities won against the argument for gambling on an occasional certainty. Whatever fighters were available were flown every day.[47]

In December 1941 Blackett was asked to explain the methods that he was using in operational research to the Advisory Committee of Sir Charles Wright, Director of Scientific Research at the Admiralty. Scientific members of the Committee included physicists Appleton and Ralph Fowler. Blackett's presentation and his memorandum "Scientists at the Operational Level" so impressed the Admiralty that in January 1942, after nine months with Coastal Command, he was asked to transfer to the Admiralty, leaving his Coastal Command group in the charge of Williams and, later, Waddington.[48] As Director of Naval Operational Research, Blackett continued to work closely with Coastal Command.

Blackett's 1941 memorandum and a second longer report of 1943, "A Note on Certain Aspects of the Methodology of Operational Research," circulated widely in Britain and the United States. Wartime memoranda in the US National Archives include sections from Blackett's reports without attribution.[49] Indeed, in his review of the postwar book *Methods of Operational Research* by Philip M. Morse and George E. Kimball, Blackett commented that "it is somewhat disconcerting to find . . . paragraphs taken almost verbatim, and without inverted commas, from one's own writing on the subject!"[50] Conant, H. P. Robertson of Princeton, and John Burchard of MIT were among American scientists who visited London in late 1940 and 1941, familiarizing themselves with operational research and its organization. Contacts were made with Desmond Bernal and Solly Zuckerman, who were doing OR work on blast damage. Robertson became deeply interested in the methods being developed by Blackett. As a result, Shirley Quimby of Columbia University was stationed in London as a liaison for the Americans, and the first US units in operational research were set up in 1942, one of them at MIT including Morse, Kimball, Francis Bitter, and John von Neumann.[51]

In Blackett's initial writings on operational research, he defined its object as the analysis of data in order to give useful advice. The data is what is found in an operational room: signals, track charts, combat reports, meteorological information, and so on. Deducing conclusions from the data often requires the highest scientific judgment and, in particular, a grasp of fluctuation phenomena, such as those following a Poisson distribution. While a commonsense view may often be the correct one, numerical proof gives added confidence to the tactics employed. Cooperation between Controllers and the OR staff can sometimes arrange operations in order to clarify doubtful points, as in the relative merits of different forms of antisubmarine sweeps by aircraft. New weapons should not automatically be assumed to be superior to old ones, but the merits of making a change should be calculated through operational research. OR staff must be in close proximity to their Command, and the OR Director must be directly responsible to the Commander-in-Chief.[52]

In practice, as in his more thorough document of 1943, Blackett distinguished different methods to use in all main fields of operational research, including the study of weapons, the study of tactics, and the study of strategy. One method is *a priori,* that is, finding general solutions to rather arbitrarily simplified problems. The more commonsense procedure is a variational method, in which the attempt is made to find, both by experimental and analytical methods, how a real operation would be altered if certain of the variables are altered, for example, tactics or weapons. Care must be exercised in choosing the order of study of a problem. First, changes of tactics should be investigated and then effects of improved weapons, not the other way round. Statistical methods, theoretical methods, and a mixture of these two methods are possibilities of procedure, depending on the quantity and diversity of available operational data.[53]

The first priority for Blackett in applying OR principles at the Admiralty was the alarming increase in U-boat sinkings of Allied merchant shipping, which reached 600,000 tons a month in the summer of 1942. German submarines were based in the Bay of Biscay, along the western coasts of southern France and northern Spain, submerging by day and surfacing at night to recharge their batteries as they moved about the Atlantic. One aspect of the research problem was analysis of the speed and size of convoys of Allied merchant ships, escort vessels, and air escorts in relation to numbers of ships lost. A surprising result of statistical analysis of data from the previous two years was that larger convoys of more than forty ships were safer than smaller ones, contrary to Navy doctrine. From the spring of 1943, the size of convoys gradually was increased.[54]

When Blackett arrived at the Admiralty, British aircraft were detecting U-boats using 1.5-meter radar, which only was effective for daytime attacks. In June 1942 a powerful searchlight was mounted in a retractable turret in Coastal Command Wellington aircraft, so that the light could be switched on and the final depth-charge attack carried out visually. This innovation increased British effectiveness until early 1943 when the Germans began fitting U-boats with a detector for the 1.5-meter transmissions.[55] About this time, American-made 10-centimeter microwave radar sets were just becoming available, which could be allocated to Coastal Command for the U-boat campaign, as well as to Air Staff for bombing in Germany.

The need for more accurate radar over Germany was a pressing concern of Bomber Command by late 1940 after Lindemann's staff established from photographs that RAF bombing was only a third or a quarter as accurate as anyone had thought, including returning combat pilots. The Butt Report of August 1941 concluded that only one-third of attacking aircraft got within five miles of their German targets. Lovell suggested that a 9-centimeter set with a radial scan might be able to provide a map on which one could see towns and big rivers. Lindemann pushed hard for such a low-centimeter radar device, known as H2S, which would give the bomber's navigator a radar picture of the ground over which he was flying.[56]

The concern that British bombers were ineffective in targeting railroads, factories, and other precise sites in Germany, along with belief that bombing German cities would bring Germans to their knees, precipitated Lindemann's inquiry into the effects of German bombing on Hull and Birmingham. Bernal and Zuckerman headed a survey, ongoing in late 1941 and completed in April 1942, and based in the Ministry of Home Security at the Princes Risborough laboratory. There were two teams of about forty workers each that investigated all details of citizen reactions, "down to the number of pints drunk and aspirins bought."[57] They concluded that bombing on Birmingham had only a small effect on production, quite outweighed by the positive effect of higher piece rates, so that more workers actually came into the city during the period of bombing than left the city, although in Hull there was a considerable exodus. There was no evidence of a breakdown of morale in either city. To Bernal's consternation, Lindemann's response was that the study might have proved that German bombing of Birmingham had little effect, but much heavier British bombing of German cities would produce a decisive result.[58]

In spring 1942 Churchill was intent upon Bomber Command's doing all that was possible to help the hard-pressed Soviet armies at Stalingrad. He wanted a report on the probable effect on Germany of the British bombing offensive in the next eighteen months. In late March Lindemann responded with a memorandum in which it was calculated, on the basis of damage in Birmingham and Hull, that 10,000 heavy bombers blitzing German cities with populations over 100,000 would destroy the homes of one-third of the German population by mid-1943. This, it was argued, would "break the spirit of the people."[59]

Blackett and Tizard each were asked their views on Lindemann's memorandum in their respective capacities as Director of Operational Research in the Admiralty and Chief Scientific Advisor to the Chief of the Air Staff. Tizard estimated that Lindemann's figures were five times too high, and Blackett estimated six times too high.[60] Indeed, Blackett and Tizard had long held severe doubts and suspicions of the bombing policy in general. An unsigned memorandum in Blackett's papers, dated 15 August 1941, written either by Blackett or Tizard, addresses the effects of bombing in Germany, noting by comparison the failure of Japanese bombing to defeat the Chinese and the rebounding of morale in British cities following German bombing. "What we want to hit is the

morale of the High Command . . . by the destruction of material resources . . . warships and merchant ships in the Channel, the North Sea,
the Atlantic and the Mediterranean."[61] Alarmed by discussions with an
RAF Group Captain and a Wing Commander, Blackett noted that they
seemed to think the bombing offensive against Germany was the only
decisive operation available. "They seem to envisage a . . . very greatly
increased fraction of bombs finding the target, e.g. up to 90% instead of
the present 10–15%."[62]

In Blackett's view, the civilian bombing policy, which was decided in
February 1942 and continued with increased fury after the spring, was
ineffective from the analysis of operational research—what he called "in-
offensive" in a memorandum of 8 April 1942 to First Sea Lord J. H.
Godfrey.[63] The bomber strategy was a "very ineffective offensive against
enemy production and civilians" in comparison to a bomber campaign
that could be a "potentially decisive offensive against one of the enemy's
strongest fighting units, the U-Boat fleet."[64] Blackett's opinions were la-
beled "defeatist" in some circles in the Air Ministry. Friends bitterly
joked that anyone who added two and two to get four was said not to be
trusted and to be hobnobbing with Tizard and Blackett.[65]

Blackett was appalled ethically by the whole bombing strategy, which,
rooted in failures to pinpoint and hit industrial and military targets, was
at best "a technically debased form of the original conception."[66]

> So far as I know it was the first time that a modern nation had deliber-
> ately planned a major military campaign against the enemy's civilian
> population rather than against his Armed Forces. During my youth in
> the Navy in World War I such an operation would have been incon-
> ceivable. . . . [Lindemann] even suggested that the building up of
> strong land Forces for the projected invasion of France was wrong.
> Never have I encountered such fanatical belief in the efficacy of bomb-
> ing.[67]

Much to Blackett's dismay, Sir Arthur Harris, Chief of Air Staff, argued
that the only relevant restriction in international law against bombing
was an agreement during the Franco-Prussian War of 1870 prohibiting
the dropping of explosive devices from dirigibles. Harris, who became
known as "Bomber Harris," was unremitting in following a plan of successive devastating strikes against German cities. Churchill, who some-

times expressed scruples, consoled doubters with the view that the Germans "who have loosed these horrors upon mankind will now in their homes and persons feel the shattering strokes of just retribution."[68]

As U-boats, fitted with 1.5-meter radar-detection devices, were an increasing menace in early 1943, Blackett prepared a paper for the Anti-U-Boat Committee, which met fortnightly at No. 10 Downing Street under the chairmanship of the Prime Minister. Aware that new, highly accurate American 10-centimeter radar sets would soon be arriving for aircraft and that they could be adapted for the needs of either Coastal Command or Bomber Command, Blackett argued that the majority of new sets should be transferred to Coastal Command, along with 190 heavy bombers to give Coastal Command a strength of 260 heavy aircraft.[69]

Blackett's action precipitated serious conflict with Coastal Command Commander-in-Chief Slessor, with whom Blackett had not vetted the memorandum. Unlike his predecessor Joubert, Slessor was a strong supporter of the bomber offensive. Slessor complained about Blackett's "slide-rule strategy" and emphasized that he wanted immediate action with well-trained crews using the 10-centimeter radar, rather than a buildup over six months of a larger Coastal Command aircraft force. The calculations Blackett used had been based on previous data for older radar sets, and Slessor was confident that the newer radar devices would make a huge difference, without large numbers of new planes. In a compromise, seventy-two heavy aircraft were added to Coastal Command for U-boat operations.[70] This fit well with the demands of Admiral of the Fleet Sir Dudley Pound for greater concentration of air power in the Atlantic.[71]

With the arrival of American Liberators—long-range antisubmarine aircraft allocated specifically by Roosevelt to Coastal Command—the U-boat menace was virtually over by summer 1943, and American supplies and troops could reach England for the invasion of Europe.[72] Between 1939 and 1945, approximately 1,200 U-boats were involved in action, 700 of which were sunk, with 32,000 German sailors drowned. On the Allied side, 2,700 Allied ships were destroyed, with 145,000 Allied sailors drowned, most of them civilians and volunteers.[73]

Bomber Harris got his way, however. At the Casablanca Conference in January 1943, a combined American and British bombing offensive was formally adopted as a major part of the British war strategy. Churchill, who had opposed a landing in France in 1942, was prepared to consider it for 1943, but continued to insist that it was wiser to wear down the Germans before launching an invasion. Among the most horrifying bombing attacks of the war was the British barrage of explosive, incendiary, napalm, and phosphorus bombs on Hamburg in late July 1943, where some 40,000 civilians died. The next wholesale destruction of a German city came in February 1945 with the bombing of Dresden, killing some 50,000 people. In September 1945 the official US Strategic Bombing Survey, whose members included John Kenneth Galbraith and Paul Nitze, estimated that about 500,000 German men, women, and children were killed in area bombing, but also 160,000 US and British airmen. Indeed, in the thirty-five major British bomber actions between November 1943 and March 1944, German night fighters destroyed the majority of the 1,047 British bombers. Blackett later described the airmen as "the best young men of both countries," noting further that "German war production went on rising steadily until it reached its peak in August, 1944. At this time the Allies were already in Paris and the Russian armies were well into Poland. German civilian morale did not crack. Perhaps it is not surprising that the [US bombing report] seems to have had a rather small circulation."[74]

The value and reliability of operational research was well established within British military commands by 1942, even thought it engendered jokes and resentments against the boffins and slide-rule strategists. Air Marshal Slessor was won over to it, despite his momentary anger at Blackett in April 1943 on the matter of bomber transfers. So were General Pile, Air Chief Marshal Joubert, and Admiral George Creasy. Statistical analysis of U-boat densities, lethality of attacks, flying hours of aircraft, and other data were part of the usual agenda for periodical joint Admiralty and Coastal Command meetings and for the fortnightly meetings of the Cabinet Anti-U-Boat Committee at 10 Downing Street. Blackett's group completed reports on such problems as enemy air raid casualties (June 1943), the use of Bomber Force in Project "Overlord" (March 1944), and a summary analysis of bombing policies and directives for all of 1939–1945.[75] Blackett's group continued to monitor and report on the situation with German U-boats, including signal detection. Leon Solomon, Evan J. Williams, and Blackett himself completed some twenty reports from 1943 to 1945 having to do with signal intelligence and codebreaking.[76] Blackett gave a talk on these subjects in December 1943 to an Intelligence Subcommittee in Washington, D.C.[77]

When Louis (Dickie) Mountbatten became Chief of Combined Operations for the Normandy invasion, Tizard recommended Bernal and Zuckerman as Mountbatten's scientific advisors for operational analysis of equipment and techniques for the landing. Mountbatten's instructions that his uniformed staff were to fully involve Bernal and Zuckerman in details of the landing, rather than simply ask them to solve preframed questions, caused some hard feelings among staff members, particularly against the outspoken Bernal and against Blackett. On the eve of D-Day, Zuckerman was in the War Room following plots of positions of ships and aircraft and recommending possible aiming points for bombers in the battle area. Zuckerman, Bernal, and Blackett all were at the general headquarters near Portsmouth as the operation began, although Zuckerman later said that he was told not to talk with Blackett about details of the impending "Overlord," the invasion of France.[78]

Bernal recalled that on 5 June he and Blackett walked through the maze of tents and huts to the Downs "and we looked out on the sea where the whole expedition lay just about to start. The air was dim and there were heavy clouds and little bits of rain. . . . We lay on the grass and talked, estimating prospects of success or failure on the different beaches." The next day, wide awake at 4 A.M. in the dormitory, Bernal and Blackett knew the planes had gone, and they waited to hear reports of the landings as messages were decoded. "P. and I went out to walk up the side of the lake, discussing the difficulties that we had as scientists in working with such a professional organization as the Navy," Bernal later wrote in his diary. He then embarked for France to follow up with operational studies of the beach landings, and Blackett returned to London.[79]

Zuckerman, like many others, later referred to Blackett as the "father of operational research" and to the London group that Zuckerman had himself convened as "Tots and Quots" as the men who largely had created operational research.[80] After the war the principles of operational research continued to be applied in British military commands, and there were attempts to promote it within government, for example in an Advisory Council on Scientific Policy and its Committee on Industrial Productivity.[81] In 1950 Blackett wrote a short article for the first issue of the new *Operational Research Quarterly,* but he took little active interest in its further development or in the establishment of operational research as an academic discipline.[82] He became deeply suspicious of the marriage of academic OR with Cold War military strategy, as can be seen in the next section of this chapter.

Blackett did support the application of OR to industry, suggesting to the Chairman of the Manchester Joint Research Council in 1949 that the Council sponsor a series of talks for local industrialists. At one of the lectures A. W. Swan of the United Steel Companies echoed other industrialists' commonsense response to the new theme: "There are many definitions of Operational Research. Mine is that Operational Research is the successor to what used to be called Scientific Management, and in my view Operational Research is Scientific Management plus the statistical approach."[83] On the occasion of another lecture, H. Bradley, Director of the British Boot, Shoe, and Allied Trades Research Association, turned to Blackett to acknowledge his impact in operational research: "his name will go down in history . . . as one who did so much to enable this country to meet and overcome the U-boat menace."[84]

The Challenge of Atomic Weapons

Many of Blackett's close friends and colleagues from Cambridge, Manchester, Liverpool, Birmingham, London, and other British universities worked in the United States on the atomic bomb. Among them were Chadwick, Peierls, and Frisch. Blackett, who formally had nothing to do with the Manhattan Project, left the Admiralty to return to Manchester in the summer of 1945, following the conclusion of the European war. He, like the general public, heard on 6 August of the bombing of Hiroshima, followed by the 9 August bombing of Nagasaki. In late August, while Blackett and his family were vacationing in Wales, confidential papers arrived, via military motorcyle dispatch, requesting Blackett to travel to London as quickly as possible. After a briefing in London, he was escorted to interview scientists who had been captured in Germany and detained at Farm Hall, a country house near Cambridge. The ten German scientists included Werner Heisenberg, who had asked to see Blackett. The two talked at length on 8 and 9 September. Informed that General Leslie Groves wanted the Germans to be treated as prisoners of war or to be settled into British universities, Blackett argued for their return to Germany. When told that Groves feared the German scientists might be highjacked by the Russians, Blackett jested that this might be a good thing, since German backwardness in atomic weaponry could slow down the advance of a Russian nuclear program.[85]

Blackett had learned of the detention of the German scientists in England only three days before his visit to Farm Hall.[86] Although he had not been involved in the development of the atomic bomb, as he told Heisenberg, Blackett had been invited in August by Prime Minister Clement Attlee to join a new Advisory Committee on Atomic Energy. This became known as the "Anderson Committee," chaired by John Anderson, a Conservative member of Churchill's Cabinet who had responsibilities for atomic affairs during the war. The Committee included Blackett, Chadwick, Appleton, Thomson, and the physiologist Henry H. Dale (who was then President of the Royal Society), as well as Sir Alan Brooke, the Chief of the Imperial General Staff; Sir Alexander Cadogan, Under-Secretary of State at the Foreign Office; and Sir Alan Barlow, Second Secretary of the Treasury.[87] The charge of the Committee was to investigate the implications of the use of atomic energy and to advise the Government what steps should be taken for its development in Britain for military or industrial purposes. The Committee also was to put forward proposals for international arrangements on atomic energy.[88]

A technical Subcommittee on Nuclear Physics was constituted in December 1945, including as members Blackett, Chadwick, Cockcroft, Oliphant, Peierls, Thomson, Charles Darwin, Norman Feather, and M. H. L. Pryce, with Chadwick as chairman.[89] A new Tizard Committee had been established following the summer elections of 1945 that precipitated Churchill's departure from Downing Street and Lindemann's return to Oxford. Tizard became head of a Chiefs of Staff Subcommittee on Future Weapons that set up, in October 1945, a Joint Technical Warfare Committee to address atomic weapons as part of its purview.

Blackett's views quickly diverged from majority opinion in both committees. He not only opposed British development of atomic weapons, but argued in favor of a neutralist foreign policy for the United Kingdom. In November 1945 Blackett wrote a detailed memorandum for the Chiefs of Staff in which he argued that a decision to manufacture or acquire atomic bombs would tend to decrease, rather than to increase, the security of Great Britain, because it likely would stimulate the USSR to an aggressive military action, not against the United Kingdom, but elsewhere in Europe. Thus research should primarily be directed toward

development of atomic power, and a separate group should conduct research on nuclear weapons but not manufacture them. A British decision not to manufacture bombs, for a specified term of years, should be
publicly announced, encouraging others to follow suit, with a program
for setting up a world system of inspection and control.[90]

The Chiefs of Staff responded that they did not accept Blackett's assumptions or conclusions. Attlee, the Prime Minister, dismissed Blackett's work as that of a "layman."[91] In January 1946 discussions about the
designation of a site for a nuclear research establishment settled on
Harwell, south of Oxford. Cockcroft was named director at Harwell,
which became an agency in the Ministry of Supply, with Lord Portal as
Controller of Atomic Energy within the Ministry.

Many British scientists worried that the United Kingdom was moving
too slowly and that British scientists' knowledge of atomic energy and
atomic weaponry was inadequate and falling further behind the Americans. There were objections that Harwell was being placed in the huge
Ministry of Supply rather than in the smaller Department of Scientific
and Industrial Research (DSIR). Oliphant reported to Blackett that some
scientists worried that Blackett's work on the atomic advisory committee
would simply fall in line with whatever Attlee's government wanted because Blackett, too, was a socialist.[92] Blackett's response to Oliphant's letter was that the "government doesn't much approve of me."[93]

Following a trip to the United States in the fall of 1946, Blackett set up
an appointment with Attlee for sometime in November to discuss the
problem of international control of atomic energy. He saw Attlee on two
occasions, but Blackett's sympathetic views toward the Soviet Union
were dismissed as "dangerous and misleading rubbish" in the Foreign
Office. In the November meeting Blackett gave Attlee a memorandum
on international control, which was circulated in February 1947. However, Blackett was not informed that January when a decision was made
to proceed with atomic weapons. Ernest Bevin, the Foreign Secretary,
was reported to have dismissed international controls and the Baruch
plan, which was under discussion at the United Nations, by commenting "Let's forget the Baroosh and get on with making the fissile." The
January decision was announced a year and a half later in Parliament, in
May 1948, but with no debate.[94] The Prime Minister dissolved the Advisory Committee on Atomic Energy in January 1948, and the Subcom-

mittee was reconstituted as the Nuclear Physics Committee responsible to the Ministry of Supply with Chadwick as Chairman and Blackett as Vice-Chairman.[95]

When he found that he was failing to sway members of the advisory atomic energy committee, including Chadwick, Blackett began to circulate his opinions publicly, first in a pamphlet published by the Fabian Society as *The Atom and the Charter* (1946), and then in the widely read book *Military and Political Consequences of Atomic Energy* (1948), which appeared in the United States under the more dramatic title *Fear, War and the Bomb* (1949).[96] It was just before his book appeared in Britain, in May 1948, that the Labour government announced in Parliament the decision of January 1947 to produce atomic weapons.

Despite growing concern in London and Washington about Soviet domestic and foreign policy, Blackett argued the need to maintain contact and cooperation with the Soviet Union.[97] His reasoning led him to criticize the plan that had been presented by Bernard Baruch to the United Nations Atomic Energy Commission in June 1946, recommending an international authority for control and inspection of all atomic materials. Blackett's objection was that the Baruch proposal included explicit penalties for violation of atomic-weapons controls, penalties that would be exempt from veto in the Security Council, where the Soviet Union was a permanent member.[98] Blackett opposed the veto exemption as impractical.

From 1946 on, while actively directing the Physics Department at Manchester, Blackett began putting together the materials that would appear in his 1948 book.[99] In a letter to his Manchester friend and colleague Michael Polanyi, Blackett had written during the war, "You speak as if it is always a duty to publish the 'truth.' If I had published the truth of what I have known of parts of our war effort, I would certainly be locked up. Should I have done so?"[100] Now, in 1948, Blackett made public his views about the military strategy that had been carried out by British and American air forces in the past war and his misgivings about present policies.

The wartime civilian bombing strategy, Blackett wrote publicly in 1948, had been arrived at because of earlier failures of the RAF to pinpoint and hit specific industrial and military targets.[101] Worse than British use of this strategy during the past war, he wrote, was the new development in American public opinion of accepting the tactics of mass destruction as a normal operation of war, a view that Blackett condemned as ethically immoral and militarily ineffective. It was his visit to the United States during the American midterm elections in 1946 that convinced Blackett of a conservative turn in American politics and an eagerness to talk about preventive war.[102] Polanyi expressed similar misgivings to Blackett after a return from the United States, despite Polanyi's longtime distrust of the Soviet Union.[103]

As he examined available US military reports on the bombing of Germany and Japan, including the official US report of September 1945, Blackett became convinced that air war had not, and could not, win a war independently of ground troops. He extended the argument to atomic weapons, warning that it was a mistake for Americans to so overestimate the decisive effects of aerial bombardment and to so fear the power of nuclear weapons that they sought absolute security from atomic weapons by the unworkable provisions of the Baruch plan.[104]

In Blackett's view, the US McMahon Act of August 1946, which created the Atomic Energy Commission and forbade any sharing of atomic information with another foreign power, including Canada and Great Britain, was a grave mistake. It reneged upon the successes of international cooperation during the past war, and it ignored the legitimate desire of the Soviet Union for the development of new sources of power from atomic energy. If the McMahon Act was to be the American position, the United Kingdom should not seek to develop atomic bombs at all, and should remain politically neutral in the growing confrontation between the United States and the Soviet Union.[105]

Most controversially of all, in 1948 Blackett expressed extreme worry that the United States had not been open to meaningful accommodations with the Soviet Union for some time. By way of supporting this point, he made an argument now familiar, but then novel, that the United States had used atomic weapons in Japan in early August 1945 "not so much as the last military act of the Second World War, but as the first act of the cold diplomatic war with Russia." The Americans, Blackett charged, made a political decision to force Japanese surrender before the mid-August date agreed upon by the Soviets and Americans for the Soviet army's invasion of Manchuria. The United States wanted to keep the Soviet Union out of Asia.[106]

Blackett's book appeared in Britain in autumn 1948 at the very time that it was announced that he was the recipient of the 1948 Nobel Prize in Physics. The Nobel award brought his book even more publicity than it might have had, especially outside Britain. Facing pages in the *Manchester Guardian* carried columns entitled "Nobel Prizes: Professor Blackett and Mr. T. S. Eliot" and "The Atomic Problem: Professor Blackett's Book."[107]

There was widespread criticism from both friends and foes that Blackett was too harsh on the Americans.[108] Frederick Osborn, who became Deputy US Representative to the United Nations Atomic Energy Commission in May 1949, debated with Blackett on the BBC in December 1948. Osborn took issue with Blackett's impugning the motives of Henry Stimson, Secretary of War under President Roosevelt and President Truman, and General George C. Marshall, the Army's Chief of Staff from 1939 to 1945. In 1948 Marshall was Secretary of State, formulating the Marshall Plan for US economic and military aid abroad. Osborn wrote Blackett that he would not discuss the matter of US motives in using atomic bombs in Japan and that he was certain that Blackett was wrong, Mr. Stimson and General Marshall being "two of the finest men I have ever known."[109]

Blackett's public charge of the inefficacy of aerial bombing during the Second World War was much disputed.[110] Blackett also was accused of giving too much credence and too much encouragement to the Russian position in the United Nations and of ignoring Deputy Foreign Minister Andrei Gromyko's rejection of any form of international ownership or supervision of atomic materials.[111] *New York Times* science correspondent Waldemar Kaempffert thought that Blackett was performing a useful service in toning down doomsday predictions, but that he had gone too far in denying the dangers of atomic weapons.[112]

By the early 1950s Blackett realized that he had misjudged the persistent lethal effects of radioactive fallout. He also was underestimating the rapidity with which missile-delivery systems would be developed and equipped with relatively small "super" or hydrogen bombs. However, Blackett continued to argue during the 1950s and early 1960s that conventional and nuclear disarmament should be negotiated in parallel.[113] Nor did he doubt his expertise in this discussion. To the comments of one reviewer that "science and politics do not readily mix together—at least not in one person,"[114] and of another that "because a man is a success in physics it does not follow that he is well qualified to elucidate political issues,"[115] Blackett's rejoinder was obvious: "Why I should stick to

Physics . . . I cannot quite conceive. Anyway I have spent eleven years of my life in warfare. That gives me a title to talk about it."[116]

A four-part series of reactions to Blackett's book appeared in the *Bulletin of Atomic Scientists* in early 1949, with comments by sociologist Edward Shils, then teaching at the London School of Economics and the University of Chicago, along with contributions by physicist Philip Morrison, US senator Brien McMahon, and Russian journalist M. Marinin.[117] The Russian's remarks put Blackett in a bad light by extolling his book's virtues and characterizing Baruch as "an old-time wily speculator from Wall Street."[118] McMahon called Blackett an apologist for the Kremlin, while Shils described Blackett as a "master of artful and intelligent distortion."[119]

Morrison had a different point of view. He deplored the *ad hominem* attacks on Blackett, supported Blackett's principal military conclusions that a major war would not be a "three-week aerial expedition," and recommended that disarmament discussions include both conventional and atomic weapons. While not accepting Blackett's characterization of the Hiroshima bomb as the first act of the Cold War, Morrison offered some personal testimony: "I can testify . . . that a date near August 10 was a mysterious final date which we, who had the daily technical job of readying the bomb, had to meet at whatever cost in risk or money or good development policy. That is hard to explain except by Blackett's thesis."[120]

However, the perspective of most American physicists, particularly those who worked on the Manhattan Project, was better represented by Columbia University physicist I. I. Rabi, who wrote a scathing attack on Blackett and on Blackett's arguments for the April 1949 issue of *Atlantic Monthly*. Rabi castigated Blackett for writing "like the amateur he is" on international affairs and for manifesting "the hopeless confusion of the average Englishman" about American attitudes and politics.[121]

Worse, Rabi wrote, Blackett had abused his responsibility as a scientist by writing so disastrously for a lay audience in a field outside his special field of competence. And, furthermore, Blackett had not worked on the atomic bomb during the war, his recent professional interests had not been primarily in nuclear physics, and the contents of his book often "show that his thinking in this is that of an outsider." In Rabi's opinion, Blackett's uninformed knowledge of atomic weapons resulted in the failure to see that the atomic bomb "has made obsolete" the methods of conventional warfare."[122] A year later the United States was in a conventional shooting war in Korea.

Politicization of a Scientific Man: Debates to the 1960s

For Blackett, his role in these debates on atomic policy gained him a reputation broadly as communist fellow traveler. In the United States this meant that the FBI kept files on him, making use of an informant's false claim that Blackett had admitted affiliation with the Communist party of Great Britain "on the occasion of the founding of the World Federation of Scientific Workers in Paris, France, in the Summer of 1946."[123] His speeches to the British Association of Scientific Workers were reported to the FBI (including Blackett's alleged remark on one occasion: "We ought not to change our present political motor car for the latest American model with its decisively right hand drive but ought to keep to our own left model"). In addition, it was reported that Blackett was a member of a delegation of scientists who called on the British Home Secretary to request clemency for Allan Nunn May, who had been arrested in March 1946 and sentenced to ten years' imprisonment. Nunn May's defense that he gave information to the USSR because he did not think development of atomic energy should be limited to the United States sounded ominously like Blackett's calls for cooperation with the Soviet Union.[124]

In May 1949 Blackett's name appeared in writer and novelist George Orwell's blacklist of thirty-eight crypto-communists or fellow travelers that Orwell sent to his friend Celia Kirwan at a semi-secret department of the British Foreign Office. Orwell seems not to have known much about Professor Blackett, identifying him as a "scientific popularizer" in physics, like the journalist J. G. Crowther, who also appeared on the list.[125] It is unclear whether Orwell's list had any impact in the British Intelligence offices of MI5 (domestic intelligence) or MI6 (foreign intelligence), but this was a period of increasing tension about espionage and communist sympathizers. After Nunn May's arrest in 1946, Klaus Fuchs fell under suspicion of giving atomic-weapons information to the Russians. Fuchs was head of the theoretical division at Harwell, working with Cockcroft, at the time that he was first questioned in 1948 and then arrested in February 1950.[126] The cosmic-ray physicist Bruno Pontecorvo, who also was working at Harwell, defected to the Soviet Union in

August 1950. The arrests in the United States of Harry Glass, David Greenglass, and Ethel and Julius Rosenberg unfolded during the spring and summer of 1950, followed by the trial of the Rosenbergs in 1951. In 1951 Blackett and Costanza were detained and questioned about his political views in Tampa, Florida, when their Canadian plane made a refueling stop en route from Mexico City to Toronto. Blackett had been attending a cosmic-ray conference in Guanajuato and was bringing back a suitcase half-full of Russian reprints on cosmic rays. Luckily, the two Pats' bags were not searched.[127] As late as 1960 Blackett had to be given a special visa at the American Embassy in London to enable him to enter the United States.[128]

Blackett's socialist views and his friendships with British communists and with Russian scientists were well known. When Heisenberg was detained at Farm Hall, he speculated in his first days there about the reasons that British scientists had not been brought immediately to see the German scientists. "It may be that the British Government are frightened of the communist professors, Dirac and so on. They say 'If we tell Dirac or Blackett where they are, they will report it immediately to their Russian friends [such as] Kapitza.'"[129] As Jeremy Bernstein notes, this is a bizarre statement in almost every way. Dirac and Blackett were not communists, and Kapitza was dismissed in 1946 from his physics institute for refusing to work on nuclear weapons development.[130]

Why did Blackett choose to spend increasing amounts of time from the late 1940s in writing essays for public affairs journals such as *The New Statesman, Encounter, Endeavour,* and *International Affairs?* By his own account Blackett began seriously to study politics, international affairs, and strategies of war following the rise of Hitler in Germany and the coming of the Spanish Civil War. In joining the Tizard Committee in 1935, Blackett realized that his early naval service had given him an understanding of the attitudes of servicemen.[131] Among his naval experiences he vividly remembered the Battle of Jutland and gazing through a periscope at the patch of oily water in which a dozen survivors were clinging to pieces of wreckage from the battle cruiser *Queen Mary.* Jutland taught him, he repeated on several occasions, the danger of assuming superiority over the enemy in military technique and the folly of failing to design defense measures against the offensive weapons in which one claims superiority.[132]

During the early 1940s Blackett felt increasing alarm at hearing BBC broadcasts that treated the bombing of German civilians as a viable and normal strategy of war. He perceived a brutalization of military and civilian attitudes about the practice of war. He came to think that the senseless destruction of refugee-swollen Dresden in February 1945 paved the way for the August bombing of Hiroshima and Nagasaki. Foreboding about a future in which military policy countenances annihilation led Blackett to devote large amounts of time to opposing emerging atomic policies, despite his desire to immerse himself in scientific research.[133]

Parallels are clear in Blackett's attitudes toward strategies of total war by conventional and nuclear bombing. In Whitehall memoranda in the 1940s, he emphasized the importance of land forces in military campaigns and the need for the Air Force to protect ground troops and supply lines, both on land and sea. In Blackett's view, the wartime Air Force was seeking to establish itself, during the early stages of the war, as a strategic offensive force, leaving the Navy with the defensive role of guarding communications and the Army with the role of occupying the enemy's country after defeat from the air.[134] In the 1950s Blackett argued that the only sensible military policy in Europe was to develop a strength in land forces that more nearly matched Soviet land forces in Europe, instead of relying on airborne nuclear weapons. It was Blackett the Royal Navy officer who decried what he called the "Jupiter complex of the airmen" threatening mankind with atomic thunderbolts.[135]

Blackett became increasingly concerned, too, about the advocacy of tactical nuclear weapons by Gordon Dean, chairman of the US Atomic Energy Commission from 1950 to 1953, and then by Henry Kissinger, professor of politics at Harvard University, in 1957.[136] As Blackett saw it, Kissinger's rules of engagement were a prescription for limited nuclear war contained in Europe.[137] In 1958 Blackett dismissed as "poppycock—and very dangerous" Kissinger's argument that American soldiers could be trained more successfully than Soviet soldiers in the use of nuclear tactical weapons.[138]

Most repugnant to Blackett were the applications of game theory to "scenarios" of nuclear war, as worked out by scholars associated with the Rand Corporation, the Hudson Institute, Princeton University, and other university and government-associated "think tanks" and operations research groups. In March 1961 Blackett delivered a speech to military officers in the Royal United Services Institution. He argued that OR groups had been able to make substantial contributions during the Second World War not only because they were in close contact with executive officers who were running the war, but because the OR group members believed their conclusions to be accurate and felt morally responsible for them.[139] Operational research cannot substitute for traditional military judgment and wisdom, he argued; rather, it provides a useful supplement.[140]

In contrast, the recent conclusions of civilian military analysts associated with the Rand Corporation, Blackett said, "seem to me wrong and dangerous." Since no large-scale nuclear war has ever occurred, there is no body of operational data on real events on which to base a common-sense analysis such as was available to wartime operational research groups. Worse, the new writings in operational research embody a "nauseating inhumanity," which, Blackett wrote, expresses a "strain of deep social pessimism combined sometimes strangely with an almost neurotic contemplation of destruction."[141]

Albert Wohlstetter's "The Delicate Balance of Terror" appeared in *Foreign Affairs* in January 1959. Wohlstetter argued that it is sane and rational for a country to initiate a first and "surprise" nuclear strike.[142] Blackett rejected these kinds of arguments as well as the conclusions of Princeton University's Oskar Morgenstern and Rand's Herman Kahn in calculating nuclear risks. Morgenstern's *The Question of National Defense* (1959) followed the Rand Corporation's classified *Report on a Study of Non-Military Defense* (1958) edited by Kahn. The Rand study, like Kahn's 1960 book *Thermonuclear War,* assumed two levels of nuclear attack and figures for civilian casualties that Kahn deemed "plausible." The conclusion was that the United States could survive nuclear war if "non-military" measures—that is, "civilian defense"—were taken immediately in preparation for war.[143] In 1962 Kahn augmented his earlier studies with the book *Thinking about the Unthinkable,* discussing both limited nuclear war and all-out nuclear war, and describing what he called "scenarios" and "games" that might be played out.[144] Rand Corporation studies argued the need for a civil defense program that was estimated to cost hundreds of billions of dollars.[145]

Dismissing American fears of a "missile gap" with the Soviet Union, a point of debate in the 1960 Kennedy-Nixon election campaign, Blackett argued, as he had done since the 1940s, for parallel reductions in conventional and nuclear weapons, noting that the growing power of China was an additional reason for urgency in this matter.[146] At a time when a partial ban on atomic testing was sporadically under negotiation, Blackett continued to focus his interest on bilateral disarmament that would lead to a reduced number of atomic weapons and provide minimum mutual deterrence.

That the alleged Russian superiority in missiles was a fiction became a matter of public discussion in late September 1961 when Joseph Alsop debunked the much publicized "missile gap" in the Paris edition of the *New York Herald Tribune.* By November, Secretary of Defense Robert McNamara revealed figures for weaponry in the US Armed Forces: 1,700 intercontinental bombers and several dozen operational ICBMs, 80 Polaris missiles in nuclear-powered submarines, 300 carrier-borne aircraft armed with megaton warheads, and nearly 1,000 supersonic land-based fighters with nuclear warheads. Now it seemed ever more clear that the Soviets' motive in shooting down an American spy-plane, the U-2, in the spring of 1960 was to ensure the secrecy of locations of their many fewer land-based missiles that constituted the Soviet retaliatory threat. Maintaining this secrecy was also a principal factor in Soviet resistance to inspections in a test-ban treaty.[147]

In autumn 1962, just after the Cuban missile crisis, Blackett's collection of military and public affairs essays written from the 1940s to the 1960s appeared under the title *Studies of War: Nuclear and Conventional.* Reaction to the book contrasted markedly with reaction in 1948 to *The Military and Political Consequences of Atomic Energy,* even though Blackett's arguments were strikingly consistent. But times had changed. Blackett's book appeared almost simultaneously with Kahn's *Thinking about the Unthinkable* and Edward Teller's *The Legacy of Hiroshima,* so that these books sometimes were reviewed together. The contrast with Kahn already has been noted. Teller, recently retired from directing the Lawrence-Livermore Laboratory for weapons research, argued the following:

> In a dangerous world we cannot have peace unless we are strong. We cannot be strong unless we are fully prepared to exploit the biggest modern power, nuclear explosives. Nuclear weapons can be used with moderation on all scales of serious conflict. . . . World War III would be much worse than anything we can remember. But it would not destroy mankind.[148]

As an anonymous reviewer wrote:

> A disenchanted observer of the strategic scene once suggested that Dr. Herman Kahn, the celebrated analyst of thermonuclear war, had been invented as some sort of cruel joke. No one with such views, it was im-

plied, could possibly be real. *The Legacy of Hiroshima* will probably give rise to similar doubts about Dr. Edward Teller. . . . Somewhere between the "father of the bomb" and the unilateral disarmer stands Professor Blackett—cool, astringent, and objective.[149]

In contrast to their reaction to Teller's book, many prominent scientists praised Blackett's collection of essays, Freeman Dyson saying, for example, that Blackett "writes with humor and grace and human wisdom, and with a deep sense of history,"[150] and Nevill Mott noting that "no review can do justice to the incisiveness of Blackett's arguments, their hard common sense and their basis in a lifetime's experience of science and war."[151]

Some reviewers attributed to Blackett a practical effect on recent developments in nuclear policy, given that the United States had substantially revised its pre-1961 policy and improved its non-nuclear resources in men and material. Nuclear weapons, for good or ill, had not made conventional weapons obsolete after all. But if Blackett was right in this result, it was land wars in Korea and Indochina that made the point, not his original arguments. A reviewer for the *Baltimore Sun* noted Blackett's disagreement with the development of small tactical nuclear weapons, adding that "he has been right before."[152] British historian A. J. P. Taylor wrote: "Blackett is asking us to believe that he is sane and that most American experts are mad. That is easy to believe. But it is unlikely that his voice of sanity will drown out American experts and air generals."[153]

One of the few thoroughly negative reviews came from Lewis Strauss, former chairman of the US Atomic Energy Commission, who ridiculed Blackett's "remoteness from reality" for proposing that impediments to disarmament in the United States might be substantially economic, political, and emotional in character rather than military.[154] To many, Blackett's position in this regard seemed common sense. In any case, his heretical views in 1948 had become familiar and debatable in mainstream politics of 1962.

Outsider and Insider in the Corridors of Power

While Blackett seems to have corresponded with surprisingly few American colleagues over these matters, he visited the United States frequently, usually on scientific matters, and he began participating in the

Pugwash Conferences on Science and World Affairs after the first Pugwash meeting in Nova Scotia in 1957. Organizing members in America included Eugene Rabinowitch, Victor Weisskopf, Bentley Glass, Hans Bethe, and Jerome Wiesner, who became President Kennedy's science advisor.[155] Blackett and Rabi both participated in the Pugwash conferences at Stowe in 1961, Cambridge in 1962, and Dubrovnic in 1963.[156]

Blackett had influential contacts in the United States, among them Henry Kissinger, another Pugwash participant, whom Blackett met first in London in the summer of 1959. Upon his return to Harvard, Kissinger wrote Blackett that he had found their views in their London conversation to be very close.[157] By this time Kissinger was moving away from advocating a flexible military strategy using both tactical nuclear weapons and conventional weapons, and he was stressing conventional weapons alone. Before Blackett was to meet Kissinger in London, Howard K. Smith, who was stationed at the CBS News bureau in London, reminded Blackett that Kissinger was one of the Harvard and MIT professors whom Senator John F. Kennedy had gathered into his "brain trust" as Kennedy prepared for the 1960 election.[158]

In 1960 C. P. Snow stirred up a storm when he gave his Godkin Lectures at Harvard University on "Science and Government."[159] Snow dramatically revived memories of the wartime disputes of Tizard and Blackett with Lindemann, as Blackett himself did on a more minor scale in his Tizard Memorial Lecture of February 1960 at the Institute for Strategic Studies. Lindemann had died in 1958 and Tizard in 1959, and so it was a time of reassessment. Reginald V. Jones had worked in scientific intelligence during the war for the British Air Staff and Secret Service Intelligence, including studies of German radar and V rockets. He was now Professor of Natural Philosophy at Aberdeen. Along with Frederick W. F. Smith, the second Lord Birkenhead, who was Lindemann's biographer, Jones rose to his former mentor Lord Cherwell's defense. Both sides who retold the story of wartime arguments between Lindemann and the Tizard-Blackett group weighed claims and counterclaims about the development of radar and about the area bombing strategy, making appeal to newly published histories of wartime campaigns, especially the official history by Sir Charles Webster and Noble Frankland of the strategic air offensive against Germany, which appeared in 1961. Bernal entered the fray with a letter to the editor of *The Times*.[160]

The old controversy resonated with the public in the early 1960s precisely because of the ongoing argument, which was coming to a head after Kennedy's election to the US presidency, about the Cold War buildup of nuclear weapons, survival in a nuclear war, and atmospheric testing of nuclear weapons. Could nuclear bombs and missiles alone win a war? Is this kind of war one worth fighting and winning? By the mid-1960s disarmament negotiations, as well as the limited test-ban treaty, were becoming part of mainstream international politics, as conventional military capabilities were expanding. Blackett's position was now both respected and respectable. The argument about American motives for use of atomic bombs in Japan also was becoming part of the mainstream of debate among historians of the Second World War.[161]

British scientists who were unsympathetic with Blackett's political views, or who disapproved of distinguished scientists engaging in public debate, particularly on their country's military strategy, mostly did not doubt Blackett's personal integrity or professional dependability, as demonstrated in Archibald Vivian Hill's remark in 1941 that the Marxist J. B. S. Haldane and socialist Blackett, "for all their queer political notions, are useful and cooperative members of the [Royal Society] Council."[162] The British intellectual and governing elite was a small group, and, as Snow put it in describing Blackett's *alter ego* Francis Getliffe in the novel *Corridors of Power*, it was a culture of insiders: "The trouble with our major allies is that they methodically read every speech Francis Getliffe has ever made, and can't believe that any of us know anything about him. One of the few advantages of living in England, is that we do know just a little about one another, don't you agree?"[163]

In this elite in Great Britain, Blackett not only was known after the Second World War as a Cambridge physicist from the glorious Cavendish circle of the 1930s, but as a founder of wartime operational research and one of the heroes of the British triumph in the U-boat campaign. His political views were controversial, maverick, and left-wing, even within his own political party, but hardly anyone within the British intellectual and governmental elite doubted his integrity or courage, even if they might question his judgment. R. V. Jones expressed his assessment of Blackett's wartime service and his postwar military views in a striking manner: "I always hoped that if the world were collapsing, Blackett and I would find ourselves fighting side by side in the last ditch, but the routes by which we got there would have been very different."[164]

4

Temptations of Theory, Strategies of Evidence: Investigating the Earth's Magnetism, 1947–1952

In late spring of 1947, Blackett succumbed to the temptations of theory. At this time, Blackett was fifty years old and resuming residence in Manchester and active direction of the Physics Department after his wartime service in operational research. Blackett's turn toward theory in 1947 involved some risk.[1] The May 3, 1947 issue of *Nature* carried an announcement of his upcoming lecture at the Royal Society:

> Professor P. M. S. Blackett, Langworthy Professor of Physics in the University of Manchester, will deliver a lecture on "The Magnetic Field of Massive Rotating Bodies" at a meeting of the Royal Society on May 15, at 4:30 P.M.[2]

Blackett circulated a preliminary draft of his paper among colleagues in several different fields, including the geophysicist Sydney Chapman and the astrophysicist Harry Plaskett, both professors at Oxford.[3] Blackett negotiated with Royal Society officers that his paper would appear immediately in *Nature,* rather than following the slower timetable of the Royal Society's *Proceedings.*[4] He arranged for notices of his lecture to be sent to a list of specified individuals, including members of the Royal Astronomical Society.[5] "Sorry, Darling, I was so grumpy over the weekend," he wrote Costanza in early April. "It was the weather and the feeling that I had only two days holiday. Also I am always a little distracted when in the process of giving birth to a paper. It is going better than ever. Plaskett had tea with me today and produced one useful idea. He is most helpful and interested."[6]

The Thursday afternoon meeting of 15 May 1947 was not a joint session of the Royal Society and the Royal Astronomical Society, as had been the case on that famous Thursday afternoon in 1919 when Astronomer Royal Sir Frank Dyson announced the results of two recent eclipse expeditions that had tested Albert Einstein's general theory of relativity.[7] But Blackett may have had that earlier occasion in mind, and journalists referred to it. Nor did Blackett, like Dyson, Sir Arthur Stanley Eddington, and C. R. Davidson in 1919, have confirming evidence for a theory in hand. But he did outline a precise plan for getting the evidence.

In his 1947 Royal Society lecture, Blackett announced what he called a new law of nature, precipitating a brief media event in science journalism. During the next month or so, reporters sought out Blackett, described as a "tall, dark, handsome scientist with a taste for natty grey suiting."[8] The weekly *News Review* headlined a report "Newton, Einstein—And Now Blackett," prominently displaying Blackett's purported new law even while misprinting it.[9] BBC listeners heard the physicist Edward N. da C. Andrade give an account of the "new discovery."[10]

Then the real work began. Blackett marshaled his considerable experimental and managerial skills across several disciplinary domains in a strategy for testing a purported new law through a network of evidence. The result was the speedy demise of the law and of the theory, largely as a result of Blackett's well-coordinated strategy.

Yet, paradoxically, Blackett's very skills as a laboratory experimentalist and a research leader extricated him from what might first appear to have been a futile leap into fundamental theory. He constructed an instrument—an improved astatic magnetometer—that outlived the physical theory that it falsified. Under Blackett's direction the instrument was used to develop new evidence in favor of a different theory, the geophysical theory of continental drift.

A Revolutionary Idea: Blackett's Fundamental Theory of Magnetism

At the close of the war, when Blackett returned from the Admiralty in London to the Physics Department in Manchester, he became Dean of Science (1948 to 1950) and Pro-Vice-Chancellor of the university (1950 to 1952). As director of Manchester's physical laboratories, Blackett reorganized laboratory work in cosmic-ray research and installed war-surplus radar equipment for detecting cosmic-ray showers at Jodrell Bank, an open field twenty miles south of Manchester. The equipment quickly became part of the tools for the new field of radio astronomy under the direction of Bernard Lovell.[11]

This is not to say that Blackett's time was spent principally in university administration in the late 1940s and early 1950s. For one thing, as discussed in Chapter 3, he was lobbying government circles on the issue of the international control of atomic energy and opposing British development of nuclear weapons. His strongly polemical book *Military and Political Consequences of Atomic Energy* appeared in 1948. In addition, Blackett was returning to his studies of cosmic rays and investigating cascade showers of electrons in the sun's magnetic field.[12] This focus led him to notice that the ratio of magnetic moment to angular momentum has a similar value for both the earth and the sun.

Where P is magnetic moment and U is angular momentum,

$$(P/U)_1 = (P/U)_E = (P/U)_S = 10^{-15}.$$

Further, he realized that the quotient of the ratio $(P/U)_1$ and the ratio $(P/U)_2$ for a Bohr magneton, where

$$(P/U)_2 = (P/U)_m = 10^7,$$

when expressed as

$$(P/U)_1/(P/U)_2 = 1.08 \times 10^{-22},$$

is remarkably close to the nondimensional ratio of gravitational mass of an electron to its charge.

$$G^{1/2} m/e = 4.90 \times 10^{-22}$$

From this numerical coincidence, Blackett derived a simple relationship among magnetic and angular moment, the gravitational constant G, and the speed of light c, employing a constant ß.

[Eq. 1] $P = ß(G^{1/2}/2c)U$

This equation, briefly known as "Blackett's equation," carried the physical meaning that a mass element in motion generates a magnetic field as a fundamental effect of the motion. The larger the mass, the more detectable the magnetic field.[13]

"The simplicity of this result . . . suggested that it must have some profound significance," Blackett wrote.[14] He inquired from the astrophysicist Subrahmanyan Chandrasekhar, who had moved from the University of Cambridge to the University of Chicago in 1937, whether there were any stars with high angular moments. In reply, Blackett received page proofs of a paper by Horace Babcock at Mount Wilson Observatory in Pasadena with evidence for polar magnetic field strength in the star 78 Virginis of 1,500 gauss.[15] With this data Blackett was satisfied that "the above equation must be taken seriously as a possible general law of Nature for all massive rotating bodies. . . . Perhaps this relation will provide the long-sought connexion between electromagnetic and gravitational phenomena."[16]

The idea of connecting magnetism and rotation was not new. Indeed, Blackett's predecessor at Manchester, the physicist Arthur Schuster, had entertained in 1912 the hypothesis that rotation might be responsible for the earth's magnetism.[17] Schuster had reasoned that since iron loses its magnetism at high temperatures, it is unlikely that the earth's magnetism is due to a ferrous core. He also dismissed electrical currents as the cause of the earth's magnetic field on the grounds that they would die out over time. After calculating the sun's magnetic intensity using the model of a rotating sphere, Schuster asked George Hale at Mount Wilson Observatory to try to detect an empirical value for the sun's magnetic field by means of the Zeeman effect. Disappointingly, Hale's figure of 50 gauss was too low to confirm the rotational hypothesis of Schuster, who was looking for a magnetic field value in the range of 62–72 gauss.[18]

In a literature search Blackett found that, following Schuster's work, there had been a good deal of work in the 1920s on the relationship between rotational and magnetic effects. For one thing, in the 1910s and 1920s the American physicist Samuel Jackson Barnett had found a gyromagnetic effect, the magnetization due to rotation that became known as the Barnett effect.[19] However, as Blackett noted in his 1947 Royal Society lecture, the gyromagnetic effect alone is inadequate to explain the earth's magnetic field. Even if the earth were composed entirely of iron, the Barnett effect would account for a magnetic field only 10^{-10} of the earth's actual field, which is on the order of 0.5 gauss. Furthermore, the uniform magnetization produced by the gyromagnetic effect gives a surface field independent of radius, which seemed unlikely for the earth.[20]

Beginning in 1915, Albert Einstein and Wander Johannes de Haas had investigated the relationship between rotation and magnetization, with an idea similar to Barnett's that orbiting or rotating electrons are responsible for permanent magnetism. They discovered what came to be called the Einstein-de Haas effect, the torque induced in a suspended cylinder as a consequence of its being suddenly magnetized.[21]

At a 1924 meeting of the Swiss Physical Society, Einstein noted the hypothesis that the magnetic fields of the earth and the sun might result from a slight difference between the charge of the proton and the electron (the proton charge being higher by an amount $\varepsilon = 3 \times 10^{-19}$). However, Auguste Piccard and E. Kessler concluded experimentally in 1925 that the excess, if it existed, must be smaller than $5 \times 10^{-21}e$.[22] Einstein continued to think that the magnetic field of the earth might be produced by some charge asymmetry and that the earth's magnetic field "is not produced by magnetic bodies, but by the entire mass of material linked to the earth's rotation."[23] In July 1947 de Haas informed Blackett that he had tried in the 1920s to test whether a rotating mass produced a magnetic field, but his results had been negative and he had published nothing on the subject.[24]

Two other earlier experiments caught Blackett's attention. In 1923 H. A. Wilson at Rice University had advanced a hypothesis linking magnetism to motion by analogy with the classical Lorentz expression for the production of a magnetic field by a moving electric charge. However, Wilson found no laboratory evidence for this conjecture in an experiment with a swinging iron bar about 200 centimeters long and 6 centimeters in diameter.[25] Blackett was not surprised at this result, arguing that only rotation, not oscillation, produces a magnetic effect. He thought Wilson's approach could be applied to the mass element of a rotating rigid body, where the velocity term is a product of the angular velocity ω and the distance R of the mass element from the center of gravity.[26]

$$v = \omega R$$

Thus Blackett began to think that what he called "the Schuster-Wilson Hypothesis" could be tested experimentally with a rotating sphere using the Wilson-based equation

[Eq. 2] $H = 1.07 \times 10^{-15} \rho \omega R^2$

where ρ is the density of the sphere.[27]

Blackett also found that the American physicists William F. G. Swann and A. Longacre had done some interesting experiments at the Franklin

Institute in Philadelphia in 1928. They put a copper sphere of 10 centimeters radius spinning at 200 revolutions per second, but they failed to measure any magnetic field.[28] Blackett calculated from his equation (Equation 2) that the magnetic field for this sphere would have been about 10^{-9} gauss, but that Swann and Longacre had claimed only to show that no field larger than 10^{-4} gauss was produced.[29] Magnetometers were better in the 1940s than in the 1920s, but Blackett saw that he needed one better still than what was currently available. He began to think, then, of constructing a sphere larger than Swann's, which could be rotated safely, while producing a field large enough to be detected by an improved magnetometer, on the order of 10^{-8} gauss. This, he told his audience at the Royal Society on 15 May, is what he would do.

The theoretical justification for Blackett's law of nature remained unclear, however. Given the irrelevance of the Barnett effect to the earth's magnetism, Blackett proposed that any proof of his equation would require "a new fundamental property of matter not contained within the structure of present day physical theory." What he had in mind was something like Einstein's asymmetry or inequality in positive and negative charges[30] and what Blackett called "the long-sought connexion between electromagnetic and gravitational phenomena."[31] He put a great deal of bearing upon the law expressed in Equation 1: "It seems extremely unlikely that the approximate validity of [this equation] could be accidental. Its simplicity, involving as it does only the two macroscopic constants G and c, is in striking contrast to the complexity and arbitrary character of all special theories hitherto put forward" for the magnetic fields of the earth and the sun. The law was phenomenological in character and, once it was more thoroughly verified, its explanation could come later.[32]

Interdisciplinary Verification for a Big Theory

Blackett's program consisted of four interlocking strategies for testing his law and the theory of the earth's magnetism. These strategies were based in three domains outside Blackett's expertise (the domains of astrophysics, theoretical quantum electrodynamics, and geophysics), supplemented by Blackett's own design of a rotating-body test, which he called a crucial experiment.[33]

In the first area of astrophysical data, Blackett initially sought evidence from Horace Babcock.[34] Observations of four stars in addition to 70 Virginis fit Blackett's equation, if adjustments were made in the value of the constant ß. However, Babcock's new data was not encouraging. His observation of the white dwarf 40 Eridani B failed to show a shift or displacement that signaled broadening due to a Zeeman effect and the existence of a high magnetic moment. Worse, Babcock wrote Blackett in October 1947, the magnetic field of BD-18°3789 not only was variable, but appeared to reverse polarity periodically. Babcock thought that this result argued against the association of the magnetic field with the star's rotating mass.[35]

Worse still, by November 1947 Babcock reported to Blackett that his father Harold Babcock's continuing work on the magnetic field of the sun, along with Georg Heinrich Thiessen's observations at Hamburg, was leading to increasing conviction among astronomers that the sun's field was smaller than the value published by Hale (and used by Blackett), and that the field varies or even reverses.[36] By 1949 the best value for the sun was down from 50 gauss, the value that Blackett had used in his equation, to 1.5 gauss.[37]

Following a second strategy, in the domain of quantum electrodynamics, Blackett asked colleagues for advice: were arguments about the effects of asymmetry of charges in relation to force fields produced by moving charges at all valid?[38] Pascual Jordan wrote Blackett that he should continue working along these lines and that Jordan, too, was trying to construct a field theory from which Blackett's law might be derived as a special case.[39] By contrast, the sentiment of most quantum physicists was negative. Word reached Blackett through his Manchester colleague Léon Rosenfeld that Wolfgang Pauli still maintained longstanding objections to the hypothesis, dating back to the versions by Schuster and by Einstein and de Haas. If a field were due to acceleration, the simple formula connecting magnetic momentum and mechanical angular momentum should not hold. If the magnetic field were a velocity effect, it should be present also for translation. These, Pauli reiterated, were ideas that had been discussed and dismissed two decades earlier.[40]

Blackett's theory became a focus of discussion at a colloquium in Niels Bohr's Institute for Theoretical Physics in Copenhagen. There Niels Arsley presented a critique and sent Blackett a typescript to be submitted to *Nature*. How, asked Arsley, would a body in motion know whether its velocity is translational or rotational? How could there be a purely magnetic field without an electric one?[41] And, Arsley reminded Blackett, relationships between rotation and magnetization had been investigated years ago with negative results.[42]

Similarly, at Brussels in the fall of 1948 at the eighth Solvay physics conference, Edward Teller, Robert Oppenheimer, and Rudolf Peierls all made objections to Blackett. They noted that current experiments in Isidor Rabi's laboratory at Columbia University seemed unlikely to corroborate the asymmetry hypothesis. At Manchester, Blackett's protégé H. Y. Tzu developed an argument that Blackett's theory could only work if some new universal constant, other than G and c, were included in the factor ß. But, Tzu suggested, the principle on which this could be done was unclear.[43]

There was enough interest in Copenhagen that talk of an experimental test occurred as late as the fall of 1949.[44] The theory was the subject of a colloquium at Princeton that same year, with generally negative opinion. S. S. Schweber, then a graduate student in physics at Princeton, recalled that Einstein made a rare appearance at the colloquium for the discussion of Blackett's theory.[45] It seemed unlikely that confirming opinions for Blackett's hypothesis would come from theoretical physicists.[46]

Even while evidence from the disciplinary domains of astrophysics and quantum electrodynamics was going against Blackett's hypothesis, geophysics was providing a third strategy of possible proof. Edward C. (Teddy) Bullard was in the audience at Blackett's May 1947 Royal Society lecture.[47] Bullard and Blackett had known each other since the autumn of 1929 when Blackett supervised Bullard's experiments on electron scattering in hydrogen gas at the Cavendish.[48] In early 1931 Bullard left physics for geophysics after he heard that there was a position open as demonstrator in the new Department of Geodesy and Geophysics at Cambridge. When Bullard had asked Rutherford about the matter, Ernest Rutherford firmly replied that there were no jobs in physics and that there were a lot of people in front of him: "If I were you I would take any job I could get."[49]

During the war Bullard worked with Blackett in Operational Research at the Admiralty. Among their tasks there was study of the earth's magnetic field in connection with work on the protection of ships from magnetic mines.[50] At the beginning of 1948 Bullard would move from the

University of Cambridge to the University of Toronto as professor of physics, returning to England in January 1950 as head of the National Physical Laboratory and taking up a position in geophysics at Cambridge in 1956. By then Bullard was known as one of Britain's leading geophysicists.[51]

At the Royal Society meeting Bullard pointed out that Blackett's hypothesis for the origins of the earth's magnetism presumed a distributed theory of the earth's magnetism, rather than a core theory. The distributed, or bulk, theory assumes that the earth's magnetic field depends on electrical currents (and magnetic rocks) distributed over the entire mass of the earth. It implies that the earth's magnetic field is larger at its surface than at its interior, a prediction that could be tested by measurements of magnetic fields in mine shafts.[52] Bullard was working with a different theory, along the lines suggested in 1946 by the German-American physicist Walter Elsasser, that the earth's magnetic field results from an electrically conducting fluid moving within the earth's interior below the earth's solid mantle and crust.[53] Thus the earth's magnetic field is rooted in a molten core, in which electrical currents work like a dynamo to create magnetic effects. Bullard was beginning to use digital computers to construct a model for generating the earth's magnetic fields using assumptions of the core, or dynamo theory, and he thought that Blackett was on the wrong track.[54]

Bullard's critique suggested an empirical test for Blackett's theory by examining magnetic fields at different depths below the earth's surface. Finding mine shafts that are free of ordinary magnetic effects is not easy, and the first results from measurements in gold-mine shafts in South Africa were encouraging but inconclusive.[55] Keith Runcorn, who was lecturing in geophysics in Blackett's physics department at Manchester, worked out formulas predicting magnetic effects from the bulk and core theories of the earth's magnetism. He also carried out field work in Lancashire that initially seemed to support the distributed, or bulk, theory.[56] However, Runcorn, who previously had studied geophysics with Bullard at Cambridge, was of two minds on the matter, and he found himself leaning more and more toward Bullard's view that the origins of the earth's magnetic field lie in a moving fluid within the interior, not in the earth's bulk.[57]

By the summer of 1950, when Bullard returned to England from three years in Toronto, Blackett was on the defensive regarding the bulk theory. A collaborative group from Cambridge and Manchester, headed by Runcorn and assisted by Blackett's Manchester undergraduate students, concluded that magnetic measurements in coal mines at three sites in Yorkshire and Lancashire favored the core theory and that the earlier South African results were compromised.[58] The data set was improved during the next year, so that by 1951 the geomagnetic evidence was failing to support Blackett's theory.

Toward the "Crucial Experiment"

And what of Blackett's own experimental work on the rotating sphere? Immediately following Blackett's lecture at the Royal Society in May 1947 there was considerable interest in his proposed laboratory test of the rotating body. Edward da C. Andrade told BBC listeners that this test was well-nigh impossible: it would require spinning a body of considerable size so fast that it inevitably would fly to pieces as a result of centrifugal forces.[59] In a popular article for the Communist *Daily Worker*, J. B. S. Haldane told readers that spinning a bronze sphere of ten yards diameter as fast as possible would result in a scarcely detectable field of 1-millionth gauss.[60]

Blackett, however, was undaunted and began consulting in June 1947 with engineers he knew at the Royal Aircraft Establishment in South Farnborough about specifications for an experimental apparatus. Blackett had in mind rotating not a sphere, but a circular disk of nonconducting material, one meter in diameter and twenty centimeters thick. The weight of the disk would be about half a ton. Subsequent experiments might employ a copper disk up to two tons in weight and elliptical in shape. Blackett was undecided whether he preferred a direct mechanical device or an air- or liquid-turbine drive.[61]

By September 1947 Blackett had in hand a three-page report assessing the conditions and feasibility for his experiment. The experiment would be tricky, indeed dangerous, since the rotational speed of 8,000 rpm, as Blackett required, meant a peripheral speed for the disk a little higher than the top speed achieved at Farnborough for wooden airplane propeller blades during overspeed tests. The engineer P. R. Martin recommended an asbestos-filled resinous material for the construction of the disk, as well as the replacement of air with hydrogen in the atmosphere surrounding the disk. This was a new technique just reported for the Oerlikon flywheel-driven railcar.

The apparatus, recommended the report, should be housed in an underground pit, sealed to contain hydrogen, with casing around the rim of the spinning wheel to protect measuring instruments from windage. The driving motor would be on the first floor above the apparatus. Preliminary tests of the rotating disk, it was suggested, could be accomplished in tunnels at the Trafford Park Works of Metropolitan Vickers in Manchester,[62] the same firm that had constructed Blackett's big electromagnet "Josephine." Blackett pursued discussions about metallic and nonmetallic disks, receiving engineering advice that led him to envision a rimless wheel of 40 inches diameter, 7.5 inches thickness, and 1.5 tons in weight.[63]

At the same time that Blackett was considering the design of a rotating sphere or cylinder, he pressed ahead with the design of a magnetometer that would have greater sensitivity than Swann and Longacre's device of 1928.[64] In August 1947 Blackett and assistants, notably J. M. Pickering, began keeping notebooks for the project, moving it from the Manchester laboratory to Jodrell Bank in January 1949.[65]

As Blackett worked on design of the magnetometer, he also began to think of substituting for the rotating-disk experiment what he eventually called "a much easier but still worthwhile subsidiary experiment." A plausible deduction from the Wilson formula was the existence of a magnetic field in the vicinity of a massive body at rest in the laboratory and in rotation with respect to the heavens. Blackett calculated that a gold cylinder of dimensions 10×10 centimeters would produce a magnetic field of approximately 10^{-8} gauss. Measurement of this effect now became his immediate goal,[66] and he arranged to borrow the gold from the Bank of England.[67]

In the course of the next three years, Blackett directed the construction of cylinders of varying materials, including gold, as well as the building and testing of different types of astatic magnetometers. In the traditional astatic magnetometer, as devised by Lord Kelvin, two equal and oppositely directed (antiparallel) magnets are fixed to a vertical rod suspended by a thin fiber (for example, silk or quartz) so that the resultant magnetic moments of the two magnets cancel each other. The system is undisturbed by a uniform magnetic field, but in a nonuniform field a rotation of the torsion fiber results with its motion dependent on the difference of horizontal field at the top and bottom magnets. The magnetic moment of each magnet depends on the fourth power of the distance from the test object. Each magnet of the pair is usually made up of three to six smaller magnets suitably spaced in a vertical direction. On the support between the pair of antiparallel magnets is fixed a mirror, from which a beam of light is reflected for viewing on a scale through a microscope. Thus deviations (in radians) of a spot of light on a scale are the measurements recorded.[68]

Blackett's task was twofold: design of the suspended system in order to give the highest possible performance, and reduction to a minimum of external disturbances so that residual error of a reading is governed only by the Brownian motion of the suspended system. Blackett's approach to the suspension design was, first, the use of small trimming magnets with carefully optimized shapes for astaticizing the suspended system and, second, increasing the periods of oscillation from approximately ten seconds to thirty seconds in order to increase sensitivity.

To deal with the problem of external disturbances, Blackett set up the laboratory apparatus in the corner of a field 200 yards from the radio-astronomy site at Jodrell Bank. His laboratory building was a copper-nailed hut on a heavy concrete foundation, with its inside walls lined with ebonite for thermal insulation.[69] Blackett did some of the work himself in the construction of the hut, assisted by his twenty-year-old son Nick in hammering copper, rather than iron, nails.[70] Some adjustments had to be made in the equipment to compensate for the change in the earth's uniform magnetic field over time. This was done by setting up a system of three Helmholtz coils mounted with their axes mutually perpendicular, a common arrangement.[71] Blackett then employed a "Flux-gate" device to detect small changes in the earth's magnetic field so that the coils then automatically compensated them.[72]

For the suspended magnets in the magnetometer, Blackett used alloys of various composition, the most successful of which, Alcomax IV, contained principally aluminum, nickel, and cobalt.[73] Blackett at first used magnets composed of iron-containing alloys, but the weaker Alcomax magnets were found to be preferable because they reduced the field of the magnetometer at the specimen. The trimming magnets were small wires made of Vicalloy, which is mainly carbon. The suspension fiber was made of fused quartz.[74]

The specimen to be studied was a cylinder mounted on a vertical hydraulic piston so that the specimen could be moved up and down below the magnetometer a distance of some twenty centimeters in five seconds or less, that is, in considerably less time than the period of oscillation of the suspended system.[75] The basic procedure was first to take a reading (d_1) of a spot of light, which was reflected off the small mirror fixed on the support tube for the magnets, with the specimen in its lowest position. Then the specimen was raised closer under the magnetometer, and a second reading (d_2) was taken after the spot of light came to rest. Then the specimen was lowered and a third reading (d_3) was taken.[76] The deflection Δ due to the specimen is then

$$\Delta = d_2 - 1/2 \ (d_1 + d_3)$$

After a set of readings, the specimen was rotated ninety degrees by a string worked from an outer room, and the process of raising and lowering the specimen was repeated. This procedure avoided measurements compromised by the eddy current disturbances caused by rotating a metallic sample.[77]

For the static-body experiments, Blackett used ten-centimeter cylinders made of gold, lead, copper, brass, and aluminum as well as five-centimeter cylinders made of lead and of an 80% tin-20% lead alloy. The gold cylinder weighed 15.2 kilograms (38.5 pounds).[78] Most of Blackett's cylinders were constructed in his laboratory, but the gold one and the five-centimeter cylinders were made by the Johnson Matthey firm.

During 1950 and 1951 a long series of measurements were made, paying increased attention to centering and leveling of the specimen. In late April 1951 experimental runs were made with the gold cylinder and Alcomax IV magnetometer, all recorded by Pickering. Measurements of a copper cylinder were recorded in the same period by Blackett himself. The sensitivity of the Alcomax IV magnetomer was 1 millimeter on the reading scale = 1.20×10^{-8} gauss, corresponding to a microscopic division of 9.8×10^{-10} gauss.[79] Blackett had funding for these experiments from the British government's Department of Scientific and Industrial Research.

Yet, even as he was beginning to run experiments at Jodrell Bank during 1950 to 1951, Blackett was losing confidence in his fundamental hypothesis. The data from stellar observations and from deep-mine observations had failed to support either Blackett's fundamental equation or the bulk theory of the earth's magnetism. Surveying the most recent literature on the earth's magnetism, Blackett began to note new work on rock magnetism published from the Carnegie Institution in Washington by Ellis A. Johnson, T. Murphy, Oscar W. Torreson, and John Graham.[80]

This work focused on the measurement of remanent or paleomagnetism in rocks, in order to study changes in the earth's magnetic field during the past millions of years of geological time. Remanent magnetism (or remanence) is found in igneous rocks that lose their magnetism when heated above the Curie temperature and regain magnetism, in the direction of the earth's magnetic field, as they cool. The Curie temperature is $760°$ centigrade for iron and $358°$ centigrade for nickel, for example. Remanent magnetism also is found in sedimentary rocks that acquire a very weak magnetism through the preferential alignment of particles of magnetic minerals as they settle in water in the presence of the earth's magnetic field.

If the value measured from a slightly magnetic rock sample for the inclination of its magnetic dipole does not coincide with the inclination expected from the rock's location on the earth's surface, then one possible inference is that the earth's magnetic pole has shifted from the position it had in paleohistoric times. Bullard's dynamo theory of the earth's core predicts that patterns of motion of electrically charged fluids inside the earth may have changed at irregular intervals, resulting in wandering of the dipole for the magnetic field, although the general orientation of the dipole would remain close to the earth's pole of rotation. In contrast, the bulk, or distribution, theory of the earth's magnetic field does not make this prediction.

It is hardly surprising, then, that Blackett paid attention to reports on rock magnetism and began to think of collecting rock samples to study with his own magnetometer. He also was fully aware of another striking conclusion that could be drawn from paleomagnetic evidence that seemed to point to a different orientation in the past of the earth's magnetic field. The shift might be apparent polar wandering, not actual polar wandering. It might be the effect of the earth's crust and its continents having shifted in relation to the earth's spin axis and its fixed geomagnetic pole. In other words, remanence might be evidence of continental drift, an old hypothesis that had broken out as the subject of heated debate at the meeting of the British Association for the Advancement of Science in Birmingham in early September 1950.[81]

In late May of 1951, as Blackett was becoming more interested in measuring magnetism in rocks, he was completing experimental runs in his magnetometer hut on a series of metallic and nonmetallic cylinders, using more and more sensitive magnetometer design. The results were negative. Blackett wrote Pascual Jordan that the rotating-body experiment still seemed a crucial experiment that he would like to carry out, but there is no evidence that Blackett ever attempted it.[82] While Blackett's results for his fixed-cylinder experiments were negative, like those of Albert Michelson and Edward Morley in their search for an ether effect in the 1880s, there is every likelihood, given the independent disconfirming evidence and the general skepticism about Blackett's theory, that any positive results would have remained unconvincing, as was the case with Dayton Miller's short-lived positive evidence for an ether effect.[83]

Blackett shortly decided to end the static-body experiments, concluding that if any magnetic field is associated with a rotating mass, its value is undetectably small.[84] Blackett published his negative results in 1952, saying that they were "in satisfactory agreement with the independent refutation of the hypothesis by . . . measurements . . . of the magnetic field of the earth underground."[85] Of his bold hypothesis, announced with so much fanfare in 1947, Blackett still expressed his regret some twenty-five years later that so attractive and simple a relationship had proven untenable.[86] Of his continued pursuit of the experiments described in the 1952 paper, he said that this work had resulted in a valuable "instrumental study on the theory and use of the magnetometer."[87]

Risking Big Theories

Why had Blackett, a consummate experimentalist, embarked in 1947 upon a grand cosmo-physical theoretical scheme? Runcorn believed that there had long been a speculative kernel in Blackett's thinking and that it had been suppressed during his early training at the Cavendish under Rutherford.[88] Runcorn later noted that, "from what he later said about Eddington, Milne, and Chandrasekhar, I think he must have followed the development of knowledge of the internal constitution of stars with wonder. . . . In his ideas on the origin of the Earth's field he gave this speculative element of his mind free reign."[89]

Yet Runcorn's statement cannot be the whole of the matter. While Blackett's interests had expanded by the late 1940s from the particle physics of cosmic rays to the cosmological physics of optical and radio astronomy, his early work hardly excluded theoretical interests and practices. Nor is theory neatly opposed to practice.[90] When Rutherford had given permission, which Blackett characterized as "grudging," for Blackett to take a brief leave from Cambridge to Göttingen in 1924, Rutherford advised Blackett "to get in touch with the methods of measurement and the ideas of Franck." Blackett returned to Cambridge in 1925 full of enthusiasm for wave mechanics and electron theory. Nor was the interest in theory new. As discussed in Chapter 2, Blackett had written theoretical papers in the 1920s and was a regular member of Paul Dirac's theoretical discussion group and an enthusiastic afficionado of Dirac's approach to quantum electrodynamics. Blackett and Giuseppe Occhialini's initial report on the positively charged electron directly linked its observation to Dirac's theoretical prediction of pair production and an antielectron.

Blackett's cosmic-ray work of the 1930s more and more engaged diverse novel theoretical interpretations of observed nuclear particles. Blackett's last publication on cosmic rays before the Second World War analyzed decay of the mesotron particle in relation to Werner Heisenberg's proposal for establishing a new fundamental constant with the dimension of length, where this fundamental length was defined in relation to the mass of the mesotron. Blackett worked out an equation for a possible connection between the mean life of the mesotron, the fundamental length, the fundamental charge e, and the gravitational constant G, trying to provide a link between atomic and gravitational phenomena.[91] In 1941, in his Guthrie Lecture, Blackett reiterated this possible connection, noting that, if the mean lifetime of the meson is related to G, it might be related through general relativity to the total mass of the universe.[92] So it was not for the first time in 1947 that Blackett had interested himself in fundamental theories on the cosmological scale.

Nor is Runcorn's remark about Arthur S. Eddington, Edward Arthur Milne, and Chandrasekhar without significance. These three astronomers all had spent time at Cambridge. Eddington was Plumian Professor of Astronomy and director of the Observatory at Cambridge. Milne worked at the Cambridge Solar Observatory from 1920 to 1924 before going to Manchester and then, in 1928, to Oxford. Chandrasekhar, educated in India, arrived in Cambridge in 1930 and was a Fellow at Trinity College from 1933 to 1937, before going to the United States. Milne briefly directed some of Paul Dirac's work in early 1925 while Ralph Fowler was away from Cambridge; Dirac worked in practice as Chandrasekhar's supervisor.[93] Eddington, Milne, Chandrasekhar, and Dirac all had interests in the 1930s in developing electrodynamical and gravitational theories on a cosmological scale.[94]

Eddington was especially well known for his interest in a kind of numerology of the universe, aimed at unification of physical theory through dimensionless ratios that are quotients of the fundamental physical constants G, m_e, m_p, h, and c (the gravitational constant, the charge of the electron, the charge of the proton, Planck's constant, and the speed of light), to which he added λ or N, the number of particles (protons) in the universe.[95] Eddington thought that the Dirac equation for the electron described not an individual electron, but the structural relation of the electron to the entire universe.[96]

In an article in *Naturwissenschaften* in 1931, Hans Bethe and German colleagues spoofed Eddington's methodology and the field of "cosmophysics." Showing suspicion of overly abstract theory, Bethe, G. Beck, and W. Riezler coauthored a prank article on a quantum theory of absolute zero, which *Naturwissenschaften*'s editor Arnold Berliner unwittingly published. The coauthors were trying to serve a humorous warning against purely speculative theories based on numerological significances. The warning proved ineffective, however, to theorists such as Dirac and Heisenberg who continued to interest themselves in fundamental numbers.[97]

Like Eddington, whose work Max Born harshly called "rubbish,"[98] Milne met unsympathetic criticism when he began to develop a theory in 1933 that the gravitation constant has a time variation for observers in a time-scale system in which mass is time-invariant. Undaunted, in 1937 Dirac offered an interpretation of the significance of a set of three dimensionless constants of nature, which are expressed in terms of the large numbers 10^{38}, 10^{39}, and 10^{78}. He proposed that these numerical values all have a time variation and that they are so large simply because the universe is so old.[99] Chandrasekhar, then at the University of Chicago's Yerkes Observatory, encouraged Dirac by sending him a calculation, based on Dirac's model, of how the number of particles in a star would increase as $t^{3/2}$. However, most of Dirac's colleagues in theoretical physics remained silent, with the notable exception of Jordan, who made the large-numbers hypothesis the starting point for a scalar-tensor theory in 1944.[100]

An unpleasant article soon appeared in *Nature* in which the astronomer and philosopher Herbert Dingle villified what he called the "pseudoscience" and "cosmythology" of Eddington, Milne, and Dirac.[101] A reproof to Dingle came from Cambridge physicist Charles Galton Darwin:

> It is surely hard enough to make discoveries in science without having to obey arbitrary rules in doing so; in discovering the laws of Nature, foul means are perfectly fair. If Dirac is not to be allowed to conjecture the age of the earth from certain curious numerical coincidences, then Maxwell committed as great a crime in conjecturing that the velocity of light was the same thing as the ratio of the electric and magnetic units.[102]

What does this have to do with Blackett? Perhaps a good deal. In the 1920s and early 1930s, while Blackett was in Cambridge, Eddington's prestige in Cambridge astronomy was dominant. Chandrasekhar and Dirac regularly came round to Cavendish Laboratory meetings in the early 1930s. Although Blackett left Cambridge for Birkbeck College in London in 1933 and then moved to Manchester in 1937, it is inconceivable that he was unaware of discussions of Cambridge cosmo-physics. The allure of fundamental constants, numerical coincidences, dimensionless constants, and simple unifying relationships is evident not just in Blackett's 1947 paper on the earth's magnetism, but in his earlier speculations on the mass increase in the penetrating cosmic radiations and on the decay of the meson. In all this, Blackett's acquaintance with the grand theoretical ambitions of Eddington, Milne, Dirac, and Chandrasekhar must have played a role, even as he was aware of the skepticism of many quantum physicists about unified grand theories.[103]

Arriving at the simple but satisfying coincidence of numbers in his 1947 equation

$$P = \beta(G^{1/2}/2c)U$$

Blackett came to recognize that there was a body of well-established theoretical objections and experimental failures that seemed to forbid the revival and pursuit of this particular theory. But, pursue it he did, along with a program of strategies for experimental verification.

Some later remarks help clarify Blackett's attitude toward forbidden experiments and theories. At McGill University in 1958, Blackett recalled the history of the proof of the nonconservation of parity in order to warn his audience about the dangers of experimentalists allowing themselves to be "deterred from making some simple but important experiments because of the predictions of a theory which they did not fully understand—for if they had, they would have realized that it was not soundly based."[104]

Reiterating this point on another occasion, Blackett said, "On the frontiers of knowledge a technically possible experiment suggested by theory should of course be performed; however, an *attractive* and *technically possible* experiment should not be omitted because existing theory suggests that it will be uninteresting. In most cases theory will prove right; in rare cases it will prove wrong and these are the great discoveries."[105] In short, Blackett expressed the need for boldness in theoretical conjectures or in experimental strategies if they could be tied rigorously to what he called phenomenological statements. Rosenfeld claimed that Blackett's genius lay precisely in his constructive use of failures: he was not deterred by flops. Blackett would just say "that's a flop. We must try to make the best of it."[106]

Systematic exploration of theory leads to productive ends, even in the refutation of the theory. The philosopher Rudolf Carnap commented in a letter to historian and philosopher Thomas Kuhn, "the development of theories is . . . a process of improvement of an instrument."[107] For Blackett, as an experimentalist, the theory of the earth's magnetism was a tool for exploring the fields of astrophysics, geophysics, and quantum physics, as well as for arriving at new knowledge of the theory and use of the magnetometer. Had Blackett's theory of the earth's magnetism met with confirmation, it would have been a great discovery.

The temptations of a fundamental and universal physical theory may have been especially appealing to Blackett after wartime service in operations research and postwar preoccupation with the development of atomic weapons. If so, for Blackett, the pursuit of his theory entailed the practical strategies of organizing collaborators and designing experiments at which he was so adept.

The search from 1947 to 1952 for corroboration of the fundamental equation relating the earth's magnetism and its motion led to an even more wide-ranging and collaborative search for corroboration of the drifting of the earth's continents. Measurements with Blackett's astatic magnetometer provided the first definite evidence from rock magnetism for a moving continent.[108] As for the Schuster-Wilson hypothesis, some theorists still have not ruled it out, at least for the magnetic fields of the very massive, very dense bodies that are black holes.[109]

5

"Reading Ourselves into the Subject": Geophysics and the Revival of Continental Drift, 1951–1965

By the time that Blackett communicated his negative results to the Royal Society on his tests for a measurable magnetic effect from a rotating cylinder, he already had embarked on a new research program in the measurement of rock magnetism. He also had learned a great deal by the spring of 1952 about the hypothesis of continental drift, saying later at a 1964 symposium sponsored by the Royal Society that it had been about fifteen years earlier that "I along with many other new workers in the field of rock magnetism, started to read ourselves into the subject of continental drift."[1]

The German meteorologist and geophysicist Alfred Wegener had outlined his proposal for continental drift in his book *Die Entstehung der Kontinente und Ozeane,* first published in 1915 and appearing in English translation in 1924.[2] After considerable debate about Wegener's data and methods, most geologists and geophysicists dismissed the hypothesis on both empirical and theoretical grounds. In 1950 Philip H. Kuenen wrote in a standard textbook that most geologists appear "to have lost faith in continental drift as a working hypothesis."[3] In the mid-1960s many American geologists still inclined against the hypothesis at a time when largely British-originated data, much of it linked directly or indirectly to the work of Blackett and his colleagues, had revived drift theory in England. When Neil Opdyke, a graduate in geology at Columbia University, arrived at Cambridge in the fall of 1955, he was astonished to find John Clegg, Mary Almond, and Peter Stubbs using data to argue for continental drift. Opdyke told them that they were "bananas" to look for continental drift.[4] By way of contrast, on the West Coast in the United States, John Verhoogen's graduate students at Berkeley were hearing favorable arguments for drift as the Belgian-born Verhoogen taught that the lack of a plausible mechanism did not preclude the continents' motions.[5]

In 1947 Blackett's research activities had turned away from nuclear physics and cosmic radiation partly because Blackett wanted an experimental project that he could do largely alone, on an odd schedule, given his frequent absences from Manchester because of responsibilities in London.[6] Blackett's final report in 1952 on his *negative* results in investigations of the origins of the earth's magnetic field was a masterful *positive* account of the theory and operation of his astatic magnetometer. At the paper's conclusion, he noted the suitability of his magnetometer for a purpose different than he had originally intended, namely measuring remanent magnetism in sedimentary rocks.[7]

On first glance, this seems a surprising transition for a nuclear physicist. Yet the move toward geophysics was a result of what Blackett himself characterized as an exploratory method of investigation and of seeing what turns up.[8] The study of magnetism had been essential to Blackett's cloud-chamber work in particle physics. Blackett's work in operational research during the war often targeted studies of magnetic effects, for example in developing magnetic mines to use against German U-boats and antimagnetic devices to mask the presence of British ships from enemy submarines. The magnetic field of the earth was an old interest: in 1936 he remarked in his Halley Lecture at Oxford on the fact that there was as yet "no satisfactory theory . . . for the phenomenon of terrestrial magnetism."[9]

Blackett also often noted in his popular lectures that the investigation of cosmic rays had to do with astronomy and geophysics no less than physics.[10] Cosmic-ray experiments demanded global networks of information, both in investigations of latitude effects and in measurements at high altitude across the world. Similarly, operational research had required global thinking. As around 1949 he turned to thinking about paleomagnetism, the history of the earth, and continental drift, Blackett faced the challenge of putting patterns of data onto a global map. What drove his new research was not simply the appeal of a theory, but rather the appeal of an experimental test. When he embarked on his fundamental theory of the earth's magnetism in 1947, Blackett had told Edward (Ted) Irving that the hypothesis of geomagnetism arising from rotation of the earth was an attractive idea because it "could be tested."[11] It turned out that continental drift could be tested too.

In addition, while particle physics by the 1950s was on its way to requiring larger and larger machines, as well as huge on-site teams of scientists, engineers, and administrative staff, the geophysical problems undertaken by Blackett were manageable enterprises within smaller laboratory frameworks. The theoretical challenge became one of piecing together new kinds of evidence in order to examine old theories, whether it was the origin of geomagnetism or the motions of the continents. Testing the commonly rejected hypothesis of continental drift with a new kind of evidence from rock magnetism, using his new astatic magnetometer, became too obvious an opportunity for Blackett to ignore.

Paleomagnetism and Geophysics at Manchester, 1951–1953

In the late 1940s there were at least two types of magnetic variation that a theory of the earth's magnetism had to explain. One was the apparent polar wandering indicated by paleomagnetism in rocks. The other was the secular, or local, variation in the earth's magnetic field that had been known since the sixteenth century, corresponding to local changes in direction and intensity of the earth's magnetic field that occur everywhere on the earth, with magnitudes that vary with place and time. The direction of the magnetic field is measured by declination (the horizontal deviation of the north end of a compass needle from the north geographic pole) and inclination (the vertical deviation or dip from the horizontal). The inclination is zero at the magnetic equator and ninety degrees at the magnetic poles. The intensity of the total field is described by horizontal intensity, vertical intensity, and the north and east components of horizontal intensity. Of long-standing interest in ocean navigation was the changing location over time of the north magnetic pole, the end of the magnetic dipole that is offset from the axis of the earth's rotation by approximately eleven degrees. The magnetic north pole is different from the geographic North Pole (at 90° north latitude at which all lines of longitude converge). In 1831 the British naval officer John Ross led an expedition in search of the Northwest Passage, and his nephew James Clark Ross located the magnetic north pole on the Boothia Peninsula in northern Canada during a sledge journey. Over the course of the next century the magnetic pole gradually moved about 1,100 kilometers northwest, accelerating more recently.[12]

As described in Chapter 4, in Edward (Teddy) Bullard's view, a dynamo, or core, theory of the earth seemed more promising than a bulk model for explaining these secular variations in the earth's magnetic field. When Blackett first proposed his rotational theory for the origin of the earth's magnetic field, Sydney Chapman wondered if Blackett's bulk, or distributed, theory for the earth's magnetism could be expected to explain secular variation. Blackett's view appears to have been that explanations of secular variation would follow eventually from whatever theory of the earth's general magnetic field turned out to be correct.[13]

During 1948 to 1950, while Bullard was working in Toronto, he regularly kept in touch with Blackett, both when he visited England and in correspondence. Bullard had interest in the mine-shaft experiments to measure changes in intensity of the earth's magnetic field at different depths, and he wrote Blackett in early 1948 of plans for aircraft to measure the vertical variation of magnetism in the atmosphere, as well as for a cable ship to measure magnetic variation undersea.[14] By mid-1951, as we have seen, the magnetic measurements in Lancashire coal mines failed to support Blackett's theory, and Blackett's approach to measurements of magnetism in the earth shifted to paleomagnetism and the capacity of his magnetometer for measuring lower levels of magnetism than had been possible previously.

In May 1951 Blackett lectured to the Cambridge Geophysical Department on the measurement of low magnetic fields and talked with Keith Runcorn about Runcorn's interest in studying secular variation in the distant past by using remanent magnetism.[15] One of Runcorn's postgraduate students was Edward (Ted) Irving, a recent Cambridge graduate in natural sciences with geology as a special subject, who was getting set to measure remanent magnetism with Runcorn in the fine-grained red beds of the Torridonian.[16] They collected a first set of rocks together in England and Scotland, and then Irving made three further trips, in April 1952, November 1952, and August/September 1953 with David Collinson.[17]

During summer 1951 Irving visited Manchester to use Blackett's Jodrell Bank magnetometer on the rock samples that he and Runcorn had collected.[18] Irving knew geology, while Blackett and Runcorn did not, and Irving had been interested in continental drift since sixth-form grammar school when he had read Wegener's *Origin of Continents and Oceans* and A. L. Du Toit's *Our Wandering Continents*.[19] When Blackett asked Irving's advice on a general text in geology, Irving suggested Arthur Holmes's *Principles of Physical Geology,* which Irving himself had just finished reading from the Manchester University library.

Holmes's book was not yet part of the standard syllabus in geophysics, even in the lecture course taught at Cambridge by Maurice Black who did tell Irving and other students that they should familiarize themselves with evidence for continental drift, especially evidence from glaciation.[20] Holmes's textbook, first published in 1944, was unusual in its strong brief for the hypothesis of continental drift.[21] Holmes, who was a professor of geology at Durham and then at Edinburgh, had studied physics at Imperial College. He had been encouraged there by R. J. Strutt (the fourth Baron Rayleigh) to construct an absolute geological timescale based on radioactivity half-lives. About 1925 Holmes concluded that the lateral motion of the continents might provide a means for discharging the heat built up under continents as a result of radioactivity and convection currents in the earth. Thus drift could be a consequence of physical processes within the earth.[22] This was a view that Holmes would argue against Cambridge mathematical physicist and geophysicist Harold Jeffreys in the next decades. One of Jeffreys's objections to Holmes's theory of subcrustal currents was that there was no "test that appears decisive for or against it."[23] As late as 1964 Jeffreys was to write that "elastico-viscous law" forbids convection and continental drift.[24]

In the summer of 1951, making his way through Irving's library copy of Holmes's book, Blackett made detailed notes covering some dozen sheets of paper, which Irving discovered afterwards in the book.[25] Blackett later said that he found especially striking Holmes's argument on glaciation: that there just was not sufficient water in the world to produce a large enough ice-cap if the continents had been in the same relative position to each other in ancient times as they are today, since the Permo-Carboniferous glaciation of the southern hemisphere occurred about the same time that the great coal deposits of the northern hemisphere were being laid down.[26] Blackett also found himself sympathetic to Holmes's arguments that it is important to decide whether continental drift "is a genuine variety of earth movement" and that "explanations may safely be left until we know with greater confidence what it is that needs to be explained."[27]

In fall 1951, John Clegg moved from Bernard Lovell's radio-astronomy group into Blackett's new rock magnetism group at Manchester that would collect rocks and study remanent magnetism in sedimentary rocks from Yorkshire and North Wales.[28] As Runcorn noted, sedimentary rocks were better dated than igneous rocks, and magnetic variations could be detailed bed by bed, layer by layer from ancient time. The difficulty is that it is more difficult to measure remanent magnetism in sedimentary rocks than in igneous rocks. Magnetic field intensities in igneous rocks range from 10^{-2} to 10^{-4} gauss, in contrast to values from 10^{-6} to 10^{-8} gauss in sedimentary rocks.[29] The new focus on remanent magnetism in sedimentary rocks would prove a masterstroke in investigations of paleomagnetism by making it possible to study a huge number of rocks and to compare these results to data for igneous rocks. If both kinds of rocks yielded the same order of quantitative data, conclusions drawn from the data would be much more credible.[30]

Using Blackett's magnetometer, the Cambridge group found that the solidly cemented, fine-grained red sandstones of the Torridonian Sandstone Series (pre-Cambrian rocks from Scotland) gave the most consistent data. The magnetization of these sandstones was directed to the southeast, strongly oblique to the earth's present field. However, the magnetization was a complex phenomenon, with some samples providing a record of the paleofield, others only of the recent field (because of overprinting, or later remagnetization), and still others a mixture of the two.

During 1952–1954 Irving established that the earth had a magnetic field as far back as the Precambrian. Rock samples from Scotland showed both reversals in the magnetic field and a direction strongly oblique to the present (normal) magnetic field.[31] The fact and meaning of reversals were hotly disputed issues throughout the 1950s and early 1960s, especially following the work of Jan Hospers, who reported reversals of the magnetic field in igneous rocks from Iceland. These were measured first with a new spinner magnetometer in J. McGarva Bruckshaw's laboratory at Imperial College and then by an astatic magnetometer in Cambridge.[32] With assistance from Sir Ronald Fisher, the Cambridge genetics professor, Hospers was able to provide a convincing interpretation on the scatters in his data using Fisher's formulation for applied statistics on a sphere.[33] Hospers subsequently showed that, irrespective of sign, the normal and reversed direction of the geomagnetic field, when averaged over tens of thousands of years, approximated closely to that of a geocentric axial dipole and that contrary results from the Carnegie Institution were the result of overprinting in sedimentary rock samples.[34]

By the time Irving completed work for his 1954 Ph.D. thesis at Cambridge, measurements were being made with a faster instrument than the original Jodrell Bank magnetometer. It was designed by Kenneth M. Creer as an instrument aimed at maximum sensitivity and minimum period rather than Blackett's design for maximum signal to noise. The Cambridge magnetometer, which could be used to make measurements much more rapidly than Blackett's, was finished in early 1953. Clegg had earlier built a similar instrument in the Manchester Physics Department, completed by April 1952.[35] Such instruments remained the workhorses of paleomagnetism until the appearance of improved spinner magnetometers in the early 1970s.[36]

When Blackett moved from Manchester to Imperial College in 1953, Clegg went with him. The next year Clegg and his Manchester colleagues Mary Almond and Peter Stubbs published a paper documenting both oblique directions and reversals in sedimentary rocks that they had collected from the Late Triassic New Red Sandstone. This was a paper that convinced many earth scientists of the importance of paleomagnetism for understanding the earth's history.[37] In another paper, in the *Journal of Geomagnetism and Geo-electricity,* Clegg, Almond, and Stubbs proposed that England had rotated some thirty-four degrees and moved toward the North Pole over geological time. However, the three coauthors did not propose drift since they had no data from other land masses.[38]

The argument was becoming common in Cambridge and London geophysics in the early 1950s that the measurements of oblique directions in the inclination of the earth's magnetic field in paleomagnetic rocks documented apparent movements of the magnetic pole relative to Britain. The motions could be explained by Britain's moving relative to the substratrum, in other words, Wegener's hypothesis of continental drift, or by apparent polar wandering (APW), or by some combination of the two.[39] In late summer 1954 Creer drew the first apparent polar wander path, by means of which quantitative testing became possible. With the APW path, it became obvious that if all continents had the same apparent polar wander path as Europe, then they had not moved relative to one another, but if each continent had its own distinctive path, then it was likely the continents had moved relative to one another. Creer taught Irving how to calculate paleopoles, as Jan Hospers was doing independently in the Netherlands, and the approach appeared in the conclusion of Irving's dissertation of 1954, along with preliminary information from the Paleocene Deccan Traps of India, which suggested that India once had been in the southern hemisphere, as Wegener had said.[40]

Indeed, Irving had realized already in 1951 that India should show the strongest paleomagnetic effects. India's motion, according to Wegener and his father-in-law, the meteorologist Wladimir Köppen, was mainly latitudinal, having moved from the southern to the northern hemisphere.[41] Given his predisposition toward drift, Irving persuaded Fisher to inquire about having rock samples sent to Cambridge while Fisher was visiting the Indian Statistical Institute in late 1951.[42] Irving was able to analyze these rock samples from the Deccan Plateau of India beginning in mid-1953, before he completed his dissertation.[43] He left England for the Australian National University in Canberra in 1954, soon adding Australian data and southern hemisphere perspectives to the study of continental drift.

Evidence and Arguments for Drift—Imperial College, 1953–1965

When Blackett moved from Manchester to Imperial College in London, he felt that he was moving back home. He had been born in Kensington, and he and Costanza now were settling nearby in Chelsea, at Paulton's Square. He saw the Imperial College position as an opportunity to implement expansion of science and technology programs in a cosmopolitan university setting and in a fashion that would make optimal use of his talents and his preference for combining scientific research with scientific administration.[44] He was closer to many of the committees on which he served and to the Athenaeum and club life in London. He felt at ease.

Blackett knew in 1953 that he likely would be a prime candidate to succeed Lawrence Bragg at the Cavendish Laboratory, but he wrote James Chadwick in 1954 that he had decided he preferred to live in London.[45] Runcorn was one of those disappointed that Blackett would not succeed Bragg, writing Blackett that Cavendish physicists were insufficiently sympathetic to geophysics or astrophysics or meterology, and that they had just refused to allow geophysics into the physics curriculum as a specialist subject.[46] Runcorn left Cambridge in 1955 for Newcastle, the King's College campus of Durham University.

By 1954 Blackett was proposing three- and four-year projects to the government's Department of Scientific and Industrial Research for the measurement of paleomagnetism around the world.[47] One of his projects was a paleomagnetic survey of the Indian subcontinent, which he first visited in 1947. His Imperial College group organized a laboratory in the Tata Institute in Bombay where they trained Indian graduates in work that was continued after the English scientists left in 1960.[48] The Indian geophysicists P. W. Sahasrabudhe and C. Radakrishnamurty spent time in London as well.[49]

In the summer of 1954, Paleozoic and Mesozoic red beds from the southwestern United States were added to the Indian and Australian data. This was the work of Richard Doell, then a graduate student at Berkeley, John Graham from the Carnegie Institution, and Runcorn.[50] A definitive survey and interpretation of British paleomagnetic data appeared in the *Philosophical Transactions of the Royal Society* in 1957, organized in a set of papers based on a conference that Blackett convened in London in 1956. The six papers were coauthored or singly authored by D. W. Collinson, Creer, Irving, and Runcorn, who attributed the work in their papers to the systematic measurement and intepretation of paleomagnetism in a program begun at Cambridge in 1951. It was, they said, the "development by Blackett of a sensitive astatic magnetometer [that] provided the incentive to extend this survey to the more weakly magnetized sedimentary rocks in order to determine the direction of the geomagnetic field in remote geological epochs and to examine whether reversals occurred in other geological periods and strata than documented by Hospers."[51]

One of the principal aims of the set of papers was to establish the reliability of remanent rock magnetism as an indicator of the orientation of magnetic particles in sedimentary rock at the time of deposition. Irving offered five different mechanisms that might be hypothesized to account for magnetization, but he demonstrated that the most plausible cause was alignment with the geomagnetic field of magnetic particles of the mineral specularite during the process of sedimentation.[52]

In 1954 Blackett presented a set of lectures on rock magnetism as the Second Weizmann Memorial Lectures in Israel, revising them for publication in 1956.[53] He emphasized that rock magnetism data might be used to "settle the long-debated and highly controversial problems of continental drift and polar wandering," noting that measurements supported the interpretation of mobilism, including a northward movement of India of some 7,000 kilometers that had resulted in India's collision with Asia as the mechanism of mountain-building of the Himalayas. Blackett also noted that palaeoclimatic arguments previously made by Wegener and others could be compared with paleomagnetic data and provide mutually supporting evidence for drift if they agreed.[54]

Comparison of paleomagnetic and paleoclimatic data appeared in a 1956 paper by Irving, who received the Walter Bucher Medal of the Australian Geological Union in 1979. (This was a paper which was rejected in 1955 by the *Journal of the Geological Society of Australia*.)[55] As he later summarized his then-controversial argument, Irving demonstrated in 1956 that

> if one took the APW path for, say, Europe, the paleolatitude variations calculated for Europe were consistent with the paleoclimatic variations within Europe inferred from geologic evidence. Coral reefs occurred in low paleolatitudes, for instance. Hence the paleomagnetically derived paleopoles coincided, at least roughly, with the paleogeographic pole as far back in time as the Late Paleozoic. . . . However, if one took the APW path for Europe and used it to calculate the paleolatitudinal variations for other continents, on the basis of fixism, then the variations were grossly inconsistent with the paleoclimatic evidence. . . . Thus the paleoclimatic argument used by Köppen and Wegener received the support of an independent geophysical test.[56]

While he had hesitated to agree with the conclusion of his students and colleagues who had begun advocating drift since the early 1950s, Runcorn became persuaded in 1956, writing:

> Probably most geologists and geophysicists feel reluctant to admit the possibility of relative displacements of the continental masses in the recent history of the earth. It is often stated that a sound reason for such

skepticism is the absence of any adequate theory of the mechanism by which such continental displacement could have taken place. This is an argument that should not be given much weight. Not until the last few years has there been an adequate theory for the existence of the geomagnetic field, but scientists did not previously disbelieve in the existence of the field for this reason.[57]

From 1954 to 1961, Blackett directed or participated in some thirteen Ph.D. theses on rock magnetism, including work originating at Cambridge.[58] A summary of work carried out in the rock magnetism group at Imperial College from 1957 to 1960 included five areas of concentration: (1) the study of the directions of magnetization of rock systems in India, Britain, and the Belgian Congo; (2) the behavior of rocks under thermal and alternating-field demagnetization treatments; (3) investigation of self-reversing mechanisms; (4) analysis of all published rock magnetic observations; and (5) experimental investigation of the effect of both hydrostatic and axial pressures on the remanent magnetization of rocks.[59]

By Clegg's account, "until 1964 at least, he [Blackett] managed to spend long periods of time—often as much as three or four half days in the week—in the rock magnetism laboratory, and he always knew exactly the state of the research of individual members of the group. He was as prolific as ever in ideas, which he offered to younger people as suggestions for research, and he was remarkably generous in allowing them to take the credit for the results."[60]

The centerpieces of Blackett's own work in these years, from 1954 until his retirement from Imperial College in 1965, were two papers written in 1960 and 1961, the first coauthored with Clegg and Stubbs, on whose data the paper largely rested, and the second singly authored. Clegg has given an account of Blackett's participation in writing the 1960 paper, one that resonates with earlier observations of Blackett's modes of reasoning and interpretation in particle physics and operational research.

The 1960 paper went through about seven typewritten drafts, with Blackett searching for reasons why the conclusions they were reaching might be subject to challenge. Clegg later remarked to Francis Everitt that this approach must have been the reason Carl Anderson beat Blackett to the positron.[61] In the final version of the 1960 paper, which analyzed rock magnetic data from Europe, North America, India, and Australia, the authors gave five possible interpretations of the data: that the direction of rock magnetization does not represent the direction of the local earth's field at the time; that geographical polar wandering has occurred; that magnetic polar wandering has occurred; that the earth's field had strong nondipole components in remote geological times; and that continental drift has occurred. The authors concluded in favor of continental drift as the most likely explanation of the data.[62]

Blackett, Clegg, and Stubbs presented no analysis of the intensity of magnetization nor of magnetic reversals in the past, while noting that there was no conclusive evidence pointing to a larger or smaller field in ancient times. Their analysis of paleomagnetic data was independent of whether reversed rocks owe their reversal to reversal of the field or to some physical or chemical mechanism. In addition, they employed a minimum of theoretical assumptions about the ways in which rocks acquire magnetization and about the mechanism in the earth that might produce the terrestrial magnetic field.[63] Thus they gave what specifically was called in the paper a mainly "phenomenological" and minimally "theoretical" analysis.[64] Rock magnetic data provided a "test" of continental drift, which could be supplemented by "another test," as already made by Irving and by Opdyke and Runcorn using the assumption that terrestrial climate had always been zoned according to geographical latitude, as in the present. One could "test in a numerical manner whether the rock magnetic latitudes are or are not consistent with the ancient climates."[65] This was the subject of Blackett's 1961 paper.

It should be noted, too, that Blackett, Clegg, and Stubbs confronted the possibility that the earth's magnetic field may not always have been an axial dipole field, that is, a simple north-south field more or less coincident with the earth's axis of rotation. They argued that none of the existing theories of the earth's magnetism are consistent with a nondipole field. Proposing a nondipole field meant accepting the improbable fact that the present alignment of the magnetic and rotational poles is purely coincidental and atypical.[66]

In his 1961 paper, Blackett supported the argument for continental drift by comparing the ancient latitudes of the various land masses, as deduced magnetically, with the evidence of ancient climates as deduced from geological and paleontological data.[67] Using data from Europe, North America, India, Australia, and South Africa, he concluded that although "legitimate doubt may be entertained about any one piece of climatic evidence, the rough agreement of so many with the magnetic data does make it rather unlikely that the agreement is purely fortuitous."[68]

At this time Allan Cox and Doell were among American geologists and geophysicists who still expressed hesitation about unreserved acceptance of paleomagnetism as evidence for drift, although they endorsed biogeographical data as a complementary line of research to paleomagnetic data.[69] When Blackett made a visit to the United States in 1960, the *New York Times* science correspondent Walter Sullivan informed the public that this British Nobel Prize winner thought it "highly probable" that the continents have drifted.[70] It appears, as the philosopher Henry Frankel has argued, that paleomagnetism had rekindled interest in continental drift but that it alone changed few minds.[71]

Theories of Magnetic Reversals

A problem that had been much discussed and that still bothered Blackett and others in the early 1960s was the degree to which rock magnetism might be altered or determined by chemical and physical processes, a question studied theoretically by the French physicist Louis Néel as early as 1951.[72] In the early 1950s Blackett showed little interest in the hypothesis of periodic reversals of the earth's general magnetic field, perhaps because of his predisposition to a bulk theory of the earth's magnetism or perhaps because he thought that reversals did not have relevance for continental drift. However, the hypothesis that reversals are a result of chemical or physical processes (self-reversals) began to attract his attention as a new project for experimental study, especially since a clear mechanism for field reversals is by no means straightforward in the dynamo theory of the earth's magnetism. From the dynamo theory it appeared that decay of the dipole field would be followed by its buildup in the reverse sense, and that this required at least some thousand years.[73]

Before Néel's work, evidence of magnetic reversals appeared in the early 1900s with reports by Bernard Brunhes and Pierre David. Paul Mercanton reported data again in 1926 and Motonori Matuyama in 1929.[74] As more evidence accumulated, there was no convincing interpretation. In the United States, Verhoogen's former students Cox and Doell conceived a project to resolve the question at the United States

Geological Survey (USGS) office in Menlo Park near Stanford. They recruited another Berkeley graduate, G. Brent Dalrymple. Cox had been studying magnetic reversal since 1956 and originally assumed that rock polarity was controlled by the mineralogy of the rocks, until he found evidence correlating direction of polarity with the age of rocks.[75] In 1963 a Canberra group (led by Irving's student Donald H. Tarling and former Berkeley postdoctoral fellow Ian McDougal) and the Cox, Doell, and Dalrymple group established two major periods of reversed magnetism in the past, with briefer reversals within each period.[76] Their method of dating depended on the fact that the radioactive isotope potassium-40 (^{40}K) constitutes approximately 0.012 of normal potassium and produces gaseous argon-40 (^{40}Ar). By looking at the amount of ^{40}Ar, one can calculate how much time has passed since the rock cooled and the magnetism became fixed.[77] This method, which works best on volcanic material, can be used for dating rocks at approximately 10,000 years to more than a billion years, depending on the rock.

In 1962 Blackett gave a paper in Japan on physical and chemical means of distinguishing self-reversed from field-reversed rocks.[78] He had been paying increased attention to the problem in the 1950s because of his student Francis Everitt's thesis work on the magnetism of baked sedimentary rocks. Everitt found two examples of igneous rock that seemed to show a physico-chemical reversal of polarity.[79] In the late 1950s Roderic Wilson and James M. Ade-Hall (later, Hall) also were writing theses at Cambridge University with some supervision by Blackett. They reported that both normal and reverse magnetization had been found in samples of the same lava flow. Cox was skeptical about these findings, based in part on his observations of oxidized and nonoxidized rock in a flow of reversed lava in the Snake River Plain in Idaho. Cox later told science writer William Glen that he found Blackett "strongly committed to self-reversal" and a "powerful and impressive man" in this period.[80] Doell wrote Blackett in 1964 that his group was sure that the existence of reversed and nonreversed samples in the same lava flow was very rare.[81]

Blackett developed a program for systematically investigating the hypothesis of self-reversal. Field-reversal assumes that the petrological (mineralogical) content of rock samples has no effect on the magnetism recorded, but self-reversal implies chemical or physical differences in the normal and reversed rock. Blackett, like others, came to argue that ferromagnetic minerals in rocks of self-reversed polarity should generally be more oxidized than normal samples from the same site.[82]

In April 1965, Doell and Dalrymple proposed to Blackett that they send him chips from some sixty-five rocks that they had studied by the K-Ar method, blind-coding the samples for Blackett so that he would not know their results on normal or reversed polarizations as correlated with time-stratigraphic measurements. Wilson spent a month or so at Menlo Park looking at thin sections of most of the rocks that Doell and Dalrymple had been studying.[83] Doell also called Blackett's attention to the "well-known tendency" of volcanoes to produce lavas of different petrological nature early and late in the eruptive cycle.[84]

Blackett used some 400 specimens from fifteen sites sent to him by colleagues. He presumed that the probability of self-reversal increases with degree of oxidation, and therefore color, of titanomagnetite grains in the rock. Observations were made using a modification of the microscopic method developed by Ade-Hall. One of Blackett's grounds for caution was his worry about the method of observation, since it was one of personal viewing. Thus differences in visual acuity or fatigue of the observer could make a difference in reported observations. There is some irony in Blackett's return to a visual method that was liable to the kinds of criticisms that had been made fifty years earlier against Rutherford's scintillation counts.[85]

The self-reversal studies proved to be inconclusive for Blackett. The results of the trial with the Menlo Park group were never published.[86] Blackett drafted a paper during the summer of 1967. Norman Watkins, who took an external Ph.D. at Imperial College and who had spent some time at Menlo Park, thought that Blackett's draft paper was too cautiously argued: "I feel that you have stated the case very fairly and accurately, and if anything tend to overemphasize the snags." [87] Blackett never published this paper.

By 1967 Wilson and Ade-Hall, who were working in Liverpool with Blackett's rock samples, doubted that they were observing evidence of self-reversals.[88] Blackett was trying to help them get funding to build their own K-Ar dating apparatus, and Wilson's student Peter Smith received a NATO Fellowship to work with Doell and Dalrymple in Menlo Park. In a letter to the Natural Environment Research Council, in which he argued the need for an outlay of £12,000 for a K-Ar instrument,

Blackett expressed astonishment that Wilson's earlier proposal had not been funded: "It is essentially about the most topical and most exciting part of rock magnetic research, and we in this country are rapidly losing the lead in this field because of inadequate dating arrangements."[89]

Blackett's investigations of self-reversals and petrology was research that he left unfinished as he increasingly lost confidence in its reliability.[90] After he retired from Imperial College in 1965, he no longer supervised a laboratory group. In a letter to Everitt, written shortly before Blackett's death in 1974, he expressed continued interest in the problem of the origins of the earth's magnetic field, while accepting the general view that the proven reversals in the magnetic poles must be dependent on reversals of the earth's core. Still, Blackett puzzled over the rock oxidations that he had taken to be evidence of self-reversals, finding it hard to believe that they were nothing but results of statistical fluctuations.[91]

In 1963 Fred Vine and Drummond Matthews, both at the Department of Geodesy and Geophysics at Cambridge, linked paleomagnetism to seafloor-spreading in an effort to explain evidence of alternating magnetic stripes parallel to an ocean ridge. "Seafloor-spreading" was a term that had been applied by R. S. Dietz in 1961 to the proposal by Princeton University geophysicist Harry Hess that ocean crust is created along ridge axes as magma is forced up from the mantle. In the paper that Vine and Matthews published in *Nature* in September 1963, Vine, who had heard Hess speak at Cambridge in early 1962, combined the seafloor-spreading mechanism with magnetic anomaly data collected by Matthews from a survey of the Carlsberg Ridge in the northwestern Indian Ocean.[92] They argued that the stripes were the result of the generation of ocean floor at the ridges, with geomagnetic field reversals documenting the alternating orientations of the geomagnetic field at the times that molten fluid cooled.[93]

Initially Vine and Matthews's publication in *Nature* was little noticed. The evidence was not compelling. They were not invited to participate in the 1964 Royal Society symposium on continental drift, organized by Blackett, Bullard, and Runcorn. In the meantime, too, the Canadian geophysicist Lawrence Morley proposed the idea of seafloor-spreading in a short paper, but it was rejected in early 1963 by *Nature* and in the summer of 1963 by the *Journal of Geophysical Research* on the grounds that it was overly speculative.[94]

In early 1965, while visiting in Cambridge, J. Tuzo Wilson of Toronto informally proposed the idea, which he published in July, of a new class of lateral faults, based on data off the Pacific Coast near the Strait of Juan de Fuca south of Vancouver Island. The "transform fault" could separate mobile belts that divide the earth's surface into large rigid plates. At the transform fault, horizontal shear motion along the fault is changed into an expanding tensional motion across the ocean ridge, accounting for seafloor-spreading. In October Wilson and Vine published their conclusion that an extension of the East Pacific Rise, the Juan de Fuca Ridge, runs through a zebra pattern of magnetic anomalies and connects with another section of the East Pacific Rise by means of the San Andreas Fault.

The data for worldwide magnetic anomalies, or field reversals, became more convincing in a November 1965 talk at the annual meeting of the Geological Society of America, where Dalrymple, Cox, and Doell reported on rock samples from Jaramillo Creek in the Jemez Mountains of New Mexico. They had found evidence of reversed magnetism in two lava flows (at 0.71 and 0.72 millions years ago), intermediate polarity (0.88 million years) in another, and normal polarity (0.89 million years) in a fourth. They placed what became known as the Jaramillo normal event at 0.9 million years ago, when the earth's magnetic field started to reverse itself. Their new polarity time-scale, which now included the Jaramillo event, provided a perfect correlation with data for seafloor magnetic anomalies showing variations in the magnetism of seafloor rock extending across hundreds of kilometers of seafloor in the East Pacific.[95] Walter Pitman and Opdyke at the Lamont Observatory of Columbia University provided independent confirmation of the Jaramillo event from deep-sea sediment cores, leading to the Lamont group's support in early 1966 for the hypothesis of seafloor-spreading.[96]

Blackett wrote Cox in late 1966 that "the new results about ocean ridges are almost too good to be true."[97] Jason Morgan of Princeton and Dan McKenzie of Cambridge presented their hypotheses of mobile terrestrial plates (plate tectonics) in 1967. J. Tuzo Wilson called the emerging consensus on a mobile earth "the current Scientific Revolution," a claim increasingly made by earth scientists in the next few years. Continental drift and plate tectonics were the Copernican revolution of the twentieth century, replacing the static earth with a mobile one.[98] Bullard wrote Blackett, in late 1968: "You, Runcorn and I are now temporary orthodoxy."[99]

Not one of the three leaders of British geophysics—Bullard, Runcorn, Blackett—had received a traditional geological education or worked in any mainline geological specialty.[100] Yet their work had helped transform geology by providing paleomagnetic evidence for continental drift, supplementing evidence from geology, geography, and paleontology. Plate tectonics now provided a plausible mechanism for the earth's mobilism.

Physicists such as Edward V. Appleton and Sydney Chapman were other twentieth-century pioneers in earth sciences, in their cases, respectively, with models of the ionosphere (50 to more than 400 kilometers) and the magnetosphere (500 to several thousand kilometers) above the earth's surface. Of physicists moving into geology, Blackett wrote Runcorn in 1961: "I do not think that one should worry with the fact that British geologists show little interest in this new work. . . . [I]t is a good tendency for physicists to widen out into borderline subjects such as geophysics, biophysics, etc. which are becoming more interesting than many of the older branches."[101]

If geophysics was a borderline subject to physics for Blackett, it was not a foreign culture. Indeed, the physicist Blackett's interest in the physics of the globe, or the *Physik der Erde,* was a long-standing preoccupation among physicists and natural philosophers. Blackett's particular interest in geomagnetism and in the earth's core lay in a tradition going back, in the nineteenth century, to the work of François Arago, Carl Friedrich Gauss, and William Thomson, among others. William Hopkins, the Cambridge tutor of James Clerk Maxwell and George Gabriel Stokes, was groundbreaking in the application of mathematical models in geology. Stokes, the Lucasian Professor of Mathematics at Cambridge from 1849 to 1903, was one of the founders of physical geodesy. He also developed mathematical techniques for studying the inner structure of the earth, as did Augustus E. H. Love, the Sedleian Professor of Natural Philosophy at Oxford. George H. Darwin, the Plumian Professor of Astronomy and Experimental Philosophy at Cambridge in the late nineteenth and early twentieth century, studied the mathematics of the earth-moon system, using the hypothesis that the moon was once part of the earth. He also was interested in the astronomical and physical causes of glacial epochs.[102]

Geophysics became professionalized as a discipline in the late nineteenth century. Georg Gerland, a member of the editorial board for Herman Wagner's *Geographisches Jahrbuch* in Königsberg, founded the first geophysical journal, the *Beiträge zur Geophysik,* in Strassburg in 1887. Emil Wiechert, a theoretical physicist trained in Königsberg, became the first chairholder in geophysics and director of the Geophysical Institute at Göttingen in 1898.[103] The Geophysical Laboratory was founded in 1905 at the Carnegie Institution with a focus on petrology and geochemistry.[104]

In 1917 the British Association for the Advancement of Science established a geophysical committee, which passed on its responsibilities to the Royal Astronomical Society. In 1922 the RAS began issuing a *Geophysical Supplement* twice a year, which became the *Geophysical Journal* in 1958.[105] When the International Research Council was founded in Brussels in 1919, its early membership included nine national delegations and two newly constituted "unions": an International Union of Astronomy and an International Union of Geodesy and Geophysics (IUGG). The IUGG had six sections: geodesy; seismology; meteorology; magnetism and terrestrial electricity; physical oceanography; and volcanology.[106]

By the 1920s and 1930s, when Blackett was working in the Cavendish Laboratory, university programs in meteorology, solid-earth geophysics, and oceanography were emerging at a scattering of universities around the world, some of them targeted for assistance from the Rockefeller Foundation, such as Percy Bridgman's high-pressure studies at Harvard.[107] At Cambridge, geological science was represented by three different departments with separate, but adjacent, laboratories: Geodesy and Geophysics; Mineralogy and Petrology; and Geology.[108] The leading geophysicist at Cambridge, Harold Jeffreys, lectured in mathematics at Cambridge from 1923 to 1932 before he became a reader in geophysics in 1932. Like George H. Darwin, Jeffreys ended his teaching career as Plumian Professor of Astronomy, yet he and Darwin were regarded as the founders of geophysics at Cambridge.

Within the British context, then, what makes Blackett's negotiation of the borderline culture of geophysics a little unusual were his solid credentials in *experimental* physics, and in nuclear physics, rather than in theoretical physics and applied mathematics. Yet, as Frankel has written in his history of continental drift: "The two major groups of paleomagnetists who developed a case for continental drift were from the U.K. and were initially housed at the University of Manchester [Blackett] and

Cambridge [Runcorn]. . . . Their work reactivated the stagnating controversy of mobilism vs. fixism."[109]

Blackett's Scientific Practice and the Methodology of Phenomenology

The Blackett-Runcorn influence spread in geophysics, as Runcorn took some of his research group from Cambridge to the University of Durham at Newcastle in 1955. Bullard replaced Runcorn at Cambridge, becoming Professor of Geophysics in the Department of Geodesy and Geophysics in 1964. Blackett had established a research program in paleomagnetism at Manchester before moving to London in 1953, but it was at Imperial College that he headed a strong research group in magnetism and geophysics for the next twelve years.[110] These were centers of experimental studies that came to support continental drift.

Of no small importance for Blackett's role in British geophysics were the organizational and administrative skills that enabled him to direct and coordinate geophysical research on both the local and global scales. Blackett was an experienced laboratory leader by the late 1930s and a coordinator of Operational Research during the war. The work in OR was a mixed-team effort, and the team element and interdisciplinary approach became characteristic of operational research and systems engineering after the war, but also, more generally, of international research.[111] The war years were ones in which Blackett mastered the organization of mixed-team effort in research, although his postwar research projects in cosmic rays, geomagnetism, and rock magnetism were small-scale research by comparison to the new big science of particle physics at national laboratories in the United States or at CERN (the European Council for Nuclear Research).

It is striking that Blackett applied methods and practices from nuclear physics to geophysics, including the approach commonly called "phenomenonological" in particle physics, meaning a way of working that is not fundamentalist or *a priori,* but aimed at finding regularities and making approximations. Everitt noted that "phenomenological" was one of Blackett's favorite words.[112] Take, for example, Blackett's characterization (which was common among nuclear physicists of his generation) of the physics of mesons and other "strange" particles as "phenomenological." Particles were differentiated by descriptions of the kinds of events that produced them, rather than by attributing fundamental essences to them.[113] In geophysics Blackett made arguments for continental drift that he, Clegg, and Stubbs explicitly characterized as "phenomenological" in their coauthored 1960 paper. The use of the term "phenomenological" created some perplexity among geologists. When Irving first heard the term, he turned to the *Encyclopedia Britannica* for a definition. Upon eventually reading the 1960 paper by Blackett and his colleagues, Irving wondered "what the fuss was about, because Blackett was really only advocating an approach that as a geologist, I took naturally."[114]

Blackett argued in the 1960 coauthored paper on "Analysis of Rock Magnetic Data," as he had in his reintroduction into physics of the rotational theory of the earth's magnetism, that continental drift had again become an attractive theory, because it now was possible to "test" the theory (by using paleomagnetic and paleoclimatic data).[115] There were no fundamental principles proposed from which to deduce the phenomenon of continental drift, but rather a systematic observational and experimental program for establishing its sufficient plausibility on the basis of paleomagnetic and paleoclimatic evidence.[116]

In both nuclear physics and geophysics, Blackett's data was instrument-driven, with emphasis on constant improvement of the apparatus in order to exploit its capacities to the utmost, in combination with unsparing collection of mountains of data. The integrity of the results rested in the maximum input of data in order to refine and eliminate alternative causal hypotheses. This was a method familiar to geophysicists and geologists.[117]

Phenomenology might also be said to be the method of operational research. In his first essay on operational research, in Admiralty documents of 1943, Blackett remarked that the initial step is to collect as much numerical data as possible, with recognition that the numerical picture is incomplete. The *a priori* method would attempt general solutions to arbitrarily simplified problems. In contrast, the more common-sense procedure is to abandon the attempt from first principles and employ a variational method that shows how a real operation would be affected by a change of variables.[118] This also was the method he had outlined in 1933 in his essay on the craft of experimental physics: "An exact mathematical solution of any problem in physics is never required, for the object of the solution is to compare it with measured quantities and these can never be exact. . . . To know where and what approximations to make is to have overcome half the difficulties."[119]

A symposium at the Royal Society in 1964 marked the public triumph of continental drift in Great Britain. On that occasion, in assessing the appropriate methodology for solving the question of drift, Blackett remarked that

> in the methodology of subjects like the Earth sciences, where the observational facts are highly complex and difficult to reduce to quantitative terms . . . a highly simplified model which can explain a large number of observed facts is invaluable, especially when it suggests new observations. When the observations are made, it is generally found necessary to make the model more complicated. However, highly simplified models which prove that some supposed phenomenon cannot have occurred, must be treated with caution, as they may discourage new observations.[120]

Historians and philosophers of science, like scientists, are familiar with the enthusiasm of British and American scientists in the 1950s and 1960s for Karl Popper's discussions of scientific method.[121] Ted Irving's 1964 book on paleomagnetism begins with a quotation from Popper, and includes in its preface a Popperian, and indeed Comtian, account of how scientists are obliged to proceed: the most simple and general explanations should be sought, until the simple ones are found wanting. It is best to give consideration only to those hypotheses that can be tested by the data that are presently available or likely to be obtained in the near future.[122] This is an approach invoking irreproachable scientific honesty and integrity, a moral theme that helps account for Popper's tremendous popularity in Great Britain and the United States in the 1950s and early 1960s.

Irving encountered Popper, not in England where Popper taught at the London School of Economics, but in July 1963 while Popper was leading a seminar at the Australian National University in Canberra. It was a small group that became progressively smaller during the term, so that there were just three participants at the end: John Eccles, who became Nobel Laureate in Physiology and Medicine in 1963, the anthropologist Derek Freeman, and Irving. Popper's emphasis on testability and falsifiability gave Irving confidence to go on with his own controversial work on mobilism because Popper captured what Irving was trying to do as a geophysicist.[123] As Irving put it, "a theory may be true even though nobody believes it, and even though we have no reason for accepting it, or for believing it is true; and another theory may be false, although we have comparatively good reasons for accepting it."[124]

Conviction grew in the 1950s that continental drift was a conjecture in geophysics that should be revived because it now could be tested. Runcorn later reflected that it had been the lack of a decisive test, in combination with strong arguments against the theory, that caused the idea of continental drift to be abandoned "until it was revived by the development of studies of rock magnetism."[125] Blackett's application of the magnetometer to the study of sedimentary rocks, along with his unflinching and enthusiastic support of empirical studies of paleolatitudes and paleoclimates, played a huge role in the revival of an often-maligned hypothesis. Championing drift required not only intellectual confidence, but also the quality that R. A. Fisher called moral courage. Writing Irving in 1956, Fisher said: "I think a lot of geologists must be timidly peering out of their holes on hearing the strange news that geophysicists are talking about continental drift, and I have often wondered how many scientific discoveries have been left unmade for lack of a quality called moral courage."[126]

6

Scientific Leadership: Recognition, Organization, Policy, 1945–1974

Patrick Blackett's career as teacher and researcher began with his education in naval colleges and developed within British universities in Cambridge, Manchester, and London. His researches from the 1920s through the 1960s spanned the areas of particle physics, cosmic-ray physics, the earth's magnetism and rock magnetism, geophysics, continental drift, and operational research, as discussed in earlier chapters. He was a fellow, professor, department head, laboratory director, dean, pro-vice-chancellor, and pro-rector. The Blackett Laboratory is his namesake at Imperial College in London. He served on advisory committees for military services, government, education, and private organizations including the Royal Society, where he was President from 1965 to 1970. His honors included foreign academy memberships and honorary university degrees. Blackett received the Royal Medal (1940) and Copley Medal (1956) from the Royal Society, the American Medal for Merit (1946), and the royally bestowed Companion of Honour (1965), Order of Merit (1967), and Life Peerage (1969), the latter giving him the title of Baron, so that he was to be addressed formally as the Lord Blackett.[1]

Lady Blackett told the historian Robert S. Anderson that Lord Blackett cared more passionately in his later years about his advisory work in India than about most other things.[2] An acquaintance of Blackett's said that Blackett was more pleased about the presidency of the Royal Society than he would have liked to admit and that his usual reserve broke down on the occasion of his first Presidential speech at the Society.[3] When approached by Harold Wilson, Blackett declined to become Minister of Technology because the office would have required him to accept a peerage, but he overcame his objections to entering the House of Lords after he became Royal Society President.[4] The honor that Blackett likely cherished the most, because of its prestige and its implications, was the award that came to him from Stockholm in 1948. The Nobel Prize in Physics conferred universal recognition from his scientific peers, as well as immediate influence among the broader public.

In examining the leadership that Blackett exercised in his scientific life, we begin with the process through which the Nobel Prize was awarded to Blackett and how his work was evaluated by colleagues over a span of thirteen years from the 1930s to the late 1940s. The chapter discusses, too, his style of leadership in laboratory research groups at different universities and his evolving roles at the national level in the planning of science and technology. His governmental advisory role expanded from informal advice to participant in a Shadow Cabinet in the 1950s to a formal role in the Ministry of Technology under Harold Wilson's government in the 1960s, coinciding with his election as President of the Royal Society. The chapter concludes with Blackett's role as scientific advisor and advocate for postcolonial development in India after 1947, when he turned his attention to the economic and technological needs of underdeveloped countries in the period of the early Cold War.

The Positron Revisited: The Nobel Award and Attribution of Scientific Achievement

In 1948 Nobel Prizes were awarded to two British intellectuals: Blackett received the Nobel Prize in Physics, and the poet T. S. Eliot received the Nobel Prize in Literature. Two British citizens could hardly have been more different. For Blackett, and for his close friend C. P. Snow, Eliot personified the self-absorbed literary intellectual whom Snow openly disdained in his "Two Cultures" lecture in 1959.[5] Snow's characterization of Eliot was hardly as acerbic as Virginia Woolf's, who had remarked: "I could wish that poor dear Tom had more spunk in him, less need to let drop by drop of his agonized perplexities fall ever so finely through pure cambric."[6]

On 10 December 1948 the American-born, traditionalist, and Anglican Tom Eliot and the internationalist, socialist, and secular Pat Blackett delivered banquet speeches at the City Hall in Stockholm. On that occasion Eliot talked briefly about the importance of poetry for the human condition, remarking on the difficulty of translating poetry from one language to another and on the small number of people who come to better understand each other through sharing the literature of poetry.[7] Blackett, in his remarks, responded to Gustaf Hellström's introduction in which Hellström mentioned both Blackett's active part in two world wars and his work in the physics that had played a devastating role in wartime. Scientific discovery, like literary creation, still is flourishing on the war-scarred continent of Europe, said Blackett, but it is the task of scientists and citizens to ensure that the new forces of atomic energy are used for the good of human beings and not for their destruction. Quoting from the early sixteenth-century poet Ludovico Ariosto's dramatization of Orlando's triumph over an enemy bearing a new firearm, Blackett recalled Orlando's sailing into the ocean and plunging the weapon into the sea:

> Oh, Cursed device, Base Implement of Death . . .
> By Beelzebub's malicious art designed
> To ruin all the race of human kind . . .
> Here lie for ever in the abyss below![8]

Letters of congratulations poured into Blackett's office and residence following the 5 November announcement of the Physics Prize. Some letters were jointly authored, such as the telegram from Princeton signed by Robert Oppenheimer, George Uhlenbeck, Albert Einstein, Hideki Yukawa, Abraham Pais, Max von Laue, Henry Placzek, and Oswald Veblen.[9] One telegram was from longtime competitor Carl Anderson: "Heartiest Congratulations on your well-deserved award."[10] Many letters were from old friends who could not help but comment on how slow they thought the Prize had been in coming: Paul Dirac ("You ought to have had it long ago"), Douglas Hartree ("I have been expecting this for some years"), Walther Heitler ("The news is none the less welcome for the fact that it is long overdue"), E. A. Milne ("I had been expecting it for some years"), Ernest Schrödinger ("long overdue"), and James Chadwick ("I hope the citation will refer adequately to the discovery of the positive electron for I have always felt that, although Anderson made the first statement, the real credit was yours").[11] One of the physicists who had nominated Blackett for the award, Charles Galton Darwin, mentioned his frustration over the delay: "It has been my opinion (in fact shared several times in the recommendation they have asked me to make) that it is long overdue."[12]

Slightly damping Blackett's euphoria was the disappointment that his dear friend Beppo (Giuseppe Occhialini) was not sharing the Prize. As an Italian citizen, Occhialini had been required to return to Italy to do military service but was able to leave Italy in 1937 for a position in physics at the University of São Paulo in Brazil and then worked for a year in a biophysics laboratory in Rio de Janeiro. In the fall of 1943, Blackett, Edward Appleton, and other friends were trying to arrange Occhialini's return to England, with clearance to do war-related work, but it was not until early 1945 that he got back to England.[13] He began to collaborate at Bristol with Cecil Powell in the work on mesons that resulted in the announcement of the discovery of the pi-meson in 1947. Occhialini would return to Italy permanently, first in 1950 to the chair in physics that his father had held in Genoa and then to a professorship at Milan in 1952. Bruno Pontecorvo was said to have made a famous toast: "I drink not to Beppo, but to us all: may we collaborate with him, it is a practically sure way of winning a Nobel Prize."[14]

In a political history of the Nobel Prizes, Robert Marc Friedman suggested that Blackett received the award in 1948 partly because of Swedish Social Democrats' sympathy with Blackett's well-publicized positions on scientific planning and international controls of nuclear weapons. It could be said, too, that Blackett was a war hero among scientists, but one free from the taint of atomic weapons and identified with the achievements of operational research. However, it was physicists, not Social Democrats, who made the Nobel award.

The physicist who made Blackett's presentation speech was Gustaf Ising, a professor at Stockholm's Högskola who had pioneered ideas on particle accelerators and became an expert in electromagnetism, including geomagnetism and rock magnetism. Ising was the member of the Nobel Physics Committee in charge of writing the committee report on Blackett in September 1948.[15] In presenting Blackett to the audience at the award ceremony in December, Ising said the following:

According to the statutes of the Nobel Foundation, the Nobel Prize for Physics may be awarded for "discovery or invention in the field of physics." The Royal Swedish Academy of Sciences in awarding this year's prize to Professor P. M. S. Blackett of Manchester, for his development of the Wilson method and his discoveries, made by this method, in nuclear physics and on cosmic radiation, indicates by the very wording of the award, that its decision is motivated on *both* the grounds mentioned in the statutes.[16]

Ising's presentation speech went on to outline Blackett's innovations in physics as a combination of discoveries and inventions that had been sustained over a considerable period of time, making him the "leading man" in the development of the Wilson cloud-chamber method going back to the 1920s. Blackett was the "first" to obtain photographs of the disruption of the atomic nucleus. Blackett had developed, with Occhialini, an automatic Wilson apparatus that "established irrefutably the existence of positive electrons" that Anderson had shown to temporarily exist in cosmic radiation. Blackett and Occhialini "discovered" positive and negative electrons appearing in pairs in cosmic radiation, and this "discovery" of pair creation led to the acceptance on the theoretical side of the transmutation of light into matter and vice versa. In the late thirties, by means of a "new" optical method, Blackett and John G. Wilson measured extremely feeble curvature of cosmic radiation and particles' energies. Ising concluded with another reference to the "discovery of pair creation," having finessed the issue of the discovery of the positron.[17]

What makes this speech significant is not so much Ising's individual evaluation of Blackett's career and achievements, but that Ising based his formal statement on a personal study of how nominations of Blackett had changed over the years since 1935. Nobel letters of nomination in physics may be submitted by members of the Nobel Physics Committee of the Royal Swedish Academy of Sciences and are also solicited from Swedish and foreign members of the Academy, professors of physics at universities that existed in 1900 in Sweden and other Nordic countries, previous Nobel Prize winners in physics, and a list of chairholders and other distinguished physicists who are asked to make recommendations in a given year. Some nominations are no more than a line; others are several or more pages, sometimes with bibliographies as appendixes. The letters are due to the committee by 1 February of the year that the Prize is to be awarded. Committee reports to the Academy usually are completed in September, followed by the Academy's discussion and vote, which are not recorded.[18]

Initial nominations of Blackett occurred in 1935, as they did for Anderson. Nominators in 1935 could also make recommendations for the reserved Prize of 1934.[19] It is not surprising that Jean Perrin nominated Blackett, since Blackett had just given a series of spectacular, beautifully illustrated lectures at the Collège de France in May 1934. Perrin reiterated his nomination in 1936, with his recommendation complemented by independent letters from Maurice de Broglie and his younger brother Louis de Broglie, the Prize winner in 1929. In 1935 Perrin gave preference to Irène and Frédéric Joliot-Curie for the Physics Prize, proposing Anderson or Anderson and Blackett for the 1934 award, arguing that the discovery of the positive electron was Anderson's, but that Blackett had made an important contribution, particularly in his discovery of cosmic showers and paired electrons. Perrin reiterated the argument for Anderson and Blackett in 1936, after the Joliot-Curies received the 1935 Nobel Prize in Chemistry, and James Chadwick the 1935 Physics award. Maurice de Broglie in 1936 nominated Anderson and Blackett, and Louis de Broglie suggested one-half to Anderson and one-half to Blackett and Occhialini.[20]

Robert Millikan took a very different point of view. In a tendentious letter nominating Anderson alone for the discovery of the positive electron, Millikan implied that there was some argument about Anderson's discovery by saying that there was no uncertainty about the fact that the discovery was made and "fully elaborated" by Anderson at least eight months before it was "*checked* [my italics] by anybody else, nor is there any doubt about the fact that all the checking that was done was the immediate result of Anderson's discovery." Millikan further stated in his letter that Anderson's second paper of 15 March 1933 on the positive electron appeared before anyone else published in the field. In fact, Blackett and Occhialini's classic paper "Some Photographs of the Tracks of Penetrating Radiation" appeared in the *Proceedings of the Royal Society of London* on 3 March 1933, having been received 7 February 1933.[21] Millikan renewed his nomination in 1936, and other brief letters of support came from Hantaro Nagaoka, Max Planck, A. Deissmann, and Max von Laue.[22] A 1935 nomination by Richard Tolman, Millikan's colleague at Caltech, primarily nominated Chadwick, but mentioned the discovery of positive electrons by Anderson, "foreshadowed by the theoretical work of Dirac" (who shared the Physics Prize in 1933 with Ernest Schrödinger) and "confirmed by Blackett."[23] Indeed, what had been decisive in the award of the Physics Prize to Dirac in 1933 was Ivar Waller's report to fellow members of the Nobel Physics Committee that Dirac's theoretical prediction of a positively charged electron had been confirmed through two independent experiments, namely by Anderson and Blackett in late 1932 and early 1933.[24]

It was letters from Jacob Clay and from Arthur Holly Compton that decided the matter for the 1936 Prize. Clay submitted a nomination of V. F. Hess for his discovery of cosmic radiation, which, Clay said, had opened up further discoveries, including ionization of the atmosphere and discovery of the positive electrons.[25] Compton was one of the leaders in latitude studies that established the particle nature of cosmic radiation, against Millikan's defense of a gamma-ray identity. Compton nominated Hess for his discovery of cosmic radiation and Clay for the discovery of the latitude effect, suggesting Anderson as a possibility for discovery of the positron and investigations of the energy loss of high-speed electrons. However, Compton complicated his nomination by saying that allocation to Anderson was in some ways inadequate because it would overlook the studies of Walther Bothe and Werner Kolhörster, Thomas Johnson, Bruno Rossi, and others using coincidence counters.[26] Studying this question for the Nobel Physics Committee in the early summer, Erik Hulthén concluded that credit for the latitude effect was too complicated to settle on Clay, and that it might be appropriate to recognize Compton and Clay for the latitude effect and Bothe and Kolhörster for discovery of the corpuscular nature of cosmic radiation. Hulthén authored a report in September summarizing the work of all nominees, including Blackett and Occhialini. The Physics Committee recommended Hess for the discovery of cosmic radiation and Anderson for discovery of the positron.[27]

Unlike Millikan, Anderson was not ungenerous to Blackett and Occhialini. In Anderson's Nobel Lecture in Stockholm, he hardly could deny that he had discovered the positron, but he generously mentioned Blackett and Blackett's colleagues several times: that Blackett and Occhialini had confirmed in the spring of 1933 the existence of the positive electron and obtained photographs of electron showers; that Blackett, Occhialini, and Chadwick were the first to show, in radiation generated by the impact of alpha particles on beryllium, that positrons could be produced by an agent other than cosmic rays; and that Blackett and Occhialini first suggested that the appearance of pairs of positive and negative electrons could be understood in terms of Dirac's electron theory.[28]

With the positron discovery now attributed to Anderson, later nominations of Blackett often referred to Blackett's "independent discovery of the positive electron" rather than its "confirmation," although both sets of terms were used. Most nominations noted Blackett's discovery, with Occhialini, of electron showers and his originality in establishing experimentally the existence of pair creation. Letters tended to mention his work with John G. Wilson on heavy electrons and the energy spectrum of cosmic radiation, noting that the interpretation of the identity and the mass of the "mesotron" was still at issue. Blackett's development of the counter-controlled cloud chamber was said to have opened up a "new world."[29] In a letter of December 1944, Max Born used all these themes, additionally describing Blackett's researches in the 1920s, including the experimental confirmation of Nevill Mott's collision theory. Blackett, said Born, had no equal in Great Britain as a physicist, except Chadwick, and Blackett had done important secret war work.[30]

By this time Millikan had launched a campaign for a second Nobel Prize for Anderson, nominating Anderson and Seth Neddermeyer in late 1940 for the "original conception" of a new particle, the mesotron or green electron, and for gathering evidence for it. Anderson himself began nominating Neddermeyer for the discovery of the mesotron.[31] Millikan would continue making his nomination, warning the Nobel Physics Committee in late 1946 that if Anderson and Neddermeyer did not receive the Prize in 1946, Millikan would repeat the recommendation.[32] A letter in early 1944 contains the first mention Millikan ever made of Blackett, criticizing Blackett's hypothesis that the highly penetrating cosmic-ray particle might be a strangely behaving electron rather than a new particle.[33]

As a result of nominations and discussions over the discovery and interpretation of the mesotron, the Nobel Physics Committee's report to the Academy for 1945 included a long section on Yukawa, Anderson and Neddermeyer, Blackett, and others.[34] Yukawa would receive an unshared prize in 1949 and Cecil Powell in 1950. Czeslaw Bialobrzoski, at the Institute of Physics in Warsaw, brought Pierre Auger's name into the list of those who should be recognized, along with Blackett, for investigations of cosmic rays, as did Jacques Hadamard and Francis Perrin.[35] Auger nominated Blackett and Rossi for the discovery and study of cosmic-ray showers.[36] Blackett also received a nomination for the 1948 award from Samuel Tolanksy, who did not stress the positron, but emphasized Blackett's discoveries made with the cloud chamber and in particular his first making visible nuclear disintegrations and cosmic-ray showers. Thus Blackett's works of discovery predated the positron.[37] What appears to have cemented the case for Blackett were two more letters, a long and impassioned one from the American physicist Compton and the other from Blackett's comrade in arms J. D. Bernal.

Compton's letter in some respects explicitly refutes Millikan's claims, made over a decade earlier, about Anderson's single priority for the positron. Compton and Millikan had long been rivals in cosmic-ray research and in leadership roles in American experimental physics.[38] However, more to the point in 1948, Compton rooted the rationale for Blackett's originality and achievement in a series of discoveries and inventions of the last twenty-five years, beginning in 1922 when Blackett was the "first" person to introduce precision techniques to cloud chambers. Blackett's article of 1929 "On the Design and Use of a Double Camera for Photographing Artificial Disintegrations," published in the *Proceedings of the Royal Society*, was a bible for all cloud-chamber workers, said Compton.[39] Blackett's photographs of the transmutation of nitrogen were the "first" clear demonstration of how the disruption of the nucleus takes place. The experimental proof of the conservation of energy and momentum, one of the commonplaces of modern physics, was "first accurately and clearly demonstrated by Blackett."

The technical advances Blackett made with the counter-controlled cloud chamber resulted in his and Occhialini's establishing the existence of particle showers. Compton went on, "In the same paper . . . [Blackett] noticed that in these many particle showers some of the particles were deviated by the magnetic field in a direction opposite that of a negative electron. This constituted an independent discovery of the positive electron which was announced in a paper by Anderson somewhat later, although it preceded the publication of Blackett's work."[40] Compton continued with an account of Blackett's demonstration of the production of electron pairs from gamma rays of thorium C and his measurement of the momentum of cosmic-ray particles, bringing Blackett's research up to date with brief mention of his recent speculation on the earth's magnetic field. Finally, as alluded to by Born in late 1944, Compton noted Blackett's recent war work and his introduction of operational research as a new field.[41]

Bernal followed a similar tack, with a résumé of Blackett's experimental techniques and investigations from the 1920s to the 1940s, including Blackett's new interest in geomagnetism, and saying by way of summary:

> Blackett's contribution to knowledge of nuclear processes and cosmic rays cannot be summed up as a single discovery made at a particular date. He has occupied a unique place in the development of this field of research and has furnished the exact data without which the work of others would have been impossible. . . . [The cloud chamber] has largely been created in its modern form through his work and it is always associated with his name. . . . Many of the most important discoveries of nuclear physics have been made possible only as a result of the use of methods for which Professor Blackett was largely responsible.[42]

Bringing to bear his knowledge of Blackett's extrapolation of his physics methodology to operational research, Bernal noted, as well, that "two features characterize his work: the importance placed on statistics of an adequate number of observations; and the minute, critical and accurate study of rare individual events."[43] Bernal addressed the positron problem by alluding to Blackett's caution and critical judgment, in combination with a penchant for exploring every possible alternative before adopting a new hypothesis, the very sort of characterization that some of Blackett's other colleagues made of him in everyday laboratory life, as discussed in earlier chapters of this book.[44]

After Ising was assigned the task of a report on Blackett, he summarized all past nominations for Blackett since 1935, and he wrote an overview of Blackett's cloud-chamber work with a section on Blackett's most recent research. Ising's report, which was one of ten reports by Physics Committee members on candidates nominated in 1948, gave the wording that was eventually used in the Nobel citation: "for his development of the Wilson cloud chamber method, and his discoveries therewith in the fields of nuclear physics and cosmic radiation."[45] Ising's summary for the Academy, which went forward with the Physics Committee's recommendation, made mention in a concluding paragraph of Blackett's revival of Arthur Schuster's old hypothesis on geomagnetism, noting that

Blackett's work now was extending into the domain of geophysics and astronomy. Perhaps this new work especially interested Ising. The Physics Committee's recommendation went forward on 16 September 1948, signed by Hulthén, Ising, Waller, Axel Lindh, and Manne Siegbahn as chair.[46] On 2 November, Darwin again mailed off a letter to Stockholm nominating Blackett, unaware that Blackett would receive the 1948 Prize.[47]

The Organization of University Research

Blackett was head of the Physics Department at Manchester in the year of his Nobel Prize. When he had returned from the Admiralty in London to the Physics Laboratory in Manchester in 1945, he found his department in need of renewal and reorganization following the war. Blackett had first arrived at Manchester in fall 1937, succeeding W. Lawrence Bragg as Langworthy Professor of Physics, a physics professorship that had been held previously by Ernest Rutherford and Arthur Schuster. Blackett was strongly mindful of this succession, as he wrote Rutherford in July 1937.[48] Whereas Bragg's physics department had focused on x-ray crystallography, Blackett's main interest was particle physics, and, in any case, some of Bragg's staff quickly dispersed, with Bragg taking away some members of his research group, as was customary.

Blackett acquired rooms adjacent to the main laboratory for the installation of his magnet and cloud chamber, which arrived from Birkbeck College along with J. G. Wilson, Lajos Jánossy, and Blackett's personal technician Arthur H. Chapman. Blackett broke with twenty-five years of Manchester tradition by moving the laboratory steward William Kay from his quarters behind the lecture room to a ground-floor room near the entrance. A departmental library was established. The message went out, too, that Saturdays now were a workday.[49] Staff members who stayed in Manchester included Tolansky, whose research was in optics, and J. M. Nuttall and E. C. Scott-Dickson, who were strong teachers. Bernard Lovell and George Rochester had recently arrived as assistant lecturers. Blackett quickly persuaded the university to create a new Chair of Theoretical Physics for Douglas R. Hartree, who had been Professor of Applied Mathematics at Manchester. In fall 1938 he hosted a weekend conference on cosmic rays and the mesotron, which brought Werner Heisenberg, Bruno Rossi, and Homi Bhabha, among others, to

Manchester. Other visitors included Occhialini, Pierre Auger, Walther Heitler, and E. J. Williams.[50]

During the war Rochester, Jánossy, Tolansky, and Nuttall remained in Manchester. When the war was over, Wilson and Lovell returned, along with Blackett. When Hartree left Manchester for Cambridge University after the war, Léon Rosenfeld came from Utrecht to succeed him as Professor of Theoretical Physics. With Blackett's strong support, Lovell located a radar facility at Jodrell Bank, twenty miles south of Manchester, that turned into a pace-setting observatory in the new field of radio astronomy. Lovell became Professor of Radio Astronomy in 1951, and Zdenek Kopal became Professor of Astronomy. Blackett's astatic magnetometer was installed in a hut at Jodrell Bank in January 1949, while equipment for observation of the new V-particles was moved to the observatory on the Pic du Midi in France late in the year.[51] Clifford Butler, who became an assistant lecturer at Manchester in 1945, was in charge of the Pic du Midi project. Keith Runcorn, who assisted Lovell as well as Rochester and Butler before he moved to the rock magnetism project, joined the department in 1946. There was turnover at Manchester as senior positions opened up elsewhere: Jánossy left for Dublin and Tolansky for Royal Holloway College in 1947; Wilson departed for Leeds in 1952, and Rochester for Durham in 1953.[52]

In the late 1940s and early 1950s, Blackett frequently had business in London, but he usually stopped in at the Physics Department on his way home and looked around the laboratory to see what was happening. It was not his practice to waste time while commuting on the train, and he traveled in a closed compartment, first class, sometimes with his Manchester colleagues, in order to be able to work. He could be irritable if he was interrupted by outsiders wanting to share the compartment, just as he could be cross on returning to the laboratory if it looked like careless mistakes had been made in his absence. But, generally, Butler recalls, Blackett was kind and encouraging.[53]

Given his schedule, Blackett had to be a good delegator of responsibilities. He tried to get maximum flexibility for managing his department's expenses, but he was unable to obtain an annual block allotment of money from the university, as he demanded.[54] He succeeded in getting funds from the Department of Scientific and Industrial Research (DSIR) to support all fields of his department's research. Other monies included a five-year grant awarded in 1945 from the Nuffield Foundation to support cosmic-ray research.[55] Among Blackett's London duties immediately after the war was his membership in a Royal Society committee, chaired by Charles G. Darwin, to furnish a report to the British Treasury's University Grants Committee on "The Balanced Development of Science in the United Kingdom."[56] The Darwin Report concluded that science was best furthered, not by redlining specific areas to be funded, but by science's "natural" development among "the most distinguished leaders."[57] There was to be no rigorous centralized scientific planning despite the fears of Michael Polanyi, John Baker, George Tansley, and other members of the Society for Freedom in Science movement.

In late 1948, as President of the Board of Trade, Harold Wilson piloted through the House of Commons a bill that set up the National Research Development Corporation (NRDC), a brainchild of Sir Stafford Cripps, who had been Minister of Aircraft Production during the war. Cripps was keen on preventing British discoveries and inventions from falling prey to foreign, especially American, patents and development. Wilson got Blackett's agreement to serve on the NRDC, although the appointment produced what Wilson later recollected as one of the most violent political fracases that he ever witnessed in Parliament, when Blackett was denounced for his views on halting nuclear weapons development and establishing cooperation in atomic policy with the Soviet Union. Blackett served on the NRDC from 1949 until 1964, but he largely remained ostracized from central advisory committees to the Government and from Whitehall council tables until the 1960s.[58]

Despite Blackett's frequent trips to London, his Manchester colleagues did not expect that Blackett would leave Manchester permanently for London or any university other than Cambridge. It was well known that Lawrence Bragg shortly would retire from the directorship at the Cavendish Laboratory.[59] Colleagues expected Blackett to be the primary candidate for the position, just as he had succeeded Bragg, and Rutherford, at Manchester. Nonetheless, Blackett began negotiating a move to Imperial College in late 1952. At this time Manchester University's support of his physics department was more than £20,000, supplemented by an annual DSIR grant for Jodrell Bank of £8,000. He expected comparable support at Imperial College and a salary something over £2,000.[60] In late July 1953 Blackett wrote Chadwick that he did not wish to be considered a candidate for the Cavendish position and that he had reached that decision when he decided the previous summer to accept the chair at Imperial College.[61] Similarly, Blackett wrote Richard Kahn in September 1953 that he did not want to be considered for the position of Provost at King's College, Cambridge, because he preferred to be in London, where a big expansion was planned at Imperial College and where Blackett's NRDC and other advisory activities were based.[62] Costanza felt the same way as Blackett and preferred London to Cambridge.[63]

Blackett brought with him to London colleagues and technicians who became known to some as the "Manchester Mafia." The Mafia group included Harry Elliot's cosmic-ray group. It also included Butler, who headed the high-energy nuclear physics group, and who has a strong memory of arriving at Imperial:

> First impressions were not encouraging. There were long, wide corridors, vast teaching labs, and the largest men's toilet I had ever seen. Research space was scattered about the building. I had an office to myself for the first time and part of an adjacent large lab. There were three chairs in the department: Blackett's; the chair in Technical Optics held by David Wright, and a Chair in Low-Energy Nuclear Physics held by Sam Devons. There were several other areas of experimental work, acoustics, spectroscopy, geophysics, and solid state physics. There had been a small cosmic-ray group led by Don Perkins who had left for Bristol. Jim McGee, a research physicist from EMI, was appointed to a Chair in Instrument Technology from October 1954. In 1955 Devons was invited to succeed Blackett at Manchester; Blackett shut down the low-energy nuclear physics activity, but encouraged some of the members to set up a new group in high-temperature physics, led by Bob Latham. From 1953 there were two separate geophysics activities in the department, Blackett's and one in applied geophysics led by [J. McGarva] Bruckshaw. In 1955 Brucksaw was appointed professor and transferred his group to the Geology Department.[64]

Blackett hoped that remodeling the Physics Department could be achieved simply by enlarging the Physics domain into Chemistry, and giving Chemistry an empty building site in Prince Consort Road that had been bombed out during the war. Instead, Imperial College's Rector, the chemist Patrick Linstead, persuaded Blackett to take the new construction site, requiring Blackett's involvement in design of the new building that opened in 1960. By then there were seven professors, a number more than double the number at Blackett's arrival in 1954, as well as twenty-seven lecturers and thirty-two research assistants in the department, divided into ten independent research groups. Students numbered some 300 undergraduates, whose program of study was directed by David Wright, and 100 postgraduates. As Lovell notes, Blackett was one of the first department heads to implement the strategy of multiprofessorial departments. In 1955 Blackett became Dean of the Royal College of Science, and he served from 1961 to 1964 as Pro-Rector.[65] It was his aim to create an urban scientific research and educational institution that equaled the old universities of Cambridge and Oxford in achievements and prestige, while opening up opportunities in science and technology to new disciplinary fields and to college students unlikely to enter the older elite establishments.

For Blackett, science and engineering went hand in hand in the ongoing development of contemporary physics. One of the new professors in Blackett's department was Dennis Gabor, who received the title Professor of Applied Electron Physics in 1958. Gabor received the Nobel Prize in Physics in 1971 for his invention and development of the holographic method. Another new position in Blackett's department was that of Abdus Salam, a Pakistani, whose tutor had been Fred Hoyle at Cambridge. Salam became Professor of Theoretical Physics in 1959 after transferring, with Paul T. Matthews, a Reader, from the Mathematics Department to the Physics Department. Salam soon established one of the most active theoretical groups in high-energy physics in the world, sharing the 1979 Nobel Prize in Physics with Sheldon Glasgow and Steven Weinberg. The three colaureates were recognized for their contributions to the theory of unified weak and electromagnetic interaction between elementary particles, which used symmetry schemes to explain the phenomenology of particles produced by accelerators.[66]

Salam was equally interested in applied physics as well as in theoretical physics. On the one hand, he was a founding director of the International Centre for Theoretical Physics in Trieste from 1964 until his death in 1993, while continuing to work in London. On the other hand, he served as personal scientific advisor to President Ayub Khan of Pakistan from 1961 to 1974 and was a member of the Pakistan Atomic Energy Commission. On political matters, especially regarding strategy for Third World development and India-Pakistan policies, he and Blackett did not always see eye to eye, as discussed further below. Devoutly religious, Salam was controversial in his religious beliefs as an adherent to the Ahmadiyah sect of Islam that accepts the claims of Mirza Ghulam

Ahmad to be a nineteenth-century prophet and a reappearance of Mo-
hammed. Salam was a formidable presence, like Blackett, at Imperial,
but he was also a colleague who said upon learning of Blackett's death in
1974 that he felt depressed and "orphaned by his demise."[67]

National Policies for Science and Technology:
Great Britain and India

In London Blackett enjoyed the sociability of the Reform Club, the
Athaeneum, and other gentleman's clubs and meeting places. He had
been a member of the Tots and Quots group, first convened by Solly
Zuckerman in 1931 and given new life during the war. The group, including Bernal, Julian Huxley, Joseph Needham, C. H. Waddington,
C. D. Darlington, Lancelot Hogben, J. G. Crowther, and Peter Ritchie
Calder, usually met in a Soho restaurant and entertained a chief guest,
who opened discussion after dinner.[68] In the earlier years Hugh Gaitskell
frequently showed up, although Crowther found him "not to be very
much at home with the atmosphere and views of most of us." On an evening in 1940, H. G. Wells was the chief guest, directing the gentlemen's
discussion to the reconstruction of the world after the war, just as bombs
suddenly began dropping across Soho.[69] It was this group that anonymously edited the Penguin book *Science in War*.[70]

A newer incarnation of the Tots and Quots group was the dinner list
put together in the mid- and late 1950s by Marcus Brumwell to meet at
the Reform Club or Brown's Hotel for discussion among distinguished
scientists and prominent members of the Labour party. Guests numbered some of the old-timers from Tots and Quots, such as Blackett,
Bernal, Zuckerman, and Ritchie Calder, as well as Snow, Jacob Bronowski, Bruce R. Williams, R. G. Forrester, George Dickson, C. F. Carter, Ben
Lockspeiser, and Harold Florey. Gaitskell, now leader of the Labour
party, attended occasionally, as did Alf Robens, the Shadow Minister for
Education and Science. Harold Wilson attended, too, and he brought
into the group Dick Crossman, who later became his spokesman on
Higher Education and Science.[71] On 27 August 1959 the scientists laid
on the dinner table a 32-page jointly authored document entitled "A
Labour Government and Science" that Gaitskell and Wilson, both of
whom were present, were prepared to accept as basic policy on science.
Wilson saw it as a strong statement that the Labour party intended to

make full use of science if returned to power, but that the party was not proposing a "soulless technocracy . . . [nor] merely gimmicks and sputniks." At dinner Snow offered to revise the document as a Labour party leaflet within fourteen days.[72]

London dinner meetings continued in the next years, although the scientists became increasingly frustrated with Gaitskell, threatening to stop dining together if he did not pay more attention to their agenda. Following Gaitskell's death early in 1963, and Wilson's becoming Labour party leader, things were looking up among the scientists, especially with the appointment of Crossman as Shadow Minister.[73] At a Labour party conference at Scarborough in fall 1963, with Blackett on the platform, Wilson gave a forceful speech that some people attributed to Blackett, although Wilson said that he wrote it himself in the small hours of the morning before he delivered it.[74]

In the months before the general election of October 1964, Wilson told Blackett that he would set up a Ministry of Technology, separate from Education, and that the Ministry would be "NRDC writ large," eventually taking over some functions from the Board of Trade, together with engineering functions from the Ministry of Aviation, and nuclear research and industry external to the military establishments. Blackett prepared a paper in September 1964 on "The Case for a Ministry of Technology" and pushed hard for efforts to save the British computer industry from IBM and other foreign competitors. Blackett was responsible for the decision to set up a National Computer Centre at Manchester. Solly Zuckerman, who had been chief scientific advisor to the Ministry of Defence since 1960, continued to serve under Wilson as scientific advisor to the Cabinet Office. It was thought that Blackett might become the new Minister of Technology (MinTech), with one of his competitors rumored to be Robert Maxwell, the wealthy publisher and Labour MP from Buckingham. Blackett declined the Ministry, but agreed to serve as MinTech's science advisor and Deputy Chairman of the Advisory Council, first under MinTech's head Frank Cousins and, then, Wedgwood (Tony) Benn.[75] Snow, who had been knighted in 1957 and who became a life peer in 1964, was Parliamentary Secretary to the new Ministry.

Blackett remained an advisor at MinTech until 1969, by which time his duties as President of the Royal Society were increasingly demanding his attention. Blackett was elected to the presidency in 1965 for a five-year term, becoming the official leader of British science for the international scientific community. With feet planted firmly in both the Royal Society and the Government, Blackett was able to strengthen ties and forge new links that ensured the Royal Society's role in education and research in the British scientific community. In 1967 the Royal Society moved from Burlington House to Carlton House Terrace, overlooking Pall Mall, with Queen Elizabeth present for the formal opening ceremony on 21 November. Blackett and Costanza moved into an apartment at Carlton House Terrace for the rest of his presidential term.[76]

At MinTech, responsibilities in administration included oversight of the National Physical Laboratory, the Atomic Energy Authority, most of the research stations that had been in the former DSIR (other than ones allotted to a new Science Research Council), and the National Research Development Corporation. MinTech had responsibilities for four industries: computers, electronics, telecommunications, and machine tools. It took over mechanical and electrical engineering and motor vehicles from the Board of Trade and, in 1967, it absorbed the Ministry of Aviation.[77]

John B. Adams, who was the first Controller for MinTech, became critical of Blackett's attempts to employ methods of operational research in the Ministry of Technology. In Adams's view, modification of British market forces through government purchasing power had been possible in wartime, but not in present circumstances.[78] MinTech had little influence over the defense industry, which consumed half of government funds for industrial research and development. In addition, in the late 1960s MinTech, like all of Wilson's government, faced a financial crisis that made cutbacks and moratoriums the order of the day rather than expansion of government initiatives and expenses. Blackett's proposal for a £5 million package in support of the British computer industry was hopelessly uncompetitive with the kind of funding being expended by computer industries overseas.[79]

Adams also disliked Blackett's greater concern with improving performance of British industry than with using scientists in the research establishments to help with industrial problems. Blackett's comment, reported in *Nature* in 1967, that British research might have taken a wrong turn after the war by concentrating talent in public laboratories rather than diffusing it through private industries surprised and angered many of his scientific colleagues and political allies. Nor was Blackett's view popular that Britain had too many small firms and that mergers were necessary.[80] Many people judged Blackett to be out of his element in MinTech's daily agenda.

Wilson gave a more sympathetic interpretation to Blackett's work at MinTech, suggesting that Blackett aimed to "break down separatisms: separatism between research and industry–indeed class distinction–between different toilers in the same vineyard. For him . . . it was . . . a question of parity of esteem between a production engineer and a theoretical physicist."[81] After winning elections in 1966, the Labour party lost in 1970 following a backlash against the government over the devaluation of the currency, trade union turmoil, and violence in Northern Ireland.

In addition to his role as science and technology advisor in Britain, Blackett became increasingly involved in Indian policy after the Second World War. Archibald Vivian Hill, with whom Blackett had served on many committees, including the Tizard Committee, had spent seven months in India during 1943–1944 to advise on the organization of science in India. He introduced Blackett to Shanti Bhatnagar, a chemist educated at Lahore and the University of London. A Fellow of the Royal Society and Director of India's Council of Scientific and Industrial Research, Bhatnagar was in London in 1946 for the Empire Scientific Conference. Soon afterwards Blackett and other prominent foreign scientists were invited to India for individual visits. Blackett was asked to speak to the 1947 meeting of the Indian Science Congress, which took place in Delhi in January, some eight months before India would become independent on 15 August 1947.

At the Indian Science Congress a British delegation was present, and Jawaharlal Nehru was to preside over the meeting, whose theme was "Research and National Planning." Blackett also was asked to address the Association of Scientific Workers (ASW) of India, a welcome venue for Blackett, who was President of the ASW in Britain from 1943 to 1947 and a leader in the formation of the World Federation of Scientific Workers (WFSW) in 1945.[82] Indeed, both Bernal and Blackett got attention from J. Edgar Hoover in one memorandum alerting the State Department to their allegedly suspicious roles in the WFSW, along with other purportedly communist activities.[83] Some of Blackett's British colleagues were hardly less critical of the ASW and boycotted the Delhi meeting. The Harvard astronomer Harlow Shapley reported to Blackett that he had been staggered in Delhi to hear Charles G. Darwin quip that the aim of the ASW was to improve the condition of the worst scientists at the expense of the best scientists.[84]

Blackett's visit to India also brought him into contact with the British soldiers and administrators whose roles in India were changing dramatically with the coming of Indian independence, and when he returned to London, Blackett met with Lord Mountbatten, who served as Viceroy of India from March to August 1947 and administered the transfer of power from Britain to the new nations of India and Pakistan. Blackett might have told Mountbatten, whom he had known since student days at Cambridge, the story that Blackett wrote his wife Costanza from his Indian sojourn. Blackett was known to be a bird-watcher. One of the British generals suggested taking him out to observe some birds.

> I went yesterday, but it had turned into a . . . shooting party with three other army people of the "it's a fine day, let's go out and shoot something" variety. They . . . had a little tiff with some villagers . . . and . . . upheld the British Raj. The tiff was over the fact that the villagers thought they had come to shoot peacocks which are considered holy. . . . But later in the day a peacock strutted across the road and the Empire builders in charge of the party . . . [were] going to shoot it when a villager turned up. . . . So we make ourselves loved.[85]

During this first visit to India, Blackett found himself on the plane with Nehru, with whom he talked en route. Blackett shortly afterwards was invited to Nehru's home, where the Acting Prime Minister asked Blackett's opinion on how long it would take India to "Indianize" the country's armed forces. Blackett replied that a war effort comparable to the one just fought by Britain would demand some twenty to thirty years of building military strength upon industrial power, but that a war on India's frontiers with a neighbor of comparable industrial strength (for example, Pakistan or China) could be prepared within two years. A few months after their first meeting, Nehru invited Blackett to spend more time in India advising him on the research and development needs of the armed forces. Gradually, Blackett's advice extended to problems of civil service and education, including visits to set up a research group on paleomagnetism at the Tata Institute for Fundamental Research in Bombay, which had opened in 1945 under the direction of Homi Bhabha with private funding from the Sir Dorab Tata Trust. Blackett frequently stayed in the Prime Minister's residence while in Delhi, often for weeks at a time, sometimes with Costanza accompanying him. Of Nehru, Blackett said: "Like so many others I fell under the spell of Nehru's charm, his luminous intelligence and his total dedication to achieving world peace, to maintaining the unity of India and to increasing the wealth and prosperity of his country by the application of modern science and technology."[86]

Robert Anderson notes that Nehru liked and trusted Blackett because of their Cambridge backgrounds, their shared enthusiasm for political socialism, and their common suspicions of US foreign policies.[87] They also seemed to agree on the need to prevent proliferation of atomic weapons, but to develop atomic energy as the source for electrical power in underdeveloped countries. In contrast to Mahatma Ghandi, Nehru believed that the well-being of India depended on the adoption of modern technology, and he favored state economic planning and investment in large industrial enterprises to bring this about. As for diversion of atomic energy into atomic weapons, Nehru consistently declared that "we will not make these bombs, even if we have the capacity to do so," while arguing for the need to acquire the scientific know-how and technology of atomic energy.[88]

Homi Bhabha, who headed the Tata Institute and the Atomic Energy Research Committee, became the leader of India's Atomic Energy Commission when it was established by the Constituent Assembly in 1948. Bhabha reported directly to the Prime Minister, with whom he had an exceptionally cordial rapport based in their shared Cambridge education, cosmopolitan culture, and dedication to India's future prosperity and prominent place in the world.[89] Bhabha was one of Blackett's closest friends. The two had known each other since the 1930s in Cambridge, where Bhabha had established himself as an outstanding theoretical physicist after having passed the Mechanical Engineering Tripos with a first in 1930. In postgraduate studies Bhabha focused on particle physics, and in late 1936 he and Walther Heitler had worked out a theoretical explanation of cascade showers in cosmic rays, about the same time as J. F. Carlson and Robert Oppenheimer. Bhabha was one of the physicists whom Blackett invited to Manchester in 1938 for his cosmic-ray conference, and Bhabha, who returned home to India in 1939, often stayed with Blackett in England. When Blackett stayed in Bhabha's family mansion in the Malabar Hills of Bombay, he stayed in a guest room below Bhabha's personal flat on the top floor where windows looked out all along one side to the harbor.[90] J. G. Crowther described Bhabha as "a handsome man, always well dressed, in perfect but expensive taste. . . . A considerable painter in the modern style, he was the only nuclear physicist who ever had one-man shows of his pictures in Paris and London. . . . He became the chairman of India's atomic energy commission, and he decorated its headquarters with his own paintings."[91] One of Bhabha's figures was a portrait of Blackett that he sketched when Blackett was in India. It was a great personal blow to Blackett when Bhabha died, on his way to an international conference, when an Air India Boeing 707 crashed into Mont Blanc in a snowstorm in January 1966. Blackett described Bhabha as "my best personal friend."[92]

Another younger Indian protégé was Vikram Sarabhai, who studied physics at Cambridge before the war and returned to complete his doctorate in 1947. There was no one at Cambridge to examine Sarabhai's thesis in cosmic-ray physics, so Blackett was asked to be the examiner, and Sarabhai traveled to Manchester for the examination. By 1958 Sarabhai was building a Physical Research Laboratory in Ahmedabad, and he succeeded Bhabha at the Department of Atomic Energy in 1966.[93] Prasanta Mahalanobis, another Cambridge-educated physicist, built the Indian Statistical Institute in Calcutta and was committed to a centrally planned state-driven economy in advice that he gave Nehru. Daulat Singh Kothari, also a Cambridge-trained physicist, became director of the Defence Science Organization, which was established in 1948 along lines of a report that Blackett prepared for Nehru. They all kept in touch with Blackett and visited him when traveling through London, and, in turn, Blackett visited their institutes, examined their doctoral students, appraised new research programs, and advised on new appointments.[94]

Blackett also met with the Chiefs of the Armed Forces and staff in the Ministry of Defence when he visited India. He toured armaments and aircraft factories and advised on military procurements, sometimes offering different advice than British military officers. "I like to think that . . . I saved India a lot of money by discouraging her from buying too much big and expensive western equipment," he said. In a 1948 report he listed weapons that India should not attempt to develop: atomic weapons, chemical weapons, supersonic jets, high performance jets, and guided missiles.[95] Blackett discussed with Bhabha, Bhatnagar, and others the organization of British atomic research and development, while continuing to argue the need for international controls.

Along with his old friend John Cockcroft, Bhabha was one of seven advisors to UN Secretary-General Dag Hammarskjöld on the organization of a conference on the peaceful uses of atomic energy. Hammarskjöld appointed Bhabha its president. Salam served as scientific secretary. Some 1,400 delegates from seventy-three nations, as well as 3,000 observers and 900 journalists, attended the meeting in the Palace of Nations in Geneva in August 1955.[96] From late 1955 on, Bhabha and Nehru made statements to the effect that India should renounce the bomb, although not the capacity to make it. By 1958, however, Bhabha seems to have told Blackett and others that he hoped to develop nuclear weapons, and he declined to participate in the Pugwash Conference of 1961, although he and Blackett both attended in 1963. Following the first Chinese nuclear test in October 1964, Bhabha likely had the go-ahead for an underground test in India as soon as possible, although the explosion did not occur until 1974, the year of Blackett's death.[97]

During many of the years that Blackett was advising Indian scientists and ministers on military and scientific matters, his Imperial College colleague Abdus Salam similarly was performing an advisory role in Pakistan, serving from 1961 to 1974 as chief scientific advisor to the President of Pakistan. There is some evidence that Bhabha's statements around 1965 that India would build a nuclear weapon within twelve to fifteen months encouraged Pakistani President Ayub Khan and Foreign Minister Zulfikar Ali Bhutto to gamble immediately on war over Kashmir, before India developed nuclear capability. Not only did Blackett and Salam thus find themselves in conflict over Indian-Pakistani allegiance, but they also often found themselves at odds over the question of how best to quickly advance Third World economic development in general.[98]

Salam argued that fundamental basic research must be supported in underdeveloped countries both to prevent the "brain-drain," of which he was an example, and to ensure that technologies are not simply purchased by their buyers as black boxes that are not understood by their users. Theoretical physics has its place in Pakistan, Turkey, and Brazil, as well as in Cambridge and London, and research centers such as Salam's international institute in Trieste could provide a meeting ground for scientists who might otherwise find themselves too isolated in their own countries. On this Blackett did not agree, and he advocated as immediate priorities the purchase of First World technologies by Third World countries and the organization in underdeveloped countries of science education and research centers closely linked to technological development, rather than to fundamental research.[99] This view laid Blackett open to the charge that he was falling prey to outmoded colonialist prejudices and imperfectly supporting the intellectual aspirations of his colleagues in the Third World.

Indeed, this charge was made. In New Delhi in 1967 Blackett gave the First Jawaharlal Nehru Memorial Lecture, which was attended by Prime Minister Indira Gandhi and reviewed widely in newspapers. In the lecture, to the consternation of many scientific colleagues, Blackett called for innovation in Indian industry through direct applications of laboratory science. He criticized the idea of the "sanctity" of basic research and argued for stronger links between research and its applications in industry, a statement that angered many Indian scientists in the very laboratories that Blackett had long been visiting since the late 1940s.[100]

In fact, Blackett's lecture to Indian colleagues in 1967 simply reiterated many themes in his lecture ten years previously to British colleagues, when he delivered the Presidential Address at the Dublin meeting of the British Association for the Advancement of Science in 1957. On that occasion, he advocated massive foreign aid to underdeveloped countries, particularly the United Kingdom's former colonies, such as India. Scientists and engineers have a particular responsibility in the matter, he urged, because "it is their genius and their skill which alone can bring the material basis of happiness within reach of all. The uneven division of power and wealth, the wide differences of health and comfort among the nations of mankind, are the sources of discord in the modern world, its major challenge and, unrelieved, its moral doom."[101]

Although Blackett had prepared this Dublin address carefully, corresponding beforehand about preliminary drafts with friends, including Bhabha (who was at the meeting) and Mahalanobis, and indeed Gaitskell, it seemed to please hardly anyone.[102] One evening paper printed the headline "Professor Go Home." *The Economist* carried a report "British Association: Rewriting Humphry Davy," summarizing Blackett's rephrasing of Davy's 1802 dictum that "the unequal division of property and labour, the differences of rank and condition among mankind, are the sources of power in civilised life, its moving causes and even its very soul." *The Economist* cynically concluded, much to Blackett's consternation, that "there is not much to be said about Professor Blackett's prescription except what he knows already: that it is unlikely to be followed. He may also reflect that Davy's opinion still rings true, economically if not morally."[103] The speech also got notice in Blackett's FBI file, where a *New York Times* clipping shows the FBI underlined Blackett's words "If the West does not help, perhaps the Soviet bloc will."[104]

Among Blackett's few sympathetic listeners was Snow, who incorporated some of their common views into his 1959 Rede Lecture on 7 May in the Senate House of Cambridge University. In what became a famous and widely debated essay on "The Two Cultures and the Scientific Revolution," Snow, himself a novelist as well as physicist and science policy advisor, distinguished the culture of literary intellectuals from that of natural scientists. According to Snow, the literary intellectual is epitomized by T. S. Eliot, whose ambitions are so narrow and self-absorbed that Eliot himself characterized his revival of verse drama as an enterprise from which, as Snow put it, "we can hope for very little, but that he would feel content if he and his co-workers could prepare the ground for a new [Thomas] Kyd or a new [Robert] Greene. That is the tone, restricted and constrained . . . it is the subdued voice of their culture. Then they hear a much louder voice, that of another archetypal figure, Rutherford, trumpeting: 'This is the heroic age of science! This is the Elizabethan age!'"[105] In Snow's estimate, it is scientists who have "the future in their bones" and "that was as true of the conservatives J. J. Thomson and Lindemann as of the radicals Einstein or Blackett." The incomprehension between the two cultures "is the kind of joke which has gone sour."[106] Or, as Snow expressed the view in an earlier article in 1958: "Between Rutherford and Blackett on the one hand, and say, Wyndham Lewis and Ezra Pound on the other, who are on the side of their fellow human beings?"[107]

In the last section of the Rede Lecture, Snow introduced the theme of "The Rich and the Poor"—a theme that was largely ignored in later polemical discussions of "the two cultures." As Blackett had done in Dublin, Snow argued in Cambridge that the gap in optimism between the two cultures leads to disheartening and dangerous consequences for the future: the result of the original scientific revolution is that "people in the industrialized countries are getting richer, and those in the non-industrialized countries are at best standing still."

This *disparity* between the rich and the poor has been noticed. It has been noticed, most acutely and not unnaturally, by the poor. . . . If we are short-sighted, inept, incapable either of good-will or enlightened self-interest, then it may be removed to the accompaniment of war and starvation: but removed it will be. The questions are, how, and by whom. . . . The scientific revolution on the world-scale needs, first and foremost, capital. . . . The capital must come from outside. . . . The second requirement, after capital, as important as capital, is men. That is, trained scientists and engineers adaptable enough to devote themselves to a foreign country's industrialisation for at least ten years of their lives.

And, Snow concluded, there is no time to lose.[108]

Thus Blackett and Snow stood side by side on the matter of the pressing need for expansion of scientific and engineering education at home, but also in underdeveloped countries. They took a rather unpopular moral position on the obligation of nonscientists and scientists alike to invest in the future of the poor. As we saw in Chapter 1, this position insisting on the social responsibility of the scientist was opposed strongly by Michael Polanyi and Edward Shils, among others. In this matter Snow saw Blackett as a model of the physicist who refused to shut himself inside the laboratory and leave social and political action to others. However, the precise method of science and technology transfer to underdeveloped countries was a seemingly intractable problem that remained in dispute, not only among western scientists but among eastern and southern scientists as well.[109]

Conclusion: Style and Character in a Scientific Life

Blackett wrote only two memorial tributes for scientists outside the Cavendish circle. These essays shed light on Blackett's feelings about what count as admirable qualities of leadership, specifically scientific leadership. In both cases Blackett's characterization of achievement goes far beyond the confines of the research laboratory. The tributes were published in 1960, one commemorating Henry Tizard, twelve years older than Blackett, and the other, Frédéric Joliot-Curie, three years younger.

Blackett had worked closely with Tizard in the 1930s and 1940s. Like Blackett, Tizard was ostracized from governmental advisory committees under Clement Attlee's government because of Tizard's skepticism about a British atomic weapons program. Like Blackett, Tizard had a reputation as a war veteran and something of a hero. He had served in combat in the First World War, and, indeed, he was legendary in some circles for a daring flight in which the guns of his new Sopwith Camel jammed as he intercepted German bombers. It was reported that Tizard recovered as best he could by following the German formation, taking notes on the speed and performance of the German Gothas, waving good-bye, and speeding home.[1]

Blackett admired Tizard for his quality of commanding respect from soldiers and scientists alike, for his evenhandedness, and for his enthusiasm: "he had a most unusual ability to establish immediate and mutually stimulating contact with anyone doing a job; he seemed as genuinely interested in talking to a college porter, an aircraftsman or a young scientist as to a crack pilot, a professor or an air marshal."[2] "A visit with

169

Tizard to an experimental establishment was an exhilarating experience," Blackett recalled; "he left behind him a new awareness of the tasks and a new keenness to get results."[3]

Joliot-Curie died in 1958 following his infamous dismissal from the French Atomic Energy Commission (CEA) in 1950 on the grounds that he was a communist; the French government had decided to embark on an atomic-weapons program, rather than continuing to focus the mission of the CEA on industrial and scientific atomic development alone. Joliot, with his wife Irène Joliot-Curie, had been one of Blackett's chief competitors in nuclear physics and cosmic-ray physics during the 1930s. Joliot was a leader in uranium fission research in 1939, and the first self-sustaining chain reaction might have occurred in Paris, had the war not intervened. Joliot and Blackett shared leftist political views and shared sympathy with the successes and failures of changes in the Soviet Union. As Blackett described it, Joliot, like himself, had an experimental philosophy of designing experiments so as to foster the greatest chance of finding something unexpected, rather than simply, and safely, confirming what already was presumed to be the case.[4]

Joliot was a man of courage. He arranged for his laboratory stock of heavy water to be smuggled to England in the charge of his coworkers Hans Halban and Lew Kowarski. He hid his stores of uranium oxide, which later were unearthed and used in the first French experimental pile in 1948. Joliot undercut, indeed sabotaged, Germans' work with his laboratory cyclotron during the years of German occupation, and he constructed radio receivers and transmitters for the French resistance and, toward the end of the war, explosives. Blackett's personal and physical description of Joliot bears repeating:

> From his earliest days Joliot was keen on sport and athletics, including Judo, tennis, skiing, sailing and above all sea fishing. . . . Joliot had debonair good looks, was gay and direct in manner and an excellent lecturer with a fine voice and command of language. In his later political days he found he also possessed the gift of mass oratory and could hold an open-air audience of hundreds of thousands of people.[5]

Michel Pinault, a biographer of Joliot, has asked the question why Joliot stayed in France during the Vichy period, the answer to which Blackett thought obvious: it was a matter of integrity and courage, as well as patriotism. In Pinault's assessment, Joliot stayed because of his conviction that he could best help the resistance to the Germans by fighting from within, in particular, fighting to retain control over his nuclear physics laboratory. Writes Pinault, Joliot "was convinced that he could put his knowledge, his competence, and his charisma in the service of . . . the State, the nation, and human progress."[6]

Among scientists of this generation, it was Blackett's American colleague Robert Oppenheimer who stands out among controversial, and charismatic, scientific leaders. After the war, Isidor Rabi wrote that Oppenheimer succeeded Albert Einstein "as the great charismatic figure of the scientific world." Glenn T. Seaborg dwelt on Oppenheimer's "magnetic, really electric, personality, [and] his charismatic presence." Even Edward Teller spoke of the "brilliance, enthusiasm and charisma" with which Oppenheimer led Los Alamos.[7] In a sociological essay, Charles Thorpe and Steven Shapin stress Oppenheimer's physical features as part of this charismatic identity: the tall and thin body frame, the blue color of his eyes, the intensity of his gaze.[8] He seemed a "disembodied spirit" carrying a moral authority associated with the ascetic way of life.[9]

In a typology of characteristics for a successful research school, the scholars J. B. Morrell and Gerald Geison each argued that an "ideal" research school requires a "charismatic" director. Few historical accounts of research schools have taken up this claim but focus instead on other characteristics of a model research school: a director establishes a research program in which a distinctive approach, often based in specific experimental techniques, is used to solve well-defined problems. Successful research groups are characterized by social cohesion, a research program, exploitable experimental techniques, pools of recruits, and access to publication outlets, as well as identifiable styles of research.[10]

In Max Weber's lectures defining "charisma" in the early 1920s, Weber explicitly dissociated charisma from the scientific profession and from expertise. Instead, Weber rooted the charismatic "gift" in "personal heroism or personal revelation" in the conduct of religion, war, and politics.[11] Weber's conception of the scientist—as a university man—argued that the scientist was the kind of man who had absolutely nothing to do with the everyday world:

> Fellow students! You come to our lectures and demand from us the qualities of leadership, and you fail to realize in advance that of a hundred professors at least ninety-nine do not and must not claim to be

football masters in the vital problems of life, or even to be "leaders" in matters of conduct. . . . [T]he qualities that make a man an excellent scholar and academic teacher are not the qualities that make him a leader to give directions in practical life or, more specifically, in politics.[12]

Clearly Blackett was a different kind of man than Weber's university scientist. Blackett cared a great deal about war and politics, and indeed sports, if not religion. He admired men, as in his tributes to Tizard and Joliot, who integrated science with affairs of war and politics. Yet how might Blackett's style of leadership be characterized, both in his laboratory research groups and in the wider scientific community? Indeed, how *was* he characterized by his contemporaries, and how did their perceptions affect judgments of his successes, or shortcomings, in scientific leadership?

As we have seen, Blackett was regarded by the Osborne Naval College admissions board as the "right sort of boy," one who was resourceful, ready to act, with a turn for practical mechanics and a mind for mathematics.[13] A veteran of wartime combat at the age of twenty-one when he entered Cambridge University, Blackett had a versatility of imagination and tough skepticism. He was fiercely independent.[14] Ivor Richards was struck by the tall and handsome appearance of Blackett in his twenties.[15] Of Blackett in his forties, a former student recalled "he was tall and strikingly handsome."[16] Later, in his sixties, Blackett was described in London as "even more handsome as an aging man than as a young one, he was as much a figure in the King's Road as he had once been in the King's Parade."[17] Some women found him irresistible. The irrepressible Ruth Nanda Anshen, a New York City patron of philosophy and religion, described her first encounter with Blackett to be an experience "like an electric shock." "There was the man," she wrote, "gaunt, tall, an element of nature." Yet, she further reflected, "The profound impression Blackett made upon me was due to his extraordinary and poignant moral conscience."[18]

In a different way, the sculptor Jacob Epstein was so struck in the late 1940s by photographs of Blackett that, after meeting Blackett's sister Marion Milner, Epstein asked her to persuade Blackett to sit for a bronze sculpture. Once the sculpture was completed, it was shown at the Tate Gallery and eventually found its place in Blackett's sitting-room.[19] Its replica was unveiled at Imperial College on the centenary of Blackett's birth. Commenting on Epstein's impressions of Blackett's appearance, Andrew Brown suggested that Epstein's "thoughts probably echoed those of the woman at Cambridge in the early 1920s who said: 'No doubt he is a very good physicist, but it is his statuesque beauty that I like.'"[20]

Good looks and seriousness of purpose did not ensure friendship or respect, and they sometimes kindled envy or suspicion. As noted earlier, Peter Kapitza was not taken with Blackett, nor Blackett with Kapitza, as they competed in the 1920s with each other for Ernest Rutherford's favor and good will. On the other hand, Mark Oliphant's reaction to Blackett was entirely different. After arriving at the Cavendish from Australia in 1927 and meeting Rutherford, Oliphant left Rutherford's office just as "two large young men strode from a room opposite, nearly colliding with the very diffident newcomer. With a charming smile, a handsome and impressive man said: 'I'm Blackett. This is Dymond. Who are you?' These members of the Laboratory were clearly friendly."[21] The Hungarian-born low-temperature physicist Nicholas Kurti first met Blackett in Berlin in the 1930s; he recalled Blackett as "a tall man, with a handsome face, horn-rimmed spectacles and a pipe. . . . I used to say to myself 'Here is the living portrait of an Englishman.'"[22]

Nevill Mott was one of Blackett's great admirers at the Cavendish, looking up to him as the skilled expert on experimental arbitration of theoretical speculations.[23] Like others at Cambridge, Mott was not surprised that Blackett felt the need to break free from his long apprenticeship under Rutherford. Blackett had learned a great deal from Rutherford, of course, and he later praised Rutherford's power of concentration and pictorial imagination, his eye for the unexpected, and his boundless enthusiasm, saying that he, Blackett, had "learnt early [from Rutherford] the vital importance of the role of the director of research in selecting promising problems for his research students." Blackett remarked that his own success in the cloud-chamber nitrogen experiments in 1924 "was an example of Rutherford's choosing the really important problems and letting a young man get on with them."[24] Blackett was proud to be associated with Rutherford and the Cavendish tradition.[25]

As director of his own laboratory at Birkbeck College, Blackett had many obstacles to overcome in a laboratory where conditions were so bad that it was hardly possible to walk between the benches. Blackett's study was the size of a telephone box.[26] As J. G. Crowther recalled, "Rutherford once said to a research student who complained of poor research conditions: 'Why, I could do research at the North Pole.' If the Birkbeck Laboratory was not quite the North Pole, it was then about the worst physical laboratory in any English university. But Blackett, like his great teacher, created a new centre of research under difficult conditions."[27]

The international research group under Blackett's tutelage at Birkbeck called itself the League of Nations.[28] The researchers found in Blackett a master craftsman of experimental physics with whom a scientific apprenticeship could be served. Blackett continued to work directly with junior colleagues, showing young Clifford Butler at Manchester, for example, how to set up the cloud-chamber control mechanism that Blackett had designed at Birkbeck College.[29] The geophysicist Ted Irving recalls working side-by-side with Blackett in the early 1950s, as Blackett demonstrated how to make adjustments to the astatic magnetometer at Jodrell Bank. On this occasion Blackett was not wearing his eyeglasses and, to Irving's horror, Blackett dropped and broke the magnetometer. It was never repaired.[30]

Skepticism and caution, as well as empiricism and theory, strongly characterized Blackett's style of work. Whatever his regrets about delaying publication on the positive electron in 1932, he did not afterwards rush into publication on subsequent research. He discouraged George Rochester and Butler from announcing the discovery of a strange particle on the basis of just one photographic event and insisted on outlining every conceivable explanation of photographic tracks until all but one had to be rejected.[31] After the ordeal of coauthoring their 1960 publication on rock magnetism and continental drift with Blackett, John Clegg chafed a bit at Blackett's perfectionist approach.[32] Blackett's method had strong British precedent. Charles Darwin, for example, wrote in his *Autobiography:* "I had . . . during many years, followed a golden rule, namely, that whenever a published fact, a new observation or thought came across me, which was opposed to my general results, to make a memorandum of it without fail and at once; for I had found by experience that such facts and thoughts were far more apt to escape from the memory than favourable ones."[33]

As a leader of research groups, whether in physics or operational research, Blackett gave his staff and coworkers considerable freedom in the ways they went about their work. He was not a constant presence. Ted Irving draws a sharp contrast between Blackett's style at Manchester and at Imperial and Keith Runcorn's style in his research group at Cambridge. Blackett managed things from the top down. In contrast, Runcorn's group was bottom-up, so that Jan Hospers, Ken Creer, David Collinson, Irving, and others in Runcorn's group talked and decided what to do without following any master plan worked out by Runcorn, who frequently was absent from the laboratory.[34]

In an interview with Brian Connell of Anglia Television, Blackett admitted that he was not sure whether it was complimentary that staff at his universities said that he ran a department like a captain runs a ship: "There is something I think in the tradition of delegating authority completely to young—junior—people and then if things go wrong, taking the blame yourself." Of the junior people working under him, Blackett said, "I once coined a slogan which has often been repeated; I defined a good laboratory as one in which ordinary people do first class work."[35] His student Francis Everitt claimed that two remarks encapsulated Blackett's outlook: "Make sure you gather plenty of data," and "You should treat your research like a military campaign."[36]

William Hunter McCrea, who worked with Blackett in operational research, confirmed the description of his officer style, also saying that Blackett believed in getting people he thought could contribute, and then leaving them to it most of the time. He would propose a problem, expect an answer pretty soon, and then sometimes forget that he had asked.[37] Blackett delegated administrative responsibilities as well as laboratory research. Butler, who worked with him at both Manchester and Imperial, was one of those who thought Blackett's naval background influenced his style of management: "some of us certainly thought of him as admiral!" Admirals are not chummy with their juniors. It was only in the 1960s, after twenty years of collaboration, that Butler and Blackett called each other by their Christian names.[38]

Blackett's physical presence clearly became one of command and authority. At Manchester a student "was awestruck by his stately procession down the main stairs for lunch. He always walked in the dead centre of the staircase, disdaining the banisters. He held his hands, naval fashion, in his jacket pockets, with thumbs protruding. He had no nickname: he was Professor Blackett."[39] Everitt recalls an occasion of student rags in the mid-1950s when King's College students invaded Imperial College, leading to defensive measures in which the science students turned hoses from fire hydrants on their adversaries. When Samuel Devons tried to calm things down, the students turned the hoses on him. At that moment Blackett appeared and stood on the steps and looked down. Within a minute, the hoses were turned off and the students were gone. Blackett had not said a word.[40]

When he was refused a visa in June 1945 to attend a conference in the Soviet Union, Blackett was one of several scientists who refused to do further war work until they had received explanation of the refusal. Mott marvelled that "to see Blackett marching out of the Admiralty was a magnificent sight."[41] "Blackett was something of a god-like figure," writes Irving. "A commanding man. Nobel laureate, politically interesting, controversial, eloquent, handsome, tough."[42] Tam Dalyell, MP for forty years in the British House of Commons, described Blackett as "quite simply, the most personally formidable man for whom I have ever worked—or, indeed, met, at close quarters."[43]

Blackett had power. Through his network of friends and acquaintances in government, industry, and military circles, Blackett could get things done. When he needed forty pounds of gold, he had contacts that enabled him to borrow it from the Bank of England. When construction of the 200-foot Jodrell Bank radio telescope began, no one knew how to make an affordable turntable for it. Blackett telephoned friends in the Navy and persuaded them to donate the bearing from the gun turret of a retired battleship.[44]

Blackett had detractors and enemies, of course. He was, after all, controversial. He was a left-winger and thought by many to be politically suspect in his sympathy for the Soviet Union and in his calls for economic aid to Britain's former colonies. He had what C. P. Snow characterized as "this extremely superior sort of personality which made people resent him, just as they resent anyone being authoritative about many things."[45]

R. V. Jones was a friend and colleague of Blackett's not only in physics but in wartime service when Jones was head of the Air Ministry's Scientific Intelligence. At the end of the European war, the two had a severe difference of opinion over postwar coordination of Intelligence among the Navy, Army, and Air Force, with Blackett insisting, against Jones, on maintaining separate Scientific Intelligence and Technical Intelligence

Sections. Coordination would come, Blackett argued, through housing the Sections in one building, and rotating the chairmanship of a joint committee every three months. Jones thought this was one of Blackett's several blunders in wartime administration.

> He tended to jump into a new field, thinking that his fresh ideas were better than those who had worked in the field for some time. Sometimes they were, but not always. He was given to "rational" solutions of problems which sometimes completely overlooked the human aspects involved, and he would then press these solutions with a fervour that belied their apparent rationalism. . . . [H]e would move from one post to another with relative ease, whereas I felt committed to whatever post I was in, to make as long-term a success of it as possible.[46]

Someone else who fell afoul of Blackett was the historian of science John Heilbron, who found Blackett busy and uncooperative when Heilbron arrived to interview Blackett in December 1962 for the Sources for History of Quantum Physics Project. Blackett, Heilbron jotted down in his notes, was not going to be immortalized in the archives since he would not allow a tape recorder or note-taking. Heilbron found Blackett sympathetic to his undertaking but at no great inconvenience to himself.[47] Blackett's research group at Imperial found it typical of Blackett's schedule that when Prime Minister Nehru visited London, Blackett was so busy that the only chance for a meeting was at breakfast.[48]

Those who worked with him knew that Blackett could have a terrible temper. One of them was his technician Arthur Chapman, who nonetheless moved with Blackett from the Birkbeck Physics Laboratory to Manchester and then to Imperial. Clifford Butler found Blackett occasionally very cross with laboratory colleagues and staff when he thought they had failed in some obvious way. Blackett could sometimes be heard using obscenities—salty language—that struck his staff as a residue from the Navy days.[49] However, the bad temper did not usually lose Blackett respect, or even affection, and he was adored by many in his laboratories. He was courteous and considerate to all his industrial staff, he presided over the local branch of the trade unionist Association of Scientific Workers in Manchester, and he and Costanza threw a party for "everybody" when he won the Nobel Prize. Gas-filled balloons floated over the garden outside their flat in a large university house, where Costanza made sure that secretaries, technicians, husbands, wives, and children all were welcome. One of the Nobel party balloons made it to the east coast of Ireland.[50]

Significantly, Blackett gained as much respect and loyalty from his failures as from his successes. While he received considerable sympathy from many British scientists following award of the 1936 Nobel Prize to Carl Anderson, Blackett also received respect because he never publicly complained about having been passed over nor ever in any way denigrated Anderson's priority for discovery of the positive electron.[51] That Blackett keenly felt the competition was registered in his writing Henry H. Dale after the 1948 Nobel award that "sometimes one has felt perhaps a little disheartened at the difficulty of competing with American competition in certain fields of pure science, where lots of money and apparatus brings big results. I do feel reasonably satisfied, however, that we in England are really pulling our weight quite well; in particular the Bristol work is very satisfying."[52]

Léon Rosenfeld remarked of Blackett that one of his strengths was that he was "not deterred by flops." After the war, when Bernard Lovell and Blackett set up war-surplus radar equipment twenty miles outside Manchester at Jodrell Bank in order to search for reflected signals from cosmic radiation, nothing seemed to work. As Rosenfeld put it, "he could have said, 'Oh well, let's drop the whole thing.' But he said, 'Well, we have the equipment. Let us try to see what we can do with it.'"[53] By chance they got hold of a signal from a radio star, and an observatory for radio astronomy came into being. Lovell told sociologist David Edge that Blackett "gave me money—eventually a separate budget—all of which he might well have said he wanted for his own cosmic ray research; he was fascinated by the techniques and by the subject matter."[54]

One of Blackett's most spectacular failures was his disproof of his restatement of the hypothesis that the magnetic fields of the sun, stars, and earth are a fundamental property of their rotating mass. Francis Everitt recalls:

> By the time I was seventeen, I had heard of Blackett, initially because of the famous cloud chamber photographs on nuclear disintegrations which were reproduced in dozens of books. My physics master in high school, E. J. Wenham, when he was teaching us about magnetism in 1951 [sic], described Blackett's hypothesis and then explained how, when the evidence told against it, Blackett had demonstrated his scien-

tific integrity by immediately acknowledging that it was wrong. Thus Blackett was held up as a high role model of the physicist by a man (Wenham) who did not in the least share Blackett's political views.[55]

In the arena of politics, Blackett risked his reputation over and again, just as he did in physics. He recognized that his political views were controversial and he understood that the very act of expressing political views—on atomic weapons, American Cold War policy, British industry, postcolonial development in India—subjected him to criticism that he was illegitimately using his reputation as a scientist to garner public favor. He did not have thin skin or prickly sensitivity in these matters, but took the hand that was dealt him, writing Rudolf Peierls in response to Peierls's concern about a newspaper article, that "one must expect that sort of thing. The article itself is not too bad."[56] Blackett was not deterred by hecklers. At a speech supporting the Labour party candidate at an election campaign in Manchester in March 1950, he spoke to a lecture hall of some 700 people. "Manchester University is one of the best universities in the country and in Europe," said Blackett. "If we appointed our professors and lecturers with as much nepotism as most of the small private firms in the country, we should be tenth rate." Some 100 people heckled and shouted questions at him during the speech.[57]

In the end, Blackett's reputation was somewhat larger than life, identified with physics, politics, and war. He had emerged in the British scientific community as a member of the well-established Cavendish school, associated with the legendary figures of J. J. Thomson and Rutherford. Blackett possessed considerable authority before he even completed his apprenticeship at Cavendish because of his status as a war veteran. In the Cambridge milieu, he was a minor hero, like any veteran who has served in combat with honor. The bearing and habits that he developed during the Navy years, which were Blackett's teenage years, reminded his contemporaries that he already had been vetted for qualities of command and leadership. In a British culture that was highly formal and formalized, Blackett the captain and later the "admiral" of the laboratory was much admired and respected. He looked the part of a leader. In an English school culture characterized by valuing manly sports, he looked the football master, too.

Blackett established an unusual expertise as a gifted experimentalist: a master craftsman in instrumentation with theoretical acumen. He was known for the phenomenology of his approach to physics, geophysics, and even operational research, as well as for his ability to teach students and colleagues using old-fashioned methods of hands-on apprenticeship. At the Cavendish, and then in the research schools that he directed at Birkbeck, Manchester, and Imperial, Blackett followed or directed groups in numerous subfields of physics, always demonstrating a commitment to the support of the mathematical theoretical physics in which Rutherford had had so little interest. Blackett's immediate research groups were distinguished by the use of key instruments: the cloud chamber, the Geiger counter, the magnetometer. He delegated research problems to his coworkers and subordinates (this he says he learned from Rutherford), but in such instances he also gave lessons and advice on instrumentation, counseled researchers on their publications, and in some cases intimately involved himself in writing up results, whether or not he put his name in as coauthor. He moved seemingly effortlessly from radioactivity physics to particle and cosmic-ray physics to geophysics and continental drift, never abandoning active scientific research until after retirement. In all these respects, Blackett exemplifies the model characteristics often attributed to a master scientist and leader of a successful research group.[58]

The research schools and physics departments that Blackett directed were relatively small and simply administered, especially in comparison to the organization of high-energy physics after the Second World War. While he was a strong advocate of the establishment of the European Council for Nuclear Research (CERN) and of British participation in CERN, Blackett did not care to administer a large bureaucratic scientific organization. This may have been a good thing, since there was considerable criticism of failures of organization and policy in the Ministry of Technology in which he was a powerful advisor. The cloud-chamber and cosmic radiation physics at which he excelled was relatively small-scale work. Similarly, Blackett's work on the earth's magnetism, rock magnetism, and continental drift in the 1950s and early 1960s was carried out in small groups with relatively simple instrumentation.

Blackett's commitment to socialism as an economic and political system, his opposition to the development of atomic weapons, his criticism of the applications of operational research to game theory for thermonuclear war, and his efforts to convince scientists and governments to make commitments of time, material, and money to build up science and technology in Britain and Third World countries, demonstrated an unflagging energy for addressing world problems. In this, he shared some of the preoccupations of his admired colleagues Tizard and Joliot. Blackett exemplifies the men and women of a new post–World War II scientific elite who took up the role of scientific advisors to political and military establishments in which science and technology were to be employed to ensure national economic development and national security.[59] Within this scientific elite, Blackett epitomizes an even smaller group of men and women who risked personal reputation among scientific peers and the larger public in order to argue the scientist's responsibility to society and the public's need to understand scientific or technical evidence supporting or calling into question public policies.

Most scientists in Britain and elsewhere continued during the 1950s and 1960s to insist that scientists maintain an ethos that science is politically neutral and value-free. In contrast, Blackett helped forge the role of the twentieth-century scientist as public citizen. Whether arguing in Whitehall against the usual strategy of small convoys or stepping forward to announce failure to confirm his theory of the earth's magnetism or openly opposing his government on the matter of British nuclear weapons, Blackett put himself at considerable risk in the interests of his convictions and integrity. The personal costs to him ranged from ridicule by fellow scientists ("mad as a hatter" said one scientist) to ostracism within Attlee's political party to suspicion from national intelligence agencies.[60] In all of this his ongoing achievements as a physicist, recognized in 1948 by the Nobel award, assured that his voice would be heard. In this conduct, his company was small, especially since outspoken scientists such as Albert Einstein or Linus Pauling took on little of the governmental responsibilities that Blackett seemed to consider his responsibility.

Especially in his later years, as remarked by Dalyell, Blackett was perceived by those who did not know him well as more formidable than charming. The impression came from his remarkable scientific intellect, his moral fervor, and his physical presence. Alan Hodgkin, who had worked with Blackett during the war, recalled an occasion when he and Lovell complained about administrative decisions in operational research, saying, "'They won't allow us to use miniature valves.' Blackett turned on me sharply, saying 'Never say "They" like that—it's a sign of frustration and wooly thinking and will get you nowhere.'"[61] Blackett was a strongly masculine man of the old-style stiff-upper-lip British tradition. His military education came often to the fore in his qualities as a leader: as one Royal Navy textbook on leadership puts it, there is no place for the expression "charm" in connection with leadership.[62]

Blackett's old friend William Cooper, who was Registrar at Manchester during the 1940s, had known both Rutherford and Blackett while Cooper was a student at Cambridge in the early 1930s. Rutherford, "big and fresh-complexioned, his spectacles shielding light, transparent eyes, was . . . boomingly Jehovianic, albeit in an attractive way." "Blackett, in later years," said Cooper, "always struck me as more Jehovianic—tall, thin, high-shouldered, with wavy hair and a flashing eye, in manner altogether loftier, nobler, graver; more of a Jehovah's Jehovah, perhaps."[63] Blackett's students resembled nothing like a cult, such as the following enjoyed by Oppenheimer at Berkeley and at Los Alamos, or by Richard Feynman, in a later generation, at the California Institute of Technology. Blackett was not a charismatic leader, in the ordinary usage of the word. In fact, one of his friends remarked to Blackett's daughter that her father had abhorred the cult of the personality.[64]

In recollections about Blackett, Butler remarked on a newspaper headline at Blackett's death describing him as the "last of the barons."[65] Toward the end of his life, Blackett became Baron Blackett of Chelsea, despite his earlier misgivings about the inegalitarian politics of the House of Lords. Blackett had never taken a Ph.D. at Cambridge, and he quipped to a friend that at least he had remained Mr. Blackett until he retired.[66] He spoke four times in the House of Lords during 1970 through 1972, once on governmental policy on research and development and three times, including his first speech, on the need for aid to underdeveloped countries. His theme of the widening gap between rich and poor was the subject of his Rede Lecture at Cambridge University in May 1969.[67] Friends saw little of him after 1972, and when they did see him, it struck them that he was frail and might have suffered a small stroke. It was unexpected to learn of his death in hospital on 13 July 1974.

What did it mean to Blackett to embark upon living a scientific life in the twentieth century? Through most of his life, even in his last public interventions, Blackett continued to demonstrate a commitment to science, reason, and social change, and he persisted in saying things that he knew many people did not want to hear. His was a life of physics, war, and politics in which one passion was never very separate from the other. When Blackett and Giuseppe Occhialini were interviewed by journalists following their announcement of the existence of the positive electron in 1933, Blackett characterized himself as "just an explorer, a traveler over an unknown field."[68] A pencilled drawing of Blackett and Occhialini depicts the two of them exploring a polar region with Rutherford looming behind them drawn as a giant tusked walrus. A new film had appeared at the Marble Arch Pavilion showing Ernest Shackleton's 1914–1916 expedition to the Antarctic. A newspaper article of early 1933 announcing the film and discussing the expedition lies next to newspaper articles about the positive electron in Blackett's family album.[69] Exploration, discovery, discipline, and courage were central to this controversial scientist's life.

NOTES

Abbreviations

BFP	The Blackett Family Papers; privately held
BJHS	*British Journal for the History of Science*
BP	The Papers of Patrick Maynard Stuart Blackett, OM FRS, Baron Blackett of Chelsea (1897–1974), Library, Royal Society of London
HSPS	*Historical Studies in the Physical and Biological Sciences*
JSI	*Journal of Scientific Instruments*
Phil. Mag.	*Philosophical Magazine*
Phil. Trans.	*Philosophical Transactions of the Royal Society*
PKVA	Protokoll vid Kungl. Vetenskapsakademiens Sammankomster för Behandling af Ärenden Rörande Nobelstiftelsen (Minutes of Meetings of the Royal Swedish Academy of Sciences, for Discussion of Matters concerning the Nobel Foundation), the Nobel Archive of the Royal Swedish Academy of Sciences, Stockholm
PP	The Papers of Michael Polanyi (1891–1976), Regenstein Library, University of Chicago
PRSL	*Proceedings of the Royal Society of London*
SHQP	Sources for the History of Quantum Physics, Niels Bohr Library, American Institute of Physics, College Park, Md.

Note: Letters written by P. M. S. Blackett that are designated as letters in the Blackett Papers at the Royal Society (BP) are carbon copies of the original letters.

Introduction

1. Edward C. Bullard, "Patrick Blackett . . . An Appreciation," *Nature,* 250 (1974), 370.
2. "Hinge of Fate: Anthony Tucker in a Unique Royal Society Tribute to the Man Whose Vision Turned the Tide of the War," *Guardian,* 20 July 1974, clipping (BFP).
3. The presentation speech and banquet remarks (as well as Blackett's lecture

and biography) can be found at http://www.nobel.se/physics/laureates/1948/blackett-bio.html.

4. T. E. Allibone, "Reminiscences of Sheffield and Cambridge," in *The Making of Physicists,* ed. Rajkumari Williamson (Bristol: Adam Hilger, 1987), pp. 21–31, esp. 30.

5. Ibid.

6. [W. E. D., I. B. N. E.], "The Nobel Prize Winners," *Discovery,* January 1948, clipping (BFP). Blackett's lecture, broadcast in 1934, appeared as Chapter 7 in *The Frustration of Science,* ed. Sir Daniel Hall, J. G. Crowther, and J. D. Bernal (London: Allen and Unwin, 1935).

7. On the scientists for social responsibility movement, see William McGucken, *Scientists, Society and State: The Social Relations of Science Movement in Great Britain, 1931–1947* (Columbus: Ohio State University Press, 1984); Gary Werskey, *The Visible College: A Collective Biography of British Scientists and Socialists of the 1930s* (London: Free Association Books, 1988). See also Brenda Swann and Francis Aprahamian, eds., *J. D. Bernal: A Life in Science and Politics* (London: Verso, 1999).

8. Blackett, "Tizard and the Science of War," in P. M. S. Blackett, *Studies of War: Nuclear and Conventional* (Edinburgh: Oliver and Boyd, 1962), p. 110.

9. James Raymond, "Qui est Blackett?" and P. M. S. Blackett, "Le savant comme citoyen" and "L'opinion de Philip Morrison, membre du Physics Department de l'Université de Cornell (USA)," in *La Tribune des Nations,* 29 (July 1949), clipping (BFP).

10. "A-Bomb Controversy," *Between the Lines,* 18 April 1949, clipping (BFP).

11. "Citation to Accompany the Award of the Medal for Merit to Patrick Maynard Stuart Blackett," The White House, 15 October 1946, signed Harry Truman (BFP).

12. Timothy Garton Ash, "Love, Death and Treachery," *Guardian,* 21 (June 2003), 4–7, and Ash, "Orwell's List," *The New York Review of Books,* 50, no. 14 (25 September 2003), 6–12.

13. Chapman Pincher, *Daily Express,* 5 September 1957, clipping (BFP).

14. "The 'Googlie' Electron: A Revolutionary Discovery," *Morning Post,* 17 February 1933, with quotation from Andrade; "Two Modest Young Scientists," *Evening Standard,* 17 February 1933; "The Nature of Electricity. A New Discovery. English Scientist's Demonstration," *Manchester Guardian,* 17 February 1933; J. D. Cockroft, "New Light on the Atom," *The Spectator,* 24 February 1933; E. N. da C. Andrade, "Last Week Another Sensational Discovery Was Announced from the Cavendish Laboratory," *Weekend Review,* 25 February 1933; "Scientific: Electron That Photographs Itself.

King's Don Discovers New Component of the Atom," *Varsity Weekly,* 25 February 1933. Clippings (BFP).

15. "The 'Googlie' Electron."

16. "Finds Cosmic Rays Have Odd Particle. British Scientist Says That They Consist in Part of 'Positive Electrons.' Credits Dr. Anderson. Dr. P. M. S. Blackett Says American Should Not Be Robbed of Leads in Discovery," *New York Times,* 17 February 1933, clipping (BFP).

17. Jacob Bronowski, "Table Talk," *Observer,* 3 September 1950, clipping (BFP).

18. Freeman Dyson, "Shock of the New Viewpoint." Extract from speech on the occasion of receiving the Britannica Award for excellence in dissemination of learning for the benefit of mankind. Unidentified clipping (BFP).

19. Comments from Giovanna Blackett Bloor to the author, 28 June 2003. Also, letter from Rod Wilson to Costanza Blackett, 22 July 1974 (BFP).

20. David Schoenberg, "Teaching and Research in the Cavendish, 1929–35," in *The Making of Physicists,* ed. Rajkumari Williamson (Bristol: Adam Hilger, 1987), pp. 101–111, esp. 104.

21. W. E. Burcham, "Some Thoughts on Physics Courses in Cambridge: 1931–7," in Williamson, ed., *Making of Physicists,* p. 164.

22. Typescript of Bernard Lovell's remarks on the occasion of Blackett's seventy-fifth birthday dinner, London, November 1972 (BFP).

23. Lord [Solly] Zuckerman, *Six Men Out of the Ordinary* (London: Peter Owen, 1992), p. 29.

24. "'Googlie' Electron. Experiments in London," *Morning Post,* 30 August 1933; [L. V. D.], "They Have Their Other Side," *The Evening News,* 25 May 1933. Clippings (BFP).

25. Letter from Blackett to Costanza Blackett, 20 September 1946, New York, on art and paintings; letter from Blackett to Costanza Blackett, 23 November 1946, Paris, on the *Mariage de Figaro* at the Comédie Française; letter from Blackett to Costanza Blackett, 2 January 1947, Cairo, on the Egyptian Museum and the Tutankhamen collection; letter from Maurice Goldsmith to Costanza Blackett, 19 July 1974, recalling Brecht Theatre performance in London (BFP). See also "Science Not Just a Matter of Brilliant Thought in an Armchair. 'Staggering Achievement'–Prof. Blackett," clipping (BFP).

26. Typescript of notes on the life of Costanza Blackett, who died 18 June 1986 (BFP).

27. Letter from Blackett to Costanza Blackett, 20 September 1946, New York (BFP).

28. G. G. Steel, V. D. Courtenay, and M. Y. Gordon, "Obituary: Nicholas M. Blackett," *International Journal of Radiation Biology,* 78 (2002), 875. Just as

his mother's name, Costanza, often was misspelled as Constanza, Nicolas Blackett's name often was misspelled as Nicholas.

29. Comments by Giovanna Blackett Bloor to the author, 20 October 2003.

30. Letter from Blackett to Costanza Blackett, 10 June 1949 (BFP). Also, Zuckerman, *Six Men,* p. 13.

31. Eric Hobsbawm, *Interesting Times: A Twentieth-Century Life* (New York: Pantheon, 2002), pp. 233–243; "How Left-Wing Was My Valley," *Sunday Telegraph,* 23 June 1996 (courtesy of Giovanna Blackett Bloor).

32. Hobsbawm, *Interesting Times,* p. 240.

33. Letter from Michael Burn to Costanza Blackett, 3 September 1974 (BFP).

34. E.g., letter from W. Ehrenberg to Costanza Blackett, 15 July 1974, and letter from George Rochester to Costanza Blackett, 16 July 1974 (BFP); Zuckerman, *Six Men,* p. 13; photo, with caption "M. Blackett aurait pu être un jeune premier de cinéma," *France Soir,* 10 September 1949 (BFP clipping).

35. Norman de Bruyne, "A Personal View of the Cavendish, 1923–1930," in *Cambridge Physics in the Thirties,* ed. John Hendry (Bristol: Adam Hilger, 1984), pp. 81–89, esp. 87.

36. [W. E. D., I. B. N. E.], "The Nobel Prize Winners."

37. Cathryn Carson, "A Scientist in Public: Werner Heisenberg after 1945," *Endeavour,* 23 (1999), 31–34. On Pauling in comparison to Blackett, see Mary Jo Nye, "What Price Politics? Scientists and Political Controversy," *Endeavour,* 23 (1999), 148–154.

38. Guy Hartcup and T. E. Allibone, *Cockcroft and the Atom* (Bristol: Adam Hilger/Institute of Physics, 1984), pp. 83–84.

39. David Wilson, *Rutherford: Simple Genius* (Cambridge, Mass.: MIT Press, 1983), p. 461; Paul Adelman, *British Politics in the 1930s and 1940s* (Cambridge: Cambridge University Press, 1987).

40. Wilson, *Rutherford,* pp. 461–463, 488.

41. Interview of David Edge with Sir Lawrence Bragg, 20 June 1969, in Sources for the History of Quantum Physics, American Institute of Physics, College Park, Md.

1. The Shaping of a Scientific Politics

1. "Nobel Prizes: Professor Blackett and Mr. T. S. Eliot," *Manchester Guardian,* 5 November 1948, p. 5. Edward A. Shils, "The Atomic Problem: Professor Blackett's Book," *Manchester Guardian,* 5 November 1948, p. 4. Other Nobel laureates were Arne Tiselius (Chemistry) and Paul Müller (Physiology or Medicine), but none for Peace.

2. [Anonymous], "Lord Blackett: Radical Nobel-Prize Winning Physicist," *The Times,* 15 July 1974, clipping (BP: A.1).

3. Noel Annan, *Our Age: Portrait of a Generation* (London: Weidenfeld and Nicolson, 1990), pp. 3, 280–281.

4. Quoted in Hilary Rose and Steven Rose, "Red Scientist: Two Strands from a Life in Three Colours," in *J. D. Bernal: A Life in Science and Politics,* ed. Brenda Swann and Francis Aprahamian (London: Verso, 1999), pp. 132–159, at 138.

5. John Stuart Mill, *Auguste Comte and Positivism* (London: N. Trübner, 1865).

6. On Wells, see Hilary Rose and Steven Rose, *Science and Society* (Harmondsworth, Middlesex: Penguin, 1970), pp. 52–53.

7. Sir Bernard Lovell, "Patrick Maynard Stuart Blackett, Baron Blackett, of Chelsea," *Biographical Memoirs of Fellows of the Royal Society,* 21 (1975), 1–115, on pp. 1–2. Also, Andrew Brown, "Patrick Blackett: Sailor, Scientist, Socialist," *Physics World,* April 1998, 35–38, on p. 35.

8. Lovell, "Blackett," p. 2; and also on Babbage, Letter from P. M. S. Blackett to D. C. Martin, 12 May 1953 (BP: A.27).

9. Rosemary Burton, "Mind of Information," *Guardian,* 3 February 1988, clipping (BFP).

10. Joanna Field, *A Life of One's Own* (Boston: Houghton Mifflin, 1981), p. 216; Marion Milner, *The Suppressed Madness of Sane Men: Forty-Four Years of Exploring Psychoanalysis* (London: Tavistock, 1987), p. 9.

11. On the gift, see Marion Milner, *The Hands of the Living God: An Account of Psycho-analytic Treatment* (London: Hogarth Press and the Institute of Psycho-analysis, 1969), p. xxiii. J. D. Bernal, for example, was much interested in sexuality and psychoanalysis; at Emmanuel College in 1920 a friend "psychoanalysed" him and suggested that "love was the cause of his despair." Quoted from Bernal's diaries by Fred Steward, "Political Formation," in Swann and Aprahamian, eds., *J. D. Bernal,* pp. 37–77, at 45.

12. Lovell, "Blackett," p. 3; Brown, "Patrick Blackett," p. 35.

13. Blackett, "The Education of an Agnostic," five-page typescript of article that appeared in *Punch,* 3 September 1958 (BP: H.77).

14. Brown, "Patrick Blackett," p. 35.

15. Blackett, "Interlude on Politics," two unnumbered pages from materials that Blackett intended for an autobiography (BP: A.10A).

16. Lovell, "Blackett," p. 2; letter from Blackett to William Archibald, former headmaster at Allen House, 14 June 1971 (BP: A.35); typescript of addresses where Blackett lived, 1897–1970, one page (BP: A.10A).

17. Lovell, "Blackett," p. 3.

18. Comments by Giovanna Blackett Bloor to the author, 28 June 2003.
19. Milner, *The Suppressed Madness of Sane Men,* pp. 1–2.
20. Blackett, "Education of an Agnostic," p. 1.
21. Lovell, "Blackett," p. 3. The source for the story is Blackett's "Biographical Notes," five-page typescript, at p. 2 (BP: A.10).
22. P. M. S. Blackett, "Atomic Heretic," *The Listener,* 60, no. 1537 (11 September 1958), 375–376, on p. 375. In fact, Blackett's family paid fees for his naval education, as was the case with most of the boys.
23. Evan Davies, "The Selborne Scheme: The Education of a Boy," in Peter Hore, ed., *Patrick Blackett: Sailor, Scientist, Socialist* (London: Frank Cass, 2002), pp. 15–37, esp. 15.
24. Lovell, "Blackett," p. 3; Davies, "The Selborne Scheme," p. 17.
25. Davies, "The Selborne Scheme," p. 17.
26. Peter Hore, "Blackett at Sea," in Hore, ed., *Patrick Blackett,* pp. 55–71, esp. 55.
27. Davies, "The Selborne Scheme," pp. 17–18; also, Geoffrey Sloan, "One of Fisher's Revolutions: The Education of the Navy," in Hore, ed., *Patrick Blackett,* pp. 38–54, esp. 40–42.
28. Sloan, "Fisher's Revolutions," pp. 45–46.
29. From *The Entry and Training of Naval Cadets* prepared by the Director of Naval Education under the Authority of the Lords Commissioners of the Admiralty, HMSO, 1914, pp. 21–22, quoted in Michael Partridge, *The Royal Naval College Osborne: A History 1903–21* (Phoenix Mill: Sutton Publishing, in association with the Royal Naval Museum, Portsmouth, 1999), p. 59.
30. Partridge, *The Royal Naval College Osborne,* pp. 60, 79.
31. On naval history, see ibid., p. 88; on ciphers, Sloan, "Fisher's Revolutions," p. 51.
32. From *The Entry and Training of Naval Cadets* (1914), pp. 1–2 and p. 4, quoted in Davies, "The Selborne Scheme," p. 24. Also partially quoted in Partridge, *The Royal Naval College Osborne,* p. 34.
33. Sloan, "Fisher's Revolutions," quoted on p. 47.
34. Partridge, *The Royal Naval College Osborne,* pp. 61, 78–79.
35. Quoted in Hore, "Blackett at Sea," p. 56.
36. John Merrill, "P. M. S. Blackett: Naval Officer, Nobel Prize Winner, Submarine Hunter," *Submarine Review* (quarterly publication of the Naval Submarine League), January 1995, 86–88, on p. 88.
37. Lovell, "Blackett," p. 3; Hore, "Blackett at Sea," p. 56.
38. Blackett, "Education of an Agnostic," p. 1.
39. Reverend Frederick Seymour Horan, "Sermon No. 3: Influence," in *A Call to Seamen and Other Sermons Preached to Naval Cadets at the Royal Naval*

College, Osborne, 2d ed. (London: John Murry, 1911), pp. 18–25, at 22–23. Horan's preface to the volume is dated May 1911.

40. Quotation from Horan, "Influence," pp. 22–23. Also, see Sermon 9, "Our Language," pp. 63–73, and Sermon 15, "Self-Control," pp. 115–121, in Horan, *A Call to Seamen.*

41. Lovell, "Blackett," p. 3.

42. Davies, "The Selborne Scheme," p. 15.

43. Blackett, "Naval Diary 1914–1918. Midshipman," p. 2 of eighty-page typescript, including patent application of 1916 (BFP). Photocopy courtesy of Captain Peter Hore.

44. On the sense of destiny, see Hore, "Blackett at Sea," p. 57; on the cadets' activities, Blackett, "Naval Diary," pp. 2–3.

45. Blackett, "Naval Diary," 8 December, p. 12; Lovell, "Blackett," p. 3.

46. Blackett, "Naval Diary," entries for 16 August 1914 (p. 3); 30 August 1914 (p. 3); 1 September 1914 (p. 4); 21 September 1914 (p. 5); 1 October 1914 (p. 6); 18 October 1914 (p. 7); 13 November 1914 (p. 9); 6 December 1914 (p. 11); 10 January 1915 (p. 15); 12 January 1915 (p. 16); 15 March 1915 (p. 22); 26 March 1915 (p. 23); 28 March 1915 (p. 24); 1 June 1915 (p. 30); 19 January 1916 (p. 46).

47. Blackett, "Education of an Agnostic," p. 2.

48. Hore, "Blackett at Sea," pp. 58, 61.

49. Evan Davies, "Patrick, Lord Blackett," 24-page manuscript (March 1998), pp. 16–17. Courtesy of Peter Hore.

50. Ibid., pp. 17–18.

51. Blackett, "Naval Diary," 31 May 1916, p. 61.

52. Ibid., 5 June 1916, p. 62; Davies, "Patrick, Lord Blackett," p. 19.

53. P. M. S. Blackett, "British Policy and the H-Bomb," in Blackett, *Studies of War: Nuclear and Conventional* (Edinburgh: Oliver and Boyd, 1962), pp. 27–46, esp. 27, originally published in *The New Statesman and Nation,* 14, 21, and 28 August 1954.

54. Blackett, "Atomic Heretic," p. 375.

55. Hore, "Blackett at Sea," p. 65.

56. Lovell, "Blackett," p. 4. A "Naval Diary" entry for 26 March 1917 (p. 73) remarks that Blackett had recently composed a letter on the subject of whether he should try to get into the RNAS or wait, but that he had not sent the letter.

57. Hore, "Blackett at Sea," pp. 66–67.

58. Ibid., p. 68.

59. Quoted in Patrick Blackett, "Boy Blackett," in Hore, ed., *Patrick Blackett,* pp. 1–14, at 10.

60. Ibid.; and Blackett, "Naval Diary," 24 April 1918, pp. 77–78.

61. Letter of Patent, Admiralty, 5 September 1919, regarding report of 7 August 1916 on instrument devised by Lieutenant Edward Bellars and Midshipman Patrick M. S. Blackett of H. M. S. *Barham,* appended to "Naval Diary," pp. 78–79. See John Brooks, "The Midshipman and the Secret Gadget," in Hore, ed., *Patrick Blackett,* pp. 72–96, esp. 93–96.

62. As noted in Captain S. W. Roskill, "The Navy at Cambridge, 1919–1923," pp. 178–193, at 179–180.

63. Its circulation around 1959 was 100,000. See *New Statesman* website at www.newstatesman.com/nsabout.htm (accessed 29 October 2003).

64. Blackett, "Biographical Notes," p. 5 (BP: A.10); Hore, "Blackett at Sea," pp. 68–69; Lovell, "Blackett," p. 5.

65. I. A. R. (Ivor A. Richards), "Professor the Lord Blackett, O. M.," three-page typescript, annotated for *Magdalene College Magazine* (BP: A3), p. 1. Also quoted in Brown, "Patrick Blackett," p. 37. Blackett's application for renewal of his exit permit (visa) in 1943 gives his height as 6 feet, $2\frac{1}{2}$ inches tall (BP: G.85).

66. Mark Oliphant, *Rutherford: Recollections of the Cambridge Days* (Amsterdam: Elsevier, 1972), p. 20, recalling their first meeting in 1927.

67. See Andrew Brown, "Blackett at Cambridge, 1919–1933," in Hore, ed., *Patrick Blackett,* pp. 97–109, esp. 100–101; Richards, "Professor the Lord Blackett," p. 2.

68. Brown, "Blackett at Cambridge," p. 98.

69. Brown, "Patrick Blackett," p. 3.

70. Interview of Blackett by Brian Connell, Anglia TV, 1971, fourteen-page typescript, p. 5 (BP: A.32). The National Film Archive, London, has a copy of the tape of this interview.

71. Blackett, "Interlude on Politics," typescript notes for autobiography (BP: A.10A).

72. Guy Hartcup and T. E. Allibone, *Cockcroft and the Atom* (Bristol: Adam Hilger/Institute of Physics, 1984), p. 22.

73. See Ann Synge, "Early Years and Influence," pp. 1–15, on 11–12, and Fred Steward, "Political Formation," pp. 36–77, esp. 39–52, in Swann and Aprahamian, eds., *J. D. Bernal.*

74. Jeffrey Hughes, "The Radioactivists: Community, Controversy and the Rise of Nuclear Physics" (University of Cambridge Ph.D. thesis, 1993), pp. 41–42.

75. David Wilson, *Rutherford: Simple Genius* (Cambridge, Mass.: MIT Press, 1983), p. 565. According to Wilson, Rutherford thought that Bernal was someone who "sprayed out ideas" and left it to others to work them out. J. G. Crowther was of the view that Rutherford tried to make sure that Bernal's laboratory did not get funds at Cambridge.

76. J. W. Boag, P. E. Rubinin, and D. Schoenberg, eds., *Kapitza in Cambridge and Moscow* (Amsterdam: N. Holland, 1990), letters from Kapitza to his mother, 19 June 1922 (p. 151) and 3 November 1922 (pp. 159–160).

77. Wilson, *Rutherford,* pp. 496–497, 505, 522.

78. Boag et al., *Kapitza,* p. 42. The two-volume minute book of the Kapitza Club exists in photocopies on microfilm in the Archive for History of Quantum Physics at the American Institute of Physics, College Park, Md., and in the Cockcroft Collection at the Churchill Archive Center, Cambridge. The original first volume is in Moscow (Boag, p. 41).

79. Helge S. Kragh, *Dirac: A Scientific Biography* (Cambridge University Press, 1990); Hartcup and Allibone, *Cockcroft,* p. 32.

80. Comments from Giovanna Blackett Bloor to the author, 28 June 2003 and 14 September 2003.

81. Interview of Thomas S. Kuhn and John L. Heilbron with Werner Heisenberg, 30 November 1962 to 12 July 1963, twelve sessions, fifth session, 15 February 1963, p. 12 (SHQP).

82. Quotation from Richards, "Professor the Lord Blackett," p. 2; "Annual Report of the Council," King's College Cambridge, November 1974 (BP: A.2). Also, comments from Giovanna Blackett Bloor to the author, 28 June 2003.

83. Blackett interview with Brian Connell, p. 6 (BP: A.32).

84. Blackett, "Interlude on Politics," p. 2 (BP: A10.A).

85. Comments from Giovanna Blackett Bloor to the author, 28 June 2003.

86. Handwritten by Blackett, from *Country Life,* 10 May 1940 (BFP).

87. Blackett, "Interlude on Politics," p. 1 (BP: A10.A).

88. Eric Hobsbawm, "Bernal at Birkbeck," in Swann and Aprahamian, eds., *J. D. Bernal,* pp. 235–254, at 237. Bernal was Blackett's successor at Birkbeck College in 1937.

89. Interview of Charles Weiner with Otto R. Frisch, 3 May 1967, in New York City (SHQP), pp. 19–25.

90. Quoted in Lovell, "Blackett," p. 76.

91. Roy and Kay MacLeod, "The Social Relations of Science and Technology, 1914–1939," in *The Twentieth Century,* ed. Carlo M. Cipolla (London: Collins/Fontana, 1976), pp. 301–363, esp. 345.

92. Boris Hessen, "The Social and Economic Roots of Newton's *Principia,*" in *Science at the Crossroads* (London: Kniga, 1932), pp. 147–212. Comments by Blackett in his Introduction to the first J. D. Bernal Lecture, given by Dorothy Hodgkin, 23 October 1969, at Birkbeck College, eight half-pages, on p. 4 (BP: H.142).

93. See Julian Huxley, *A Scientist among the Soviets* (London: Harper, 1932). On Blackett's visits and Kapitza's comments, see Boag et al., *Kapitza,*

pp. 253 and 306. On the successes of the Soviet system as well as the enormities of the purges, see Loren R. Graham, *What Have We Learned about Science and Technology from the Russian Experience?* (Stanford: Stanford University Press, 1996), and Paul Josephson, *Totalitarian Science and Technology* (Atlantic Highlands, N.J.: Humanities Press, 1996).

94. See Huxley, *A Scientist among the Soviets* (London: Harper, 1932).

95. Quoted by Eric Hobsbawm, "Preface," in Swann and Aprahamian, eds., *J. D. Bernal*, pp. ix–xx, at xii. Also, see Hilary Rose and Steven Rose, "Red Scientist: Two Strands from a Life in Three Colors," in ibid., pp. 132–159, esp. 139. See also J. D. Bernal, "The Scientist and the World Today: The End of a Political Delusion," *Cambridge Left*, Winter 1933–1934, pp. 36–45.

96. Langevin's well-known remark is quoted in Ivor Montagu, "The Peacemonger," in Swann and Aprahamian, eds., *J. D. Bernal*, pp. 212–234, at 212. Perrin's remark was made in his speech in London at the Rassemblement universel pour la Paix in 1938; see Mary Jo Nye, "Science and Socialism: The Case of Jean Perrin in the Third Republic," *French Historical Studies*, 9 (1975), 141–169, on p. 163. Also, Bernadette Bensaude-Vincent, *Langevin: Science et Vigilance* (Paris: Belin, 1987).

97. Peter Ritchie Calder, "Bernal at War," in Swann and Apahamian, eds., *J. D. Bernal*, pp. 161–190, esp. 161.

98. Hobsbawm, "Preface," p. xii; Rose and Rose, "Red Scientist," p. 141.

99. Sir Nevill Mott, *A Life in Science* (London: Taylor and Francis, 1986) p. 53.

100. Ibid., p. 51.

101. See Christopher Lawrence and Anna-K. Mayer, "Regenerating England: An Introduction," in *Regenerating England: Science, Medicine and Culture in Inter-War Britain*, ed. Christopher Lawrence and Anna-K. Mayer (Amsterdam: Rodopi, 2000), pp. 1–23, esp. 4–5. Also Asa Briggs, *The History of Broadcasting in the United Kingdom*, 2 vols. (Oxford: Oxford University Press, 1995).

102. See Gary Werskey, *The Visible College: A Collective Biography of British Scientists and Socialists of the 1930s* (London: Free Association Books, 1988), p. 170; Julian Huxley, *Scientific Research and Social Needs* (London: Watts, 1934), foreword by Hyman Levy at p. v, and author's preface by Julian Huxley at p. x.

103. Blackett, "Pure Science: Discussion with Professor P. M. S. Blackett," in Huxley, *Scientific Research and Social Needs*, pp. 203–224.

104. Ibid., p. 224.

105. See *The Next Five Years: An Essay in Political Agreement* (London: Macmillan, 1935). The Macmillan family publishing house also published *Nature*. See Werskey, *The Visible College*, p. 238, note.

106. Blackett, "The Frustration of Science," thirteen-page typescript based on BBC broadcast in 1934 (BP: H.1). Appeared as Chapter 7 in *The Frustration of Science,* ed. Sir Daniel Hall, J. G. Crowther, and J. D. Bernal (London: Allen and Unwin, 1935).

107. Robert E. Filner, "The Roots of Political Activism in British Science," *Bulletin of Atomic Scientists,* 32 (1976), 25–29, on p. 26.

108. Letter from Beatrice Webb to Blackett, 2 May 1935 (BP: A.26).

109. See Letter from Alex Wood to Blackett, 5 February 1935 (BP: A.26). Wood was a Fellow at Emmanuel College, Cambridge.

110. *New Statesman* bought *The Nation* in early 1931, and the new weekly used the name *The New Statesman and Nation* from 1931 to 1957.

111. See Helge Kragh, *Quantum Generations: A History of Physics in the 20th Century* (Princeton University Press, 1999), p. 252; and Charles Weiner, "A New Site for the Seminar: The Refugees and American Physics in the Thirties," in Donald Fleming and Bernard Bailyn, eds., *The Intellectual Migration: Europe and America, 1930–1960* (Cambridge, Mass.: Harvard University Press, 1969), pp. 190–234, esp 211–212. For a list of those dismissed in April 1933 from government-funded positions, see the article "Nazi 'Purge' of the Universities," *Manchester Guardian,* 19 May 1933, reprinted in Weiner, p. 234. See also Montagu, "The Peacemonger," pp. 214–215, and William McGucken, *Scientists, Society and State: The Social Relations of Science Movement in Great Britain, 1931–1947* (Columbus: Ohio State University, 1984), pp. 80–81.

112. Annan, *Our Age,* p. 193.

113. Erik P. Rau, "Technological Systems, Expertise, and Policy Making: The British Origins of Operational Research," in *Technologies of Power: Essays in Honor of Thomas Park Hughes and Agatha Chipley Hughes,* ed. Michael Thad Allen and Gabrielle Hecht (Cambridge: MIT Press, 2001), pp. 215–252, esp. 220.

114. Ibid., pp. 220–222.

115. Calder, "Bernal at War," pp. 162–163.

116. McGucken, *Scientists, Society and State,* p. 128.

117. Neil Cameron, "The Politics of British Science in the Munich Era," in *Otto Hahn and the Rise of Nuclear Physics,* ed. William R. Shea (Dordrecht: Reidel, 1983), pp. 181–200, esp. 187.

118. Rose and Rose, "Red Scientist," pp. 140–141; McGucken, *Scientists, Society and State,* p. 132.

119. Calder, "Bernal at War," pp. 163–164.

120. McGucken, *Scientists, Society and State,* p. 156.

121. Rose and Rose, *Science and Society,* pp. 67–68.

122. Calder, "Bernal at War," p. 171.

123. J. G. Crowther, *Fifty Years with Science* (London: Barrie and Jenkins, 1970), pp. 210–218, at 217.

124. Ibid., p. 172; *Science in War* (Harmondsworth, Middlesex: Penguin, 1940), "written by 25 scientists," p. 137.

125. Rose and Rose, *Science and Society,* pp. 69–71; McGucken, *Scientists, Society and State,* pp. 185, 190–216.

126. Magda Kemeny Polanyi was an advanced student in chemistry who stopped short of writing a doctoral dissertation at the Karlsruhe Technische-Hochschule. She enrolled at the Berlin Technische-Hochschule after her marriage to Michael Polanyi in 1921 but did not complete the Ph.D. Their son John Polanyi shared the Nobel Prize in Chemistry in 1986 with Dudley Herschbach and Y. T. Lee. Correspondence in the collected papers of P. M. S. Blackett includes a lively letter from Magda Polanyi, dated 13 June 1965, on the occasion of Blackett's receiving the "Companion of Honour," and a seventieth birthday card and congratulations on Blackett's receiving the "Order of Merit" in November 1967 (BP: A.61, A.79). Also, see handwritten draft of letter from Blackett to Polanyi, 11 March 1939, and letter from Polanyi to Blackett, dated 28 October 1941 (BP: J.65).

127. Handwritten letter to Magda Polanyi from Costanza ["Pat"] Blackett, from Penparc, Llanfrothen, Penrhyndeudraeth, Wales, 28 March 1939; handwritten note from Costanza Blackett ["Pat"] to Michael Polanyi ["Misi"], from Penparc, 5 September 1939 (PP: 3.14).

128. Patrick Blackett to Michael Polanyi ["Mischi"], from the Admiralty, 28 June 1945, saying that he was arriving by night train Tuesday and looking forward to seeing Polanyi at the committee on Wednesday afternoon "and to stay with you in the evening. Pat is coming up on Thursday" (PP: 4.13).

129. Letter from Michael Polanyi to Patrick Blackett, from Department of Chemistry at Manchester, 28 October 1941, signed "Love to you and Pat, Misi" (BP: J.65).

130. Letter from Patrick Blackett to Michael Polanyi ["Mischi"], from Pitcullen, Middlesex, 3 November 1941. The letter is signed "With love to Magda, Patrick" (PP: 4.7).

131. Michael Polanyi, *The Tacit Dimension* (Garden City, N.Y.: Doubleday, 1965), pp. 3–4.

132. Michael Polanyi, "U.S.S.R. Economics—Fundamental Data, System, and Spirit," *Manchester School of Economic and Social Studies,* 6 (November 1935), pp. 67–89 (published as the third essay in Polanyi, *The Contempt of Freedom* [London: Watts, 1940]).

133. Letter from the Film Centre to Polanyi, 9 May 1938 (PP: 3.11), followed by letter from Michael Polanyi to Mr. Sale, 28 April 1939, reporting that he

had received £1,000 from the Rockefeller Foundation in order to release the film for general instructional purposes; see also letter from John Jewkes of the Economics Research Section of the University of Manchester to Robert Letort, Rockefeller Foundation in Paris, 18 May 1939, regarding support for continuing experimental work on the production of diagrammatic films illustrative of economic processes (PP: 3.15).

134. Typescript, "Memorandum on Economic Films," six pages (PP: 3.6), and carbon copy of letter from Michael Polanyi to Charles Vale in London, 4 September 1937 (PP: 3.9). Hayek, who received the Nobel Prize in Economics in 1974, published *The Road to Serfdom* in 1944, arguing against government intervention in the free market and suggesting that government manipulation of the economy leads to totalitarianism, as in Germany. In the late 1930s and 1940s Hayek taught at the London School of Economics; he taught at the University of Chicago as Professor of Social and Moral Science during 1950–1962.

135. Letter to Polanyi from Association of Scientific Workers, 24 August 1938; and letter to Polanyi from J. D. Bernal, 10 September 1938 (PP: 3.12).

136. Note from Patrick Blackett to Michael Polanyi, from Penparc, 26 August 1939 (PP: 4.1).

137. On Polanyi's naturalization papers, see Costanza Blackett to Michael Polanyi, from Penparc, 5 September 1939 (PP: 4.1).

138. McGucken, *Scientists, Society and State,* p. 272.

139. Letter from Max Born to Blackett, 22 July 1941, from Edinburgh (BP: J. 9). Also see McGucken, *Scientists, Society and State,* pp. 266–275. See John Baker, "Counterblast to Bernalism," *The New Statesman and the Nation,* 29 (July 1939), 174–175; also Michael Polanyi, "Rights and Duties of Science," *Manchester School of Economics and Social Studies,* 19 (October 1939), 175–193; also published in *The Contempt of Freedom.*

140. Letter from Michael Polanyi to Patrick Blackett, from Manchester, 28 October 1941 (BP: J.65).

141. E.g., Polanyi, in *Manchester Guardian,* 7 November 1942, where the science correspondent was J. G. Crowther. See also Polanyi, "Autonomy of Science," *Memoirs and Proceedings of the Manchester Literary and Philosophical Society,* 85 (1943), 19–38.

142. Darlington reported to the editor of *The New Statesman* in 1949 that members of the British delegation to the Soviet Union in 1945 were given two accounts of the disappearance of Nikolai Vavilov, the geneticist and brother of the President of the Soviet Academy. One story was meant, they were told, for internal dissemination. It claimed that he had been shot during the war while trying to escape from Russia. The second story, for external consumption, was that Vavilov had died at Magadan during the war

"while breeding frost-resistant plants." H. J. Muller published a report in the *Bulletin of the Atomic Scientists* in December 1948 on the repression of the Soviet geneticists, and Sir Henry Dale resigned from the Soviet Academy when its secretary never replied to the request from the Royal Society for the time and place of death of Vavilov. In C. P. Darlington, "Letter to the Editor: The Lysenko Controversy," *New Statesman and the Nation,* 37 (22 January 1949), 81–82. See Greta Jones, *Science, Politics and the Cold War* (London: Routledge, 1988), pp. 23–24.

143. Quoted from letter from A. V. Hill to Tansley, 6 June 1941, in McGucken, *Scientists, Society and State,* p. 288. See also Rose and Rose, *Science and Society,* pp. 61, 63–64.

144. Quoted in McGucken, *Scientists, Society and State,* pp. 350–351, from letter by Blackett, May 1944 (BP: H.9).

145. Memos A, B, and C from 1945–1946 (PP: 22.11).

146. Typescript of five pages, undated, but following 11 March 1946 meeting, entitled "The Balanced Development of Science in the Universities of U.K." (PP: 22.11).

147. Tom Wilkie, *British Science and Politics since 1945* (Oxford: Blackwell, 1991), pp. 47–53. Clement Attlee's postwar government also acted positively upon Blackett's recommendation for the establishment of a National Research Development corporation with right of first refusal for patenting results of research supported by public funds.

148. Phil Mullins, "Michael Polanyi and J. H. Oldham: In Praise of Friendship," *Appraisal,* 1, no. 4 (October 1997), 179–189, on p. 182.

149. Frances Stonor Saunders, *The Cultural Cold War: The CIA and the World of Arts and Letters* (New York: New Press, 1999), p. 82. George Kennan memorably commented in 1967 that "this country has no Ministry of Culture, and CIA was obliged to do what it could to fill the gap." Quoted in Stephen Turner, "Obituary for Edward Shils," *Tradition and Society,* 22, no. 2 (1995–1996), 5–9, on p. 5.

150. Edward Shils, "Thirty Years of *Minerva*," *Minerva,* Index to Volumes 1–30 (1962–1992), pp. iii–viii, esp. vii; Turner, "Obituary for Edward Shils," p. 8; Shils, "Robert Maynard Hutchins," in Shils, ed., *Remembering the University of Chicago* (University of Chicago Press, 1991), pp. 191–192.

151. Letter from John Polanyi to Costanza Blackett, 2 October 1974 (BFP).

2. Laboratory Life and the Craft of Nuclear Physics

1. Jeffrey Alan Hughes, "The Radioactivists: Community, Controversy, and the Rise of Nuclear Physics" (University of Cambridge Ph.D. thesis, 1993). See, e.g., pp. 25, 29. Also see Hughes, "Radioactivity and Nuclear Physics," in *The Cambridge History of Science,* vol. 5, *Modern Mathematical and Physi-*

cal Sciences, ed. Mary Jo Nye (Cambridge: Cambridge University Press, 2003), 350–374; and Helge Kragh, *Quantum Generations: A History of Physics in the Twentieth Century* (Princeton University Press, 1999), p. 313, where Kragh notes the distinction made by George Gamow and Charles Critchfield in *Theory of Atomic Nucleus and Nuclear-Energy Sources* (1949): "a convenient, even though not very sharply defined, boundary between *nuclear physics proper,* and the next, as yet rather unexplored, division of the science of matter which can be called tentatively the *physics of elementary particles.*"

2. On this, see Edward Crisp Bullard, typescript of obituary essay for *Nature,* 18 July 1974 (Bullard Papers, Churchill College Archives, Cambridge: G.111).

3. Blackett's handwritten manuscript, undated (BFP).

4. Hughes, "The Radioactivists," pp. 42–44. On Chadwick's role and career at the Cavendish, see Andrew Brown, *The Neutron and the Bomb: A Biography of James Chadwick* (Oxford: Oxford University Press, 1997), e.g., p. 55 on the "nursery."

5. On radio sets, see Sir Bernard Lovell, "Patrick Maynard Stuart Blackett, Baron Blackett, of Chelsea," *Biographical Memoirs of Fellows of the Royal Society,* 21 (1975), 1–115, esp. pp. 2–3.

6. Alice Kimball Smith and Charles Weiner, eds. *Robert Oppenheimer: Letters and Recollections* (Cambridge, Mass.: Harvard University Press, 1980), pp. 91, 93. Also see S. S. Schweber, *In the Shadow of the Bomb: Bethe, Oppenheimer, and the Moral Responsibility of the Scientist* (Princeton, N.J.: Princeton University Press, 2000), pp. 55 (quoting from Smith and Weiner, pp. 90–92), and 63.

7. P. M. S. Blackett, "On the Analysis of Alpha-Ray Photographs," *PRSL,* A102 (1922), 294. See also Blackett, "The Old Days at the Cavendish," *Rivista del Nuova Cimento,* 1 (1969), xxxii–xl.

8. Rutherford first used the term "proton" at the Cardiff meeting of the British Association for the Advancement of Science in 1920 (Hughes, "The Radioactivists," p. 22). Rutherford also proposed the existence of a "neutral hydrogen atom" in which a nucleus of unit positive charge has an electron attached at a distance. Thus a charged hydrogen atom or an electron or both might escape from this particle, or as separate components from the nucleus (ibid., pp. 57–58). Also see Roger H. Stuewer, "Rutherford's Satellite Model of the Nucleus," *HSPS,* 16 (1986), 321–352.

9. J. W. Boag et al., *Kapitza in Cambridge and Moscow* (Amsterdam: N. Holland, 1990), pp. 151, 156, 159–160, 169. Also, J. G. Crowther, *The Cavendish Laboratory 1874–1974* (New York: Science History Publications, 1974), pp. 190–191.

10. Boag et al. *Kapitza,* pp. 169–170, 172.

11. Quoted in Stuewer, "Rutherford's Satellite Model of the Nucleus," p. 334. At this time Rutherford's model of the atomic nucleus, which he was developing in experimental work with Chadwick, proposed that nuclear protons orbit the interior core of the nucleus. An alternative hypothesis that an incident alpha particle might be captured by the nucleus, rather than colliding with a proton and flying off, had been proposed by Jean Perrin in 1921 and by Hans Pettersson in 1924 (Stuewer, ibid.).

12. Stuewer, ibid.; P. M. S. Blackett, "The Old Days," p. xxxiv.

13. P. M. S. Blackett, "The Birth of Nuclear Science," *The Listener,* March 1954, pp. 380–382, one of three BBC talks (BP: B.116); Blackett, "The Ejection of Protons from Nitrogen Nuclei, Photographed by the Wilson Method," *PRSL,* A107 (1925), 349–360. On the instrument's design, see Blackett, "An Automatic Cloud Chamber for the Rapid Production of alpha-Ray Photographs," *JSI,* 4 (1927), 433. In the Blackett Papers (B.8), there is a reddish and blue and gold notebook with photographs pasted in it of particle disintegration tracks with records of their measurements.

14. Helge S. Kragh, *Dirac: A Scientific Biography* (Cambridge University Press, 1990).

15. Boag et al., *Kapitza,* p. 42.

16. P. M. S. Blackett, "Angular Momentum and Electron Impact," *Proceedings of the Cambridge Philosophical Society,* 22 (1924), 56–66. See Lovell, "Blackett," p. 11.

17. Typescript by John L. Heilbron of his interview with P. M. S. Blackett, 17 December 1962, Imperial College, p. 3 (SHQP).

18. Smith and Weiner, *Robert Oppenheimer,* p. 96.

19. Interview by Thomas S. Kuhn and John L. Heilbron of Werner Heisenberg, 30 November 1962 to 12 July 1963, twelve sessions, fifth session, 15 February 1963, p. 12 (SHQP).

20. Quoted from [Sir] Edmund Hudson in Lovell, "Blackett," p. 12, note.

21. Heilbron interview with Blackett, p. 3.

22. P. M. S. Blackett, "The Limits of Classical Scattering Theory," *Proceedings of the Cambridge Philosophical Society,* 23 (1927), 698, discussed by Lovell, "Blackett," p. 13.

23. Blackett published definitive descriptions of the cloud chamber, including "An Automatic Cloud Chamber for the Rapid Production of Alpha-Ray Photographs"; "On the Automatic Use of the Standard Wilson Chamber," *JSI,* 6 (1929), 184–191; and "On the Design and Use of a Double Camera for Photographing Artificial Disintegrations," *PRSL,* A123 (1929), 613–629. See, too, P. M. S. Blackett and E. P. Hudson, "The Elasticity of the Collisions of Alpha-Particles with Hydrogen Nuclei," *PRSL,* A117 (1927), 124.

24. See Kragh, *Quantum Generations,* p. 179; P. M. S. Blackett and F. C. Cham-

pion, "The Scattering of Slow Alpha-Particles by Helium," *PRSL,* A130 (1931), 380.

25. Heilbron interview with Blackett, p. 3. At a conference in Florence, Blackett said that "the majority of work at the Cavendish was not directed in detail by abstract theoretical considerations. I personally did one experiment to test a prediction of wave mechanics by Mott." Blackett, "The Old Days," p. xxxv.

26. Heilbron interview with Blackett, p. 3.

27. Millikan's view was that cosmic radiation is composed of high-energy photons that constitute the "birth cries of the universe," namely energy emitted during processes of creation of atomic nuclei in space from the combination of protons and electrons. On experimental researches on cosmic rays, see Martha Cecilia Bustamante, "Blackett's Experimental Researches on the Energy of Cosmic Rays," *Archives Internationales d'Histoire des Sciences,* 47 (1997), 108–141; and Bustamante, "Bruno Rossi and the Cosmic-Ray Physics in the Thirties," *Conference Proceedings,* vol. 42, *History of Physics in Europe in the 19th and 20th Centuries,* ed. F. Bevilacqua (Bologna: SIF, 1993), pp. 247–252.

28. Hughes, "The Radioactivists," pp. 28, 150. How the Geiger-Müller counter replaced the microscopic scintillation counter is a main theme of Hughes's Ph.D. thesis.

29. Ibid., p. 235. On de Broglie's laboratory, see Bruce Wheaton, *The Tiger and the Shark: Empirical Roots of Wave-Particle Dualism* (Cambridge: Cambridge University Press, 1983); and Mary Jo Nye, "Aristocratic Culture and the Pursuit of Science: The de Broglies in Modern France," *Isis,* 88 (1997), 397–421.

30. Dmitry Skobeltzyn, "The Early Stage of Cosmic-Ray Research," pp. 111–119, Pierre Auger, "Some Aspects of French Physics in the 1930s," pp. 173–176, and Louis Leprince-Ringuet, "The Scientific Activities of Leprince-Ringuet and His Group on Cosmic Rays: 1933–1953," pp. 177–182, in Laurie M. Brown and Lillian Hoddeson, eds., *The Birth of Particle Physics* (Cambridge: Cambridge University Press, 1983). Skobeltzyn was among those Soviet scientists in the early 1950s who rejected the Copenhagen interpretation of quantum mechanics and favored the Bohm and de Broglie interpretations of causality, determinism, and realism.

31. See Martha Cecilia Bustamante, "Les travaux de Bruno Rossi au début des années trente: une étape décisive dans la physique des rayons cosmiques," *Archives Internationales d'Histoire des Sciences,* 44 (1994), 92–115; Louis Leprince-Ringuet, "Notice nécrologique sur le duc Maurice de Broglie," *Comptes Rendus Hebdomadaires de l'Académie des Sciences,* 251 (1960), 297–303, on p. 301; and Hughes, "The Radioactivists," p. 241.

32. Hughes, "The Radioactivists," p. 241.
33. Letter from P. M. S. Blackett to Lise Meitner, 27 April 1930, Meitner Archives, Churchill College, Cambridge.
34. Peter Galison, "The Discovery of the Muon and the Failed Revolution against Quantum Electrodynamics," *Centaurus,* 26 (1983), 262–316, on pp. 282–284.
35. Schweber, *In the Shadow of the Bomb,* p. 97.
36. Blackett, "The Old Days," p. xxxvii.
37. Comments from Giovanna Blackett Bloor to the author, 28 June 2003.
38. Ibid.
39. Ibid.
40. Heilbron Interview with Blackett, p. 3.
41. Quoted in Lovell, "Blackett," on pp. 18–19, from G. P. S. Occhialini, *Notes and Records of the Royal Society of London,* 29 (1975), 144.
42. John Hendry, ed., *Cambridge Physics in the Thirties* (Bristol: Adam Hilger, 1984), p. 25.
43. Quoted in Norwood Russell Hanson, *The Concept of the Positron: A Philosophical Analysis* (Cambridge University Press, 1963), pp. 216–217. Also see Hughes, "The Radioactivists," pp. 250–251. An interview by Charles Weiner of James Chadwick, 15–20 April 1969, Cambridge, p. 66 (SHQP), notes that Millikan came to visit the Cavendish in 1932 and showed Anderson's photographs that, Chadwick remembers, Millikan said were tracks that he could not explain. Chadwick further recalled that he then talked to Occhialini and Blackett about doing the experiments more properly than Caltech was doing, "but that was already too late" (ibid., SHQP).
44. Account in Robert Andrews Millikan, *Electrons (+ and -), Protons, Photons, Neutrons, and Cosmic Rays* (Chicago: University of Chicago Press, 1935), pp. 323–327.
45. P. M. S. Blackett and G. Occhialini, "Photography of Penetrating Corpuscular Radiation" (in "Letters to the Editor"), *Nature,* 130 (3 September 1932), 363 (dated 21 August 1932).
46. Ibid.
47. On the discovery ("A cosmic ray had apparently picked off from a proton the disembodied positive unit of electrical charge, the twin of the negative electron") and Aston's visit, see Millikan, *Electrons,* pp. 321 and 331. See also Carl D. Anderson, "The Apparent Existence of Easily Deflectable Positives," *Science,* 76 (9 September 1932), 238–239 (dated 1 September 1932).
48. Anderson, "Apparent Existence," p. 239.
49. Millikan, *Electrons,* p. 333.
50. Comments by Subrahmanyan Chandrasekhar in interview by Spencer Weart, 17 May 1977, pp. 23 and 38 (SHQP).

51. S. S. Schweber, *QED and the Men Who Made It: Dyson, Feynman, Schwinger, and Tomonaga* (Princeton, N.J.: Princeton University Press, 1994), p. 67.

52. Paul Dirac, "Blackett and the Positron," in Hendry, *Cambridge Physics,* pp. 61–62. Dirac also wrote Louis Alvarez that Blackett had told Dirac privately that he and Occhialini had evidence for the positive electron a year before Anderson published the September 1932 paper. Dirac said that Blackett admitted being overly cautious in drawing conclusions, even though he had been familiar with Dirac's new theory of negative energy holes that might be physically manifested as positive electrons. Kragh, *Dirac,* p. 220. Kragh later notes that M. De Maria and A. Russo deny that Dirac's recollection could be correct, in "The Discovery of the Positron," *Rivista di Storia della Scienza,* 2 (1985), 237–286. Also see Heilbron interview with Blackett, p. 3.

53. P. M. S. Blackett and G. P. S. Occhialini, "Some Photographs of the Tracks of Penetrating Radiation," *PRSL,* A139 (1933), 699–726 (communicated by Lord Rutherford, received 7 February 1933). The long quotation is taken from p. 714. Also see J. Chadwick, P. M. S. Blackett, and G. Occhialini, "New Evidence for the Positive Electron," *Nature,* 131 (1933), 473; P. M. S. Blackett, "The Positive Electron," *Nature,* 132 (16 December 1933), 917–919.

54. Carl D. Anderson, "Cosmic-Ray Positive and Negative Electrons," *Physical Review,* 44 (1933), 406–416; see also Anderson, "The Positive Electron," *Physical Review,* 43 (1933), 491. On "positron," see interview by Charles Weiner of Carl Anderson, 30 June 1966, Pasadena, pp. 16–17 (SHQP).

55. Peter Galison, *How Experiments End* (Chicago: Chicago University Press, 1987), p. 95; see pp. 75–133 for Galison's perceptive discussion of cosmic rays. The paper is Carl Anderson, R. A. Millikan, Seth Neddermeyer, and William Pickering, "The Mechanism of Cosmic-Ray Counter Action," *Physical Review,* 45 (1934), 352–363. In 1935 Millikan wrote that effects that he and his coauthors had found "are only with some difficulty reconciled with the Dirac theory. . . . Rather they might indicate the existence of a nuclear reaction of a type in which the nucleus plays a more active role than merely that of a catalyst" (Millikan, *Electrons,* p. 349).

56. Bustamante, "Blackett's Experimental Researches," p. 127.

57. Charles Weiner interview of Carl Anderson, pp. 13–14.

58. Carl D. Anderson, with Herbert L. Anderson, "Unravelling the Particle Content of Cosmic Rays," in Brown and Hoddeson, eds., *Birth of Particle Physics,* pp. 131–154, at 140–141.

59. Hanson, *Concept of the Positron,* p. 3.

60. Letter from Robert Oppenheimer to P. M. S. Blackett, 14 December 1956, Oppenheimer Papers, from Collections of the Manuscript Division, Library of Congress; and Letter from Blackett to Oppenheimer, 7 January

1957, ibid. Courtesy of S. S. Schweber. Although Hanson's book on the positron was not published until 1963, he began work on the project at least as early as 1953, including interviews or correspondence with Blackett and Oppenheimer. In October 1956 Dirac showed Skobeltzyn a prospectus of the book. See Hanson, *Concept of the Positron,* Acknowledgements section, and Appendix IV, Letter from D. Skobeltzyn to N. R. Hanson, 10 October 1956, pp. 180–181.

61. J. P. Kunze, "Positives Elektron," *Physikalische Zeitschrift,* 34 (1933), 849–857. Thanks to Dieter Hoffmann for information about Kunze.

62. Letters from Jean Perrin to the Nobel Committee for Physics, 27 January 1936 (p. 69), Maurice de Broglie to the NCP, 21 January 1936 (p. 71), and Louis de Broglie to the NCP, 16 January 1936, (p. 73), in PKVA, 1936.

63. Handwritten letter from H. H. Dale to Blackett, 5 November 1948 (BP: A.46).

64. H. Pleijel, "Presentation Speech: Nobel Prize in Physics 1932 and 1933," *Nobel Lectures: Physics, 1922–1941,* http://www.nobel.se/physics/laureates/1933/press.html (accessed 13 January 2001).

65. In a letter from James Chadwick to Blackett, 18 November 1971 from Cambridge, Chadwick wrote of Rutherford's reluctance to develop nuclear physics in the 1930s (BP: J.18). Also see Jeffrey A. Hughes, "'Brains in Their Fingertips': Physics at the Cavendish Laboratory, 1880–1940," in Richard Mason, ed., *Cambridge Minds* (Cambridge: Cambridge University Press, 1995), pp. 160–176, esp. 172–175; and Brown, *The Neutron and the Bomb,* p. 146.

66. Quoted in Lovell, "Blackett," p. 22.

67. In letter from Garrett Birkhoff, in Cambridge, 9 March 1933, to Edwin Kemble, quoted in Kragh, *Dirac,* p. 110.

68. As it turned out, Blackett stayed at Birkbeck College only five years, succeeding Lawrence Bragg at Manchester in 1937, when Bragg was called to direct the Cavendish Laboratory following Rutherford's sudden death after operation for a hernia. Kapitza, having returned to the Soviet Union for his usual summer vacation in 1934, was not allowed to leave. Alexander Wood, *The Cavendish Laboratory* (Cambridge University Press, 1946), pp. 51–52. See also Crowther, *The Cavendish Laboratory.* Edward Bullard noted after Blackett's death that Blackett thought Rutherford gave a disproportionate share of Cavendish funds to Kapitza. See Bullard, "Patrick Blackett . . . An Appreciation," *Nature,* 250 (2 August 1974), p. 370.

69. See Lovell, "Blackett," p. 24; and Bustamante, "Blackett's Experimental Researches," p. 124, citing *The Daily Express,* 8 June 1934. On the name of the electromagnet, comments from Francis Everitt to the author, September 2003.

70. Andrew Brown, "Patrick Blackett: Sailor, Scientist, Socialist," *Physics World*, April 1998, 35–38, on p. 37.

71. Letter from Peter Astbury to Costanza Blackett, 13 October 1979 (BFP).

72. Lovell, "Blackett,", p. 24.

73. Interview by Charles Weiner of Otto R. Frisch, 3 May 1967, p. 19 (SHQP).

74. Typescript of Bernard Lovell's remarks on the occasion of Blackett's seventy-fifth birthday dinner, London, November 1972 (BFP).

75. Interview by Charles Weiner of Otto R. Frisch, pp. 19–25.

76. P. M. S. Blackett, "Cosmic Radiation," Royal Institution Evening Discourse, *Proceedings of the Royal Institution of Great Britain*, 28 (1934), 312; and *La radiation cosmique* (Conférences du Collège de France, in three parts) (Paris: Hermann, 1935).

77. P. M. S. Blackett, *Cosmic Rays: Being the Halley Lecture, 5 June 1936* (Oxford: Clarendon Press, 1936), p. 3.

78. Blackett, *La radiation cosmique*, pt. 1, pp. 11–12. Also Blackett, "Cosmic Radiation," *Scientific American*, November 1938, 246–249.

79. See David C. Cassidy, "Cosmic Ray Showers, High Energy Physics, and Quantum Field Theories: Programmatic Interactions in the 1930s," *Historical Studies in the Physical Sciences*, 12 (1981), 1–39, at p. 15.

80. Bustamante, "Blackett's Experimental Researches," p. 129; Hans Bethe and Walther Heitler, "On the Stopping of Fast Particles and on the Creation of Positive Electrons," *PRSL*, A146 (1934), 83–112.

81. Bethe and Heiter, "On the Stopping of Fast Particles," p. 112.

82. Galison, "Discovery of the Muon," p. 294.

83. Kragh, *Quantum Generations*, p. 19; Galison, "Discovery of the Muon" and *How Experiments End*. See discussion in Blackett, *La radiation cosmique*, pt. 4, pp. 15–16. Note: the average cosmic ray energy is of order 1,000 MEV in comparison to 1–10 MEV for naturally radioactive substances, according to Blackett, p. 6 in sixteen-page typescript "The Place of Cosmic Ray Research in the Physical Sciences (1946)" (BP: B.90).

84. See Bustamante, "Blackett's Experimental Researches," p. 129; C. D. Anderson and S. H. Neddermeyer, "Fundamental Processes in the Absorption of Cosmic-Ray Electrons and Photons," *International Conference on Physics, London, 1934* (Cambridge, 1935), 171–187; E. J. Williams, "Nature of the High Energy Particles of Penetrating Radiation and Status of Ionization and Radiation Formulae," *Physical Review*, 45 (1934), 729–730; A. H. Compton and H. A. Bethe, "Composition of Cosmic Rays," *Nature*, 134 (1934), 734–735.

85. C. D. Anderson and S. H. Neddermeyer, "Cloud Chamber Observations of Cosmic Rays at 4300 Meters Elevation and Near Sea-Level," *Physical Review*, 50 (15 August 1936), 263–271, on p. 268.

86. Bustamante, "Blackett's Experimental Researches," p. 131; P. M. S. Blackett with R. B. Brode, "The Measurement of the Energy of Cosmic Rays, II: The Curvature Measurements and the Energy Spectrum," *PRSL*, A154 (1936), 573–587; P. M. S. Blackett, "Further Measurements of the Cosmic-Ray Spectrum," *PRSL*, A159 (1937), 1–18.

87. R. B. Brode, H. G. MacPherson, and M. A. Starr, "The Heavy Particle Component of the Cosmic Radiation," *Physical Review*, 5 (1 October 1936), 581–588, on p. 588.

88. H. J. Bhabha and Walther Heitler, "The Passage of Fast Electrons and the Theory of Cosmic Showers," *PRSL*, A159 (1937), 432–458; J. F. Carlson and J. R. Oppenheimer, "On Multiplicative Showers," *Physical Review*, 57 (1937), 220–231. See Lovell, "Blackett," p. 27.

89. Neil A. Porter, *Physicists in Conflict: From Antiquity to the New Millenium* (Bristol: Institute of Physics, 1998), pp. 189–191. Porter did his doctoral work in physics at Manchester.

90. Quoted from Smith and Weiner, *Robert Oppenheimer*, p. 197. The Anderson colloquium at Caltech was reported publicly in *Science*, p. 9 of the supplement, 20 November 1936.

91. Carl D. Anderson, "The Production and Properties of Positrons," *Nobel Lectures: Physics, 1922–1941* (Amsterdam: Elsevier, 1965), 364–376, on p. 372.

92. P. M. S. Blackett and J. G. Wilson, "The Energy Loss of Cosmic Ray Particles in Metal Plates," *PRSL*, 160 (1937), 304–323; Bustamante, "Blackett's Experimental Researches," p. 133.

93. Galison, *How Experiments End*, pp. 119–122.

94. Typescript (blue ink, likely a carbon) of P. M. S. Blackett, "On the Nature of the Heavy Component of Cosmic Rays," five pages, dated in pencil 1937–1938 (BP: B.86).

95. Bustamante, "Blackett's Experimental Researches," p. 134; L. W. Nordheim, "Probability of Radiative Processes of Very High Energies," *Physical Review*, 49 (1936), 189–191, discussed in Cassidy, "Cosmic Ray Showers."

96. Blackett, "The Nature of the Penetrating Component of Cosmic Rays," *PRSL*, 165 (1938), 11–31, on p. 27; and Blackett and J. G. Wilson, "The Scattering of Cosmic Ray Particles in Metal Plates," *PRSL*, 165 (1938), 209–215.

97. David C. Cassidy, *Uncertainty: The Life and Science of Werner Heisenberg* (New York: W. H. Freeman, 1992), p. 406.

98. Kragh, *Quantum Generations*, pp. 195–196.

99. Bustamante, "Blackett's Experimental Researches," p. 137.

100. Cassidy, *Uncertainty*, pp. 404–407; Schweber, *QED*, pp. 100–101.

101. P. M. S. Blackett, "High Altitude Cosmic Radiation," *Nature,* 142 (15 October 1938), 692–693. Also see his summary "Cosmic Rays: Recent Developments," The 24th Guthrie Lecture, 26 February 1940, *Proceedings of the Physical Society,* 53 (1 May 1941), 203–213.

102. Smith and Weiner, *Robert Oppenheimer,* p. 206.

103. P. M. S. Blackett, "Further Evidence for the Radioactive Decay of Mesotrons," Letter to the Editor, *Nature,* 142 (3 December 1938), p. 992, dated 7 November from Manchester, followed on p. 993 by a letter from Bruno Rossi, Universitetets Institut for Teoretisk Fysik, Kobenhavn, dated 4 November.

104. Bernard Lovell, *The Story of Jodrell Bank* (New York: Harper and Row, 1968). Also, interview by David Edge of [Sir] Bernard Lovell, 6 July 1971, at Jodrell Bank, pp. 13–14 (SHQP).

105. See Clifford Butler, "Recollections of Patrick Blackett 1945–1970," *Notes and Records of the Royal Society of London,* 53 (1999), 143–156, on p. 144.

106. As noted by Francis Everitt, in e-mail communication to the author, 11 April 2001, especially regarding comments by physicist Frank McDonald.

107. G. D. Rochester and C. C. Butler, "Evidence for the Existence of New Unstable Particles," *Nature,* 160 (1947), 855–857.

108. Butler, "Recollections," pp. 144–145. Also see interview by Charles Weiner of Léon Rosenfeld, 3 September 1968, Copenhagen, p. 35 (SHQP), and, on leadership style in operational research, interview by Robert Smith of William Hunter McCrea, 22 September 1978, p. 22 (SHQP).

109. Rochester and Butler, "Evidence for the Existence," p. 855.

110. Butler, "Recollections," pp. 146–147.

111. Kragh, *Quantum Generations,* pp. 313–315.

112. See Lovell, "Blackett," p. 31, note. Also, Porter, *Physicists in Conflict,* p. 187.

113. Robert E. Marshak, "Particle Physics in Rapid Transition: 1947–1952," in Brown and Hoddeson, eds., *Birth of Particle Physics,* pp. 376–401, at 385.

114. P. M. S. Blackett, "The Craft of Experimental Physics," in Harold Wright, ed., *University Studies: Cambridge 1933* (London: Ivor Nicolson and Watson, 1933), pp. 67–96, at 67.

115. P. M. S. Blackett, "The Rutherford Memorial Lecture, 1958," *PRSL,* A251 (1959), 293–305, on p. 299. On particle physics and phenomenology, see Silvan S. Schweber, Hans A. Bethe, and Frederic de Hoffmann, *Mesons and Fields,* 3 vols. (Evanston, Ill.: Row, Peterson and Co., 1955–1956): Bethe and Hoffmann, vol. 2, *Mesons* (1955), pp. 373–376 on "Phenomenology."

116. Blackett, "Rutherford Memorial Lecture," p. 293.

117. Ibid., esp. pp. 297, 298, 299, 305.

3. Corridors of Power

1. C. P. Snow, *Corridors of Power* (London: Macmillan, 1964; Penguin, 1966), pp. 42–43.

2. In an interview with John Halperin, Lord Snow explained that it was Blackett's politics that were given to Getliffe. Another character, David Rubin, was based on I. I. Rabi. In John Halperin, *C. P. Snow: An Oral Biography* (New York: St. Martin's Press, 1983), pp. 201, 192.

3. Ibid., pp. 17–18, 201; David Shusterman, *C. P. Snow* (Boston: Twayne Publishers, 1991).

4. BP: E.24–E.34. It was Lord Snow, along with Lord Chalfont of the Foreign Office, who formally introduced Blackett to the House of Lords on the occasion of his first sitting in 1969. Letter from Charles (C. P. Snow) to Blackett, 24 January 1969, and letter from Alun Chalfont to Blackett, 28 January 1969 (BP: A.84).

5. See Alice K. Smith, *A Peril and a Hope: The Scientists' Movement in America, 1945–1947* (Chicago: University of Chicago Press, 1968), and Robert Gilpin, *American Scientists and Nuclear Policy* (Princeton: Princeton University Press, 1962). More recently, Paul Forman, "Behind Quantum Electrodynamics: National Security as a Basis for Physical Research in the United States, 1940–1960," *HSPS,* 18 (1988), 149–229; Barton J. Bernstein, "Four Physicists and the Bomb: The Early Years, 1945–1950," *HSPS,* 18, no. 2 (1988), 231–263; Lawrence Badash, *Scientists and the Development of Nuclear Weapons: From Fission to the Limited Test Ban Treaty 1939–1963* (New York: Humanities Press, 1995).

6. David Edgerton, "British Scientific Intellectuals and the Relations of Science, Technology and War," in Paul Forman and J. M. Sánchez-Ron, eds., *National Military Establishments and the Advancement of Science and Technology,* vol. 180, *Boston Studies in the Philosophy of Science* (Dordrecht: Kluwer, 1996), pp. 1–35, esp. 16, 18, 25; Greta Jones, "The Mushroom-Shaped Cloud: British Scientists' Opposition to Nuclear Weapons Policy, 1945–1947," *Annals of Science,* 43 (1986), 1–26, on pp. 5–6.

7. The best study is Thomas Hager, *Force of Nature: The Life of Linus Pauling* (New York: Simon and Schuster, 1995). Pauling, a Nobel Laureate in Chemistry in 1954, received the 1962 Nobel Peace Prize in 1963 for his efforts toward a nuclear test-ban treaty, which was signed as a limited ban in 1963. See also Cathryn Carson, "A Scientist in Public: Werner Heisenberg after 1945," *Endeavour,* 23 (1999), 31–33, on p. 32; and "New Models for Science in Politics: Heisenberg in West Germany," *HSPS,* 30 (1999), 115–171, on pp. 155–163.

8. M. Fortun and S. S. Schweber, "Scientists and the Legacy of World War II:

The Case of Operations Research (OR)," *Social Studies of Science,* 23 (1993), 595–642, on p. 598.

9. See Paul Crook, "The Case against Area Bombing," in Peter Hore, ed., *Patrick Blackett: Sailor, Scientist, Socialist* (London: Frank Cass, 2002), pp. 167–186, esp. 167–168.

10. See P. M. S. Blackett, "Tizard and the Science of War," Tizard Memorial Lecture, *Nature,* 185 (5 March 1960), 647–653, in sixteen-page reprint (BP: H.83); also published in Blackett, *Studies of War: Nuclear and Conventional* (Edinburgh: Oliver and Boyd, 1962), pp. 101–119. See also Ronald W. Clark, *The Rise of the Boffins* (London: Phoenix House, 1962), pp. 61–62; and Erik P. Rau, "Technological Systems, Expertise, and Policy Making: The British Origins of Operational Research," in *Technologies of Power: Essays in Honor of Thomas Park Hughes and Agatha Chipley Hughes,* ed. Michael Thad Allen and Gabrielle Hecht (Cambridge: MIT Press, 2001), pp. 215–252, esp. 220.

11. Daniel J. Kevles, *The Physicists: The History of a Scientific Community in Modern America,* 2d ed. (Cambridge, Mass.: Harvard University Press, 1987), pp. 290–291.

12. Rau, "Technological Systems," pp. 221–224; Blackett, "Tizard and the Science of War," reprint, pp. 2–3.

13. Clark, *Rise of the Boffins,* p. 90; Mark Oliphant, *Rutherford: Recollections of the Cambridge Days* (Amsterdam: Elsevier, 1972), p. 60.

14. Ronald W. Clark, *Tizard* (London: Methuen, 1965), p. 168, note.

15. Sir Bernard Lovell, "Patrick Maynard Stuart Blackett, Baron Blackett, of Chelsea," *Biographical Memoirs of Fellows of the Royal Society,* 21 (1975), 1–115, at pp. 50–53. Lord Swinton was Sir Philip Cunliffe-Lister, former Secretary of State for the Colonies before he became Secretary of State for Air.

16. George P. Thomson, "Frederick Alexander Lindemann, Viscount Cherwell 1886–1957," *Biographical Memoirs of Fellows of the Royal Society,* 4 (1958), 44–71, on p. 58.

17. See Roy Forbes Harrod, *The Prof: A Personal Memoir of Lord Cherwell* (London: Macmillan, 1959), e.g., pp. 29–30, 91, 98; the introduction, esp. pp. 12 and 15, in Jeannine Alton and Julia Latham-Jackson, eds., *Catalogue of the Papers of Frederick Alexander Lindemann, Viscount Cherwell of Oxford (1886–1957)* (deposited Nuffield College, Oxford; Contemporary Scientific Archives Centre, 1981); and Thomson, "Lindemann," p. 67. On Rutherford's opinion, see David Wilson, *Rutherford: Simple Genius* (Cambridge, Mass.: MIT Press, 1983), p. 565.

18. See Lovell's analysis, "Blackett," p. 52, drawing upon R. V. Jones, "Scientists at War," *The Times,* 6, 7, 8 April 1961; see also Clark, *Tizard,* p. 138.

19. Lovell, "Blackett," pp. 52–53.

20. Twenty-page typescript, with three-page appendix, titled "Confidential," enclosed with letter to Blackett from R. V. Jones, 5 December 1962. This is a copy of Jones's article to be published in the *Oxford Magazine* (BP: J.44).

21. Alan Hodgkin, *Chance and Design: Reminiscences of Science in Peace and War* (Cambridge: Cambridge University Press, 1992), p. 141.

22. See, e.g., L. C. B. Seaman, *Post-Victorian Britain 1902–1951* (London: Routledge, 1966), pp. 328–341.

23. Hodgkin, *Chance and Design*, pp. 141–152.

24. Quoted in Carroll Pursell, "Science Agencies in World War II: The OSRD and Its Challengers," in Nathan Reingold, ed., *The Sciences in the American Context: New Perspectives* (Washington, D.C.: Smithsonian Institution Press, 1979), pp. 359–378, on 361.

25. Blackett, "Tizard and the Science of War," reprint, p. 7.

26. Quoted in Hodgkin, *Chance and Design*, p. 155. See David A. Mindell, "Automation's Finest Hour: Radar and System Integration in World War II," in *Systems, Experts, and Computers: The Systems Approach in Management and Engineering, World War II and After,* ed. Agatha C. Hughes and Thomas P. Hughes (Cambridge, Mass.: MIT Press, 2000), pp. 27–56, esp. 28–29. Also David Zimmerman, *Top Secret Exchange: The Tizard Commission and the Scientific War* (London: A. Sutton Publishing, 1996).

27. Seaman, *Post-Victorian Britain*, p. 340.

28. Letter from Blackett to George P. Thomson, 28 July 1941; and Thomson's reply, 31 July 1941 (BP: J.104). See Margaret Gowing, *Britain and Atomic Energy, 1939–1945* (London: Macmillan, 1964), and Margaret Gowing and Lorna Arnold, *Independence and Deterrence: Britain and Atomic Energy, 1945–1952,* 2 vols. (New York: St. Martin's, 1972 and 1974).

29. Guy Hartcup and T. E. Allibone, *Cockcroft and the Atom* (Bristol: Adam Hilger/Institute of Physics, 1984), p. 122; Clark, *Tizard*, pp. 221–222.

30. Robert Jungk, *Brighter Than a Thousand Suns: The Moral and Political History of the Atomic Scientists,* trans. James Cleugh (New York: Harcourt Brace, 1958), pp. 69–70.

31. Spencer Weart, *Scientists in Power* (Cambridge, Mass.: Harvard University Press, 1979).

32. Thomson, "Lindemann," p. 64; Seaman, *Post-Victorian Britain,* p. 412.

33. Lovell, "Blackett," p. 70.

34. Seaman, *Post-Victorian Britain,* pp. 412–413; Thomson, "Lindemann," p. 65.

35. Andrew Brown, "Patrick Blackett: Sailor, Scientist, Socialist," *Physics World,* April 1998, 35–38, at p. 38.

36. See M. Moore, "Forty Years of Pugwash," *Bulletin of Atomic Scientists,* No-

vember/December 1997; and J. Rotblat, *Pugwash—The First Ten Years: History of the Conferences of Science and World Affairs* (London: Heinemann, 1967).

37. Lovell, "Blackett," p. 56.

38. Ibid.; Hodgkin, *Chance and Design,* p. 141.

39. Clark, *Rise of the Boffins,* pp. 144–145; Fortun and Schweber, "Scientists and the Legacy of World War II," p. 601.

40. Blackett, "Science and Government," in *Studies of War,* pp. 120–127, at 123 (originally in *Scientific American,* 1961).

41. Lovell, "Blackett," p. 58; Rau, "Technological Systems," pp. 233–234; Blackett, "Recollections of Problems Studied, 1940–1945," in *Studies of War,* pp. 205–234, esp. 214 (originally in *Brassey's Annual,* 1953); Oliphant, *Rutherford,* p. 60.

42. Guy Hartcup, *The Challenge of War: Britain's Scientific and Engineering Contributions to World War Two* (New York: Taplinger Publishing Co., 1970), p. 78.

43. Clark, *Rise of the Boffins,* p. vii. The Boffin Books series for children portrayed a fictional family having an air of owlish wisdom.

44. Blackett, *Studies of War,* p. 215.

45. Hartcup, *Challenge of War,* p. 80.

46. Ibid., pp. 216–218. Also, comments from Giovanna Blackett Bloor to the author, 28 June 2003.

47. Hartcup, *Challenge of War,* pp. 219–220.

48. Lovell, "Blackett," p. 60.

49. Robin E. Rider, "Operational Research," in *Companion Encyclopedia of the History and Philosophy of the Mathematical Sciences,* ed. Ivor Grattan-Guinness (London: Routledge, 1994), pp. 837–842, esp. 837–838.

50. Blackett, "Operational Research," review of Philip M. Morse and George E. Kimball, *Methods of Operational Research* (Cambridge, Mass.: MIT Press, 1951), in *Physics Today,* November 1951, 18–20, on p. 18.

51. Fortun and Schweber, "Scientists and the Legacy of World War II," p. 603; Rau, "The Adoption of Operations Research in the United States during World War II," in *Systems, Experts, and Computers,* ed. Hughes and Hughes, pp. 57–92, on 62.

52. Blackett, "Document I. Scientists at the Operational Level (1941)," pp. 171–176 in *Studies of War,* pp. 171–176.

53. Blackett, "Document II. A Note on Certain Aspects of the Methodology of Operational Research (1943)," in *Studies of War,* pp. 176–187.

54. Lovell, "Blackett," pp. 66–67; Blackett, "Appendix B (Document II): Examples from the Convoy Battle," in *Studies of War,* pp. 192–195.

55. Lovell, "Blackett," pp. 62–63.

56. Crook, "The Case against Area Bombing," p. 169; Thomson, "Lindemann," p. 62; Hodgkin, *Chance and Design,* pp. 200–224.

57. Carbon copy of letter from J. D. Bernal to the editor of *The Times,* 27 April 1961 (BP: J.44); also quoted in Crook, "The Case against Area Bombing," p. 181.

58. Bernal to the editor of *The Times,* 1961 (BP: J.44). See discussion of the survey, too, by Solly Zuckerman, *From Apes to Warlords: The Autobiography of Solly Zuckerman* (New York: Harper and Row, 1978), pp. 140, and 139–148.

59. Quoted from Lindemann, 20 March 1942 memo, in Sir Charles Webster and Noble Frankland, *The Strategic Air Offensive against Germany,* vol. I, *Preparation* (London, 1961), in Crook, "The Case against Area Bombing," p. 177; see also pp. 171–172. Crook notes the inconsistencies of some details in Lindemann's memorandum with Blackett's memories of it in Blackett's Tizard Memorial Lecture.

60. Rau, "Technological Systems," p. 239; Blackett, "Tizard and the Science of War," reprint, p. 9.

61. Carbon copy of unsigned paper, Whitehall, 15 August 1941, stamped "Most Secret" (BP: D.61).

62. Unsigned carbon copy of one-page "Notes on Conversation with Group-Captain Odbert and Wing-Commander Molesworth," 16 February 1942, with "Secret" typewritten in upper right corner (BP: D.62).

63. Blackett, three-page typescript "Note on the Use of the Bomber Force," repeated in Top Secret Document to J. H. Godfrey, 8 April 1942 (BP: D.64).

64. Blackett, "Effect of Bombing Policy," marked "Most Secret" and downgraded to "Restricted" 26 July 1962 (BP: D.62).

65. Blackett, "Tizard and the Science of War," in *Studies of War,* p. 110. Also, C. P. Snow, *Science and Government* (New York: Mentor, 1962), p. 48.

66. P. M. S. Blackett, *The Military and Political Consequences of Atomic Energy* (London: Turnstile Press, 1948), pp. 9, 14–15.

67. Quoted in Lovell, "Blackett," p. 65, from Blackett, "Science and Government," *Scientific American,* April 1961, reprinted in *Studies of War,* pp. 123–124.

68. Neil A. Porter, *Physicists in Conflict: From Antiquity to the New Millenium* (Bristol: Institute of Physics, 1998), pp. 162–163. Quotation in W. G. Sebald, "Reflections: A Natural History of Destruction," *The New Yorker,* 4 November 2002, 66–77, on p. 70.

69. Lovell, "Blackett," pp. 62–63; Rau, "Technological Systems," pp. 240–241.

70. Lovell, "Blackett," pp. 63–64.

71. Crook, "The Case against Area Bombing," p. 169.

72. Blackett, "Recollections of Problems Studied," in *Studies of War,* pp. 227–228.

73. Porter, *Physicists in Conflict,* p. 169.
74. Blackett, "Science and Government," in *Studies of War,* pp. 124–125. See also Seaman, *Post-Victorian Britain,* p. 368; and N. Frankland, *The Bombing Offensive against Germany* (London: Faber and Faber, 1965), p. 73.
75. Blackett, "Evan James Williams, 1903–45," in *Studies of War,* pp. 235–239, on 238; reports in BP: D.67, D.73, D.75.
76. Jock Gardner, "Blackett and the Black Arts," in Hore, ed., *Patrick Blackett,* pp. 126–137, esp. 134–135.
77. Blackett, "Operational Analysis: Its Relation to Intelligence and Plans," seven pages, for Talk Given to Combined Intelligence Subcommittee, Washington, 13 December 1943 (BP: D.90).
78. Lord Zuckerman, *Six Men Out of the Ordinary* (London: Peter Owen, 1992), p. 25.
79. Quotations are from J. D. Bernal, "D-Day Diaries," in *J. D. Bernal: A Life in Science and Politics,* ed. Brenda Swann and Francis Aprahamian (London: Verso, 1999), pp. 196–211, on 196–197, 198; also Earl Mountbatten of Burma, "Memories of Desmond Bernal," in ibid., pp. 191–195; Zuckerman, *Apes to Warlords,* pp. 266–267.
80. Zuckerman, *Apes to Warlords,* pp. 266, 371.
81. Lovell, "Blackett," pp. 68–69; Fortun and Schweber, "Scientists and the Legacy of World War II," pp. 614–615; see also Jonathan Rosenhead, "Operational Research at the Crossroads: Cecil Gordon and the Development of Post-war OR," *Journal of the Operational Research Society,* 40 (1989), 3–28.
82. Blackett, "The Scope of Operational Research," in *Studies of War* pp. 199–204 (originally in *Operational Research Quarterly,* 1 [March 1950]).
83. In *Operational Research: Its Application to Peace-Time Industry* (Manchester: Manchester Joint Research Council, 1953), p. 89, quoted in Fortun and Schweber, "Scientists and the Legacy of World War II," p. 617.
84. *Operational Research,* p. 18.
85. From Blackett's one-page typescript "German Scientists Brought to England after the War," part of materials intended for his autobiography (BP: A.10A).
86. Jeremy Bernstein, ed., *Hitler's Uranium Club: The Secret Recordings at Farm Hall* (Woodbury, N.Y.: American Institute of Physics, 1996), pp. 241–259.
87. A letter, dated 17 August 1945, from the Office of the Prime Minister invited Blackett to join the Advisory Committee (BP: D.184). On the Committee, see Andrew Brown, *The Neutron and the Bomb: A Biography of Sir James Chadwick* (Oxford: Oxford University Press, 1997), p. 304.
88. Jeannine Alton, Harriot Weiskittel, and Julia Latham-Jackson, eds., *Patrick Maynard Stuart Blackett, OM FRS Baron Blackett of Chelsea (1897–1974)* (Contemporary Scientific Archives Centre, 63/1/79), p. 199.

89. Memorandum by James Chadwick, 11 December 1945 (BP: D.190).
90. "Atomic Energy. An Immediate Policy for Great Britain. Memorandum by P. M. S. Blackett," ten-page typescript dated November 1945 (BP: D.167), published in Gowing and Arnold, *Independence and Deterrence,* vol. 1, pp. 194–206, esp. 203–204. See also Hartcup and Allibone, *Cockcroft,* p. 138.
91. Gowing and Arnold, *Independence and Deterrence,* vol. 1, p. 172.
92. Letter from Mark Oliphant to Blackett, from University of Birmingham, 22 January 1946 (BP: D.192).
93. Blackett, handwritten notes, one page (BP: D.192).
94. Letters from Blackett to R. Hon. C. R. Attlee, Prime Minister, 21 October 1946 and 11 November 1946 (BP: D.174); see Gowing and Arnold, *Independence and Deterrence,* vol. 1, pp. 115–116, 183–184; Brown, *The Neutron and the Bomb,* p. 305, note.
95. Brown, *The Neutron and the Bomb,* p. 315.
96. *The Military and Political Consequences of Atomic Energy* (London: Turnstile Press, 1948) was published in a slightly revised and less caustic version, *Fear, War and the Bomb* (New York: Whittlesey House, 1949), for an American audience. It was distributed by the Book Find Club, the predecessor of Book of the Month Club. Paul Jarrico, chairman of the Film Division of the National Council of the Arts, Sciences, and Professions in Los Angeles, contacted Blackett about making a documentary film based on the book. He proposed including among the film technicians some of the men blacklisted from Hollywood film work and known as "The Hollywood Ten." Blackett declined, finding it hard to imagine how the subject could be properly tackled in a film. See letter from Paul Jarrico, Los Angeles, to Blackett, 4 May 1949; and letter from Michael Hodson to Blackett, 13 June 1949 (BP: H.29). The chairman of the National Council of the Arts was the Harvard University astronomer Harlow Shapley and the regional chairman in California was Linus Pauling.
97. Blackett was one of eight British scientists refused permission to visit the Soviet Academy of Sciences in mid-June 1945, on the grounds that they could not be spared from war work, although the German surrender had occurred the previous May. The eight were Blackett, Bernal, Darwin, Mott, P. A. M. Dirac, E. A. Milne, R. G. W. Norrish, and E. K. Rideal. See typed press release from the Association of Scientific Workers, dated 16 June 1945 (BP: G.91).
98. See Badash, *Scientists and the Development of Nuclear Weapons,* pp. 68–70.
99. During the period 1946–1952 Blackett was director of the physical laboratories, dean of the faculty of sciences (1950–1952), and pro-vice-chancellor (1950–1952) at the University of Manchester.

100. Blackett to Polanyi, 3 November 1941 (BP: J.65).

101. P. M. S. Blackett, *Military and Political Consequences,* pp. 9, 14–15.

102. Gowing and Arnold, *Independence and Deterrence,* vol. 1, p. 115.

103. Mentioned in a letter from Blackett to Nevill Mott, 14 November 1946 (BP: D.175).

104. Blackett, *Military and Political Consequences,* p. 145.

105. Reiterated in Blackett, "The First Real Chance for Disarmament," 37-page typescript for *Harper's* magazine, November 1962, on p. 29 (BP: F.72).

106. Blackett, *Military and Political Consequences,* p. 120. Gar Alperovitz revived the argument in his dissertation and book of 1965. "I think the only way you can understand why Nagasaki was tripped off, automatically, bing-bing, just like that, with no consideration, is this tremendous rush to end the war–*not* just to end the war before an invasion, but *immediately!* . . . What was the rush? Well, P. M. S. Blackett, another Nobel prize winner, saw in 1945 that the only way you could explain that immediate, fast one-two punch, was the fact that the Russians were in fact scheduled to enter the war on August 9." Quoted in Jerome R. Ravetz, *Scientific Knowledge and Its Social Problems* (Oxford University Press, 1979), p. 64, note. See Alperovitz, *Atomic Diplomacy: Hiroshima and Potsdam. The Use of the Atomic Bomb and the American Confrontation with Soviet Power* (New York: Simon and Schuster, 1965), and more recently, Alperovitz, *The Decision to Use the Atomic Bomb and the Architecture of an American Myth* (London: Harper-Collins, 1995). Also, John Lewis Gaddis, *What We Know: Rethinking Cold War History* (Oxford: Clarendon Press, 1997), pp. 86–88; and Walter LaFeber, *America, Russia and the Cold War, 1945–1966,* 8th ed. (New York: McGraw-Hill, 1997), p. 25.

107. "Nobel Prizes: Professor Blackett and Mr. T. S. Eliot," *Manchester Guardian,* 5 November 1948, p. 5; and Edward Shils, "The Atomic Problem: Professor Blackett's Book," ibid., p. 4.

108. E.g., letter from H. T. Tizard to Blackett, 10 August 1948, who nonetheless considered it a thoughtful and well-written book manuscript (BP: H.37); and letter from George Thomson to Blackett, 16 October 1948, who thought it a "grand book" but that the Americans are "fundamentally right in the things that matter" (BP: H.37).

109. Letter from Frederick Osborn, London, to Blackett, 26 November 1948; Frederick Osborn, "The United Nations and Atomic Control," 15 December 1948, five-page carbon-copy typescript; and Blackett's reply, six-page carbon-copy typescript (BP: H.34).

110. E.g., letter from Edward Mead Earle, Institute for Advanced Study, to Blackett, 1 July 1949 (BP: H.36).

111. E. M. Friedwald, "Blackett's Book Dissected," *Discovery,* 9 (November

1948), 352; Lord Cherwell, "Atomic Bombing the Decisive Weapon—and Deterrent," *Daily Telegraph and Morning Post,* 9 December 1948, p. 4.

112. Waldemar Kaempffert, "The Atom's Power in War and Peace: A Famous British Physicist Champions Russia's Side in the Momentous Debates," *The New York Times Book Review,* sec. 7, *New York Times,* 13 February 1949, pp. 1, 32.

113. P. M. S. Blackett, "Steps toward Disarmament," *Scientific American* 206, no. 4 (April 1962), 45–53, on p. 51.

114. Friedwald, "Blackett's Book Dissected," p. 352.

115. Kaempffert, "The Atom's Power," p. 32.

116. Letter from Blackett to J. Langdon-Davies, n.d. (BP: H.37).

117. See letter from Edward Shils to Blackett, 17 December 1948; letter from Blackett to Shils, 23 December 1948 (BP: H.41). See also Edward A. Shils, "Blackett's Apologia for the Soviet Position," *Bulletin of Atomic Scientists,* 5 (February 1949), 34–37; Philip Morrison, "Blackett's Analysis of the Issue," ibid., 37–40; Brien McMahon, "Comment on Blackett's Book," 40–43; and M. Marinin, "An English Scientist Exposes Atomic Diplomacy" (translation from review in *Pravda,* 22 November 1948), 43 and 50. The editor of the *Bulletin of Atomic Scientists,* H. H. Goldsmith, inquired of Blackett whether he would like to reply to Shils's review in the April issue (letter of 14 February 1949), but Blackett declined, saying that it was impossible, but that someday he might write a review of reviews and he would not forget Mr. Shils. Letter of 26 February 1949 (BP: H.41). Shils's scathing review of Blackett's 1948 book appeared in the *Manchester Guardian,* 5 November 1948, p. 4.

118. Marinin, "An English Scientist," p. 43.

119. Shils, "Blackett's Apologia," p. 35; McMahon, "Comment on Blackett's Book," p. 43.

120. Morrison, "Blackett's Analysis," p. 40.

121. I. I. Rabi, "Playing Down the Bomb: Blackett vs. the Atom," *Atlantic Monthly,* 183 (August 1949), 21–24, on p. 21.

122. Ibid., pp. 21, 23, 24.

123. Formerly confidential document, dated 11 May 1951, cc: Legal Attaché, London, England/Secret Air Courier, and cc: Foreign Service Desk, File no. 100-354-451-5; formerly confidential document, dated 22 November 1952, no. 100-354451-6 in Federal Bureau of Investigation File no. 100-354451. Thanks to Ronald E. Doel for copies of the copies.

124. Memorandum from J. Edgar Hoover to Jack D. Neal, Chief, Division of Foreign Activity Correlation at the State Department, 9 February 1948, File no. 100-354451.

125. Timothy Garton Ash, "Love, Death and Treachery," *The Guardian Review,* 21 June 2003, 4–7.
126. Hartcup and Allibone, *Cockcroft,* pp. 133–134, 159.
127. One-page typescript, "Cosmic Ray Conference 1951" (BP: A.10A).
128. Letter of 17 August 1960 to Blackett from Thomas H. Osgood, attaché at the American Embassy in London (BP: A.36).
129. Bernstein, *Hitler's Uranium Club,* p. 79.
130. Ibid.
131. Six-page handwritten and unpublished "Preface" for *Studies of War,* on p. 2 (BP: H.93).
132. P. M. S. Blackett,"British Policy and the H-Bomb," in *Studies of War,* pp. 27–46, on 27, originally published in *The New Statesman and Nation,* 14, 21, and 28 August 1954.
133. Blackett, handwritten and unpublished "Preface."
134. Three-page typescript, "Note on the Use of the Bomber Force," with Blackett's initials at the top in his hand. Follows unsigned note of 16 February 1942 (BP: D.62).
135. P. M. S. Blackett, "Thoughts on British Defense Policy," reprinted from *The New Statesman,* 5 December 1959, eight pages, on p. 6 (BP: D.112). Blackett's opposition to a military strategy of destroying population centers was not unshared in America. US Admiral William Leahy, Chief of Staff to Presidents Roosevelt and Truman, concluded his war memoir by saying that "these new concepts of 'total war' are basically distasteful to the soldier and sailor of my generation." William T. Leahy, *I Was There: The Personal Story of the Chief of Staff to Presidents Roosevelt and Truman Based on His Notes and Diaries Made at the Time* (London: Victor Gollancz, 1950), p. 514.
136. Barton Bernstein notes that Robert Oppenheimer and Enrico Fermi began to counsel the development of tactical nuclear weapons and preparations for limited nuclear war in late 1947. See Bernstein, "Four Physicists and the Bomb," p. 253.
137. P. M. S. Blackett, "America's Atomic Dilemma," in *Studies of War,* pp. 17–26, on 17–20 (originally published in *The New Statesman,* 13 February 1954), and "Nuclear Weapons and Defence: Comments on Kissinger, Kennan, and King-Hall," in ibid., pp. 54–72, on 54–55 (originally published in *International Affairs,* October 1958). Among George Kennan's writings, see *The Nuclear Dilemma: Soviet-American Relations in the Atomic Age* (New York: Pantheon, 1982); more generally, David Rees, *The Age of Containment: The Cold War, 1945–1965* (London: St. Martin's, 1967), and Walter LaFeber, *America, Russia and the Cold War.*
138. Blackett, "Nuclear Weapons and Defence," p. 62.

139. P. M. S. Blackett, seventeen-page typescript, "Operational Research and Nuclear Weapons" (BP: D.109), which is an earlier version of "Critique of Some Contemporary Defense Thinking" (1961), in *Studies of War,* pp. 128–146.

140. Blackett, "Critique of Some Contemporary Defense Thinking," p. 129.

141. Ibid., pp. 128, 145.

142. Discussed in ibid., p. 130.

143. Oskar Morgenstern, *The Question of National Defense* (New York: Random House, 1959); Herman Kahn, ed., *A Report on a Study of Non-Military Defense* (Rand Corporation, 1958); Herman Kahn, *On Thermonuclear War* (Princeton: Princeton University Press, 1960). See also John Strachey, *On Prevention of War* (London: Macmillan, 1962), pp. 13–15.

144. Herman Kahn, *Thinking about the Unthinkable* (London: Weidenfeld and Nicolson, 1962), with an introduction by Raymond Aron who, like Kahn, defends the importance of this kind of thinking.

145. On Rand, see David Hounshell, "The Cold War, RAND, and the Generation of Knowledge, 1946–1962," *HSPS,* 27 (1997), 237–267. In 1950 Blackett wrote a preface for the pamphlet "Atomic Attack: Can Britain Be Defended?" which enraged John Anderson and others by arguing that civil defense in Britain against nuclear war was impracticable. In 1957 a Government White Paper reached the same conclusion. See Jones, "The Mushroom-Shaped Cloud," pp. 11–12.

146. Blackett, "The Real Road to Disarmament," in *Studies of War,* pp. 147–166, on 160–166, originally published in *The New Statesman,* 2 March 1962, with shorter version appearing under title "Steps toward Disarmament," *Scientific American,* April 1962.

147. On Alsop's article, see letter from Captain J. P. Wright, Ministry of Defence, to Blackett, dated 23 November 1961, on first- and second-strike doctrine (BP: F.84). See also Blackett, "Steps toward Disarmament," pp. 45, 49–50.

148. Edward Teller with Allen Brown, *The Legacy of Hiroshima* (London: Macmillan, 1962), p. viii.

149. Unsigned review, clipping with no source, entitled "More Than One Approach to Thermonuclear Chauvinism," dated 6 December 1962 (BP: H.95).

150. Freeman Dyson, review of Blackett's *Studies of War* and Ralph Lapp's *Kill and Overkill: The Strategy of Annihilation* (1962), photocopied review without attribution of source (BP: H.95).

151. Sir Nevill Mott, "Nuclear Weapons: Playing It Cool," *New Scientist,* 25 October 1962, clipping (BP: H.95).

152. Mark S. Watson, "Views on Military Trends," *Baltimore Sun,* 23 December 1962, clipping (BP: H.95).

153. A. J. P. Taylor, "City of Destruction," *New Statesman,* 26 October 1962, clipping (BP: H.95).

154. Lewis Strauss, "Lucid Essays on Disarmament, Not Entirely Realistic," *Chicago Sunday Tribune Magazine of Books,* 9 December 1962, clipping (BP: H.95).

155. Correspondence and Pugwash organizational materials in Blackett Papers (J.66–J.71). Active members in the United Kingdom included Powell, Rotblat, Mott, Cockcroft, Peierls, Kathleen Lonsdale, Waddington, Edward (Teddy) Bullard, and William Penney. Rotblat started to become disillusioned with the Manhattan Project in March 1944 when General Groves told him that the real purpose of the bomb would be to counter the Soviet Union. After the war Rotblat became a British citizen, having worked at the University of Liverpool under a postdoctoral fellowship in 1939. Rotblat was president of Pugwash when he received the Nobel Peace Prize in 1995. Richard W. Stevenson, "Peace Prize Goes to A-Bomb Scientist Who Turned Critic," *New York Times,* 14 October 1995, p. 3.

156. J. Rotblat, *Pugwash—The First Ten Years: History of the Conferences of Science and World Affairs* (London: Heinemann, 1967).

157. Letter to Blackett from Henry A. Kissinger, Harvard University Center for International Affairs, 10 July 1959 (BP: F.80).

158. Letter to Blackett from Howard K. Smith, Washington Bureau of CBS News, 3 April 1959 (BP: F.82).

159. Charles Percy Snow, *The Two Cultures* (Cambridge: Cambridge University Press, 1959), and *Science and Government* (Cambridge, Mass.: Harvard University Press, 1961).

160. Blackett, review of Snow's *Science and Government,* in *Studies of War* (1962), pp. 120–127, originally in *Scientific American,* 1961; carbon copy of letter from J. D. Bernal to the editor of *The Times,* dated 27 April 1961 (BP: J.44); letters from R. V. Jones to Blackett, 28 April 1961 and 5 December 1962, the latter including typescript by Jones for the *Oxford Magazine,* and 4 January 1963 (BP: J.44); letter from Blackett to Jones, 4 January 1963, saying he will not comment publicly or privately on what Jones had written about Blackett's having failed to look again at some of the original documents at issue (BP: J.44). Jones's "Lord Cherwell's Judgement in World War II" appeared in *Oxford Magazine,* 9 May 1963, 279–286. The official history is Sir Charles Webster and Noble Frankland's *The Strategic Air Offensive against Germany,* note 59 above.

161. See, e.g., the use of Blackett's arguments in Louis Morton, "The Decision to Use the Atomic Bomb," *Foreign Affairs,* 35 (January 1957), 334–353. And William Appleman Williams, *The Tragedy of American Diplomacy,* 2d ed. (New York: Dell, 1972; 1st ed. 1959), on p. 253.

162. Quoted from letter from A. V. Hill to Tansley, 6 June 1941, in William McGucken, *Scientists, Society and the State: The Social Relations of Science Movement in Great Britain 1931–1947* (Columbus: Ohio State University Press, 1984), p. 288; Hilary Rose and Steven Rose, *Science and Society* (Harmondsworth, Middlesex: Penguin, 1970), pp. 61, 63–64. Also see Robert Filner, "The Roots of Political Activism in British Science," *Bulletin of Atomic Scientists*, 32 (1976), 25–29, and Gary Werskey, *The Visible College: A Collective Biography of British Scientists and Socialists of the 1930s* (London: Free Association Books, 1988).

163. Snow, *Corridors of Power,* p. 229.

164. R. V. Jones, *Most Secret War* (London: Hamish Hamilton, 1978), p. 493.

4. Temptations of Theory, Strategies of Evidence

1. On Paul Dirac's move from quantum theory to cosmological theory, see Helge Kragh, *Dirac: A Scientific Biography* (Cambridge: Cambridge University Press, 1990), esp. pp. 223, 233.

2. *Nature* 159 (1947), 601.

3. Handwritten draft of letter from P. M. S. Blackett to "Paul," 28 March 1947, saying copies of the paper have been sent to Plaskett and Chapman as well (BP: C.41). Handwritten letter from Sydney Chapman to Blackett, 18 April 1947 (BP: A.41). In the *Catalogue* of Blackett's papers, compiled by Jeannine Alton et al. (Oxford: Contemporary Scientific Archives Centre, 1979), "Paul" is identified as Paul Ehrenfest. However, Paul Ehrenfest died in 1933, and his son Paul Ehrenfest, Jr., died in 1939 (thanks to Martin J. Klein for this information). "Paul" might be Paul Dirac.

4. Letter from Thomas Merton, Treasurer, Royal Society, to Patrick Blackett, 17 April 1947, and letter from Blackett to Merton, 21 April 1947 (BP: C.65).

5. Letters from Blackett to Assistant Secretary, Royal Society, dated 25 April 1947 and 28 April 1947 (BP: C.65).

6. Letter from Blackett to Costanza Blackett, 9 April 1947 (BFP).

7. Ronald W. Clark, *Einstein: The Life and Times* (New York: Avon, 1972), p. 289; Abraham Pais, *Einstein Lived Here* (Oxford: Oxford University Press, 1994), p. 145.

8. "Newton, Einstein—and Now Blackett," *News Review,* 29 May 1947, pp. 14–15, on 14.

9. Ibid; Ritchie Calder, "A New Law of the Universe: Professor Blackett Offers a Theory," *Daily News—Chronicle* (London), 16 May 1947, clippings (BP: C.68).

10. E. N. da C. Andrade, "A New Discovery in Magnetism," *The Listener,* 29 May 1947, p. 837 (BP: C.68).

11. Sir Bernard Lovell, "Patrick Maynard Stuart Blackett, Baron Blackett, of Chelsea, 18 November 1897–13 July 1974," *Biographical Memoirs of Fellows of the Royal Society,* 21 (1975), 1–115, at p. 39; see also Lovell, *The Story of Jodrell Bank* (Oxford: Oxford University Press, 1968), and interview of David Edge with Sir Bernard Lovell, 6 July 1971, at Jodrell Bank (SHQP).

12. Blackett, "On Pomeranchuk's Theory of the Radiation by Ultra-relativistic Electrons in the Earth's Magnetic Fields," *Physical Society Cambridge Conference Report* (1947), 79–85. See Lovell, "Blackett," p. 39.

13. See handwritten draft paper, "A Possible Re-interpretation of Wilson's Postulate" [n.d.] (BP: C.5); and Blackett, "The Magnetic Field of Massive Rotating Bodies," *Nature,* 159 (17 May 1947), 658–666 (read at Royal Society 15 May 1947), on p. 658. On the recognition of the simple formula, see letter from Horace Blackett to Babcock, 17 July 1947 (BP: C.46).

14. Blackett, "Magnetic Field," p. 658.

15. Letter from Blackett to S. Chandrasekhar at University of Chicago's Yerkes Observatory (in Williams Bay, Wis.), 14 November 1946; letter from S. Chandrasekhar to Blackett, 10 January 1947 (BP: C.41).

16. Blackett, "Magnetic Field," p. 658.

17. Blackett turned up Schuster within a few days of beginning a literature search. See letter from Blackett to Walter Sullivan, 20 February 1972 (BP: A.34).

18. Arthur Schuster, "A Critical Examination of the Possible Causes of Terrestrial Magnetism," *PRSL,* 24 (15 April 1912), pt. III, pp. 121–137, abstracted in four-page typescript (BP: C.17); and Arthur Schuster, "Terrestrial Magnetism—Past, Present, and Future," possibly given as Halley Lecture at Oxford in 1913, typed abstract of four pages (BP: C.17). See Peter Galison, *How Experiments End* (Chicago: University of Chicago Press, 1987), pp. 52–56.

19. S. J. Barnett, "Gyromagnetic Effects: History, Theory and Experiments," *Physica,* 13 (1933), 241–268, and *Physikalische Zeitschrift,* 35 (1934), 203–205. See Galison, *How Experiments End,* pp. 52–72. Barnett became familiar with Schuster's hypothesis on the earth's magnetism in 1915 (ibid., p. 54), although this was not his main interest.

20. Blackett, "Magnetic Field," p. 659, drawing upon Sydney Chapman and Julius Bartels, *Geomagnetism,* 2 vols. (Oxford: Clarendon Press, 1940), p. 705. Also see W. F. G. Swann and A. Longacre, "An Attempt to Detect a Magnetic Field as the Result of the Rotation of a Copper Sphere at High

Speed," *Journal of the Franklin Institute,* 206 (1928), 421–434, on pp. 421–422.

21. See discussion in Abraham Pais, *'Subtle Is the Lord . . .': The Science and the Life of Albert Einstein* (Oxford: Oxford University Press, 1982), pp. 245–249. And in Galison, *How Experiments End,* pp. 34–74.

22. A. Piccard and E. Kessler, "Détermination du rapport des charges électrostatique du proton et de l'électron," *Archives des Sciences Physiques et Naturelles,* 7 (1925), 340–342. I am grateful to Helge Kragh for this reference.

23. Quoted in Walter Sullivan, *Continents in Motion: The New Earth Debate,* 2d ed. (New York: American Institute of Physics, 1991), p. 89.

24. W. J. de Haas to Blackett, 9 July 1947 and 25 July 1947 (BP: C.49).

25. H. A. Wilson, "An Experiment on the Origin of the Earth's Magnetic Field," *PRSL,* 104 (1923), 451–455, discussed in Blackett, "Magnetic Field," p. 660, and in Blackett, "The Magnetic Field of Massive Rotating Bodies," in *Les particules élémentaires. Rapports et discussions. Huitième conseil de physique tenu à l'Université de Bruxelles du 27 septembre au 2 octobre 1948* (Bruxelles: Stoops, 1950), 21–53, on p. 23.

26. Blackett, in *Les particules élémentaires,* pp. 22–23.

27. Anonymous typescript entitled "The Magnetic and Rotational Characteristics of Cosmic Bodies" [n.d.] (BP: C.6). This typescript also refers to Eddington's *Relativity Theory of Protons and Electrons* (1936) and Einstein's *General Theory of Relativity* (1933). Blackett, "Magnetic Field," p. 665.

28. Swann and Longacre, "An Attempt to Detect a Magnetic Field"; Swann, "A Generalization of Electrodynamics, Consistent with Restricted Relativity and Affording a Possible Explanation of the Earth's Magnetic and Gravitational Fields, and the Maintenance of the Earth's Charge," *Phil. Mag.,* 3 (1927), 1088–1136.

29. Swann and Longacre, "An Attempt to Detect a Magnetic Field," p. 433; Lovell, "Blackett," pp. 40–41.

30. Blackett, "The Magnetic Field of Massive Rotating Bodies," *Phil. Mag.* [series 7], 40 (February 1949), 125–150, on p. 125; and in *Les particules élémentaires,* p. 46.

31. Blackett, "Magnetic Field," p. 658.

32. Ibid., p. 660. Francis Everitt, who worked with Blackett at Imperial College from 1955 to 1960, has noted that "phenomenological" was one of Blackett's favorite words. Letter from Francis Everitt to the author, 5 June 1997; and Everitt, "The Creative Imagination of an Experimental Physicist," in *Near Zero: New Frontiers of Physics,* ed. J. D. Fairbank et al. (New York: Freeman, 1988), pp. 19–64, on 62.

33. Letter from Blackett to Pascual Jordan, 1 February 1951 (BP: C.55).

34. Interview by Spencer Weart of Horace W. Babcock, 25 July 1977, at Pasadena (Niels Bohr Library, American Institute of Physics Archives, College Park, Md.), p. 36 of typescript.

35. Letter from Horace Babcock to Blackett, 6 October 1947 (BP: C.46).

36. Letter from Horace Babcock to Blackett, 20 November 1947 (BP: C. 46.)

37. Harold Spencer Jones, "The Magnetism of the Earth, Sun, and Stars," *The Times Science Review* (Summer 1952), pp. 3–4, clipping (BP: C.17). Jones noted that observations at Mount Wilson for the sun's field during 1940–1947 did not give consistent results, with eighteen sets indicating a field with intensity at the pole ranging from 6 to 60 gauss and twenty-four sets showing no field or a small negative field. Thiessen first got the value of 53 gauss in 1945, but no more than 2–3 gauss during 1947–1948.

38. Letter from Blackett to "Paul," 28 March 1947 (BP: C.41).

39. Letters from Pascual Jordan to Blackett, 15 July 1947 and 1 July 1949 (BP: C.55).

40. Letter from Wolfgang Pauli to L. Rosenfeld, 21 June 1948 (BP: C.57).

41. Letter from Niels Arsley to Blackett, 11 February 1948 (BP: C.45); Niels Arsley, "Blackett Hypothesis of the Magnetic Field of Rotating Bodies," *Nature,* 161 (17 April 1948), 598–599.

42. Arsley cites S. J. Barnett, *Reviews of Modern Physics,* 7 (1935), 129.

43. H. Y. Tzu, "Universal Constants in Blackett's Formula," *Nature,* 16 (19 November 1947), 746–747. Also see J. Fuch, "Blackett's Hypothesis of the Magnetic Field of Rotating Bodies," *Nature,* 161 (17 April 1948), 599. Fuch argued that Blackett's formula could not be correct, but must require a more general form including Planck's constant.

44. Letter from V. Bjerknes to Blackett, 6 October 1949, and letter from Blackett to V. Bjerknes, 11 October 1949 (BP: C.49).

45. S. S. Schweber, personal remarks, 8 November 1996, at annual meeting of the History of Science Society, in Atlanta. It is not unlikely that Einstein also wanted to show solidarity with Blackett's current opposition to nuclear weapons policy in the United States and Great Britain.

46. See David Kaiser on the evolving disciplinary dynamics between particle physics and cosmology, in "A 'Psi Is Just a Psi'? Pedagogy, Practice, and the Reconstitution of General Relativity, 1942–1975," *HSPS,* 29 (1998), 321–338.

47. See Jeannine Alton and Peter Harper, compilers, "Report on the Correspondence and Papers of Sir Edward Crisp Bullard (1907–1980)," 2 vols. (Oxford: Contemporary Science Archives Centre, 1984), in Churchill College Archives.

48. Letter from Edward C. Bullard to Bernard Lovell, 19 March 1976 (photocopy of handwritten notes), p. 18 (Bullard Papers/Churchill College, G.111).

49. D. P. McKenzie, "Edward Crisp Bullard, 21 September 1907–3 April 1980," *Biographical Memoirs of Fellows of the Royal Society,* 33 (1987), 67–98, on p. 72.

50. Letter from Bullard to Lovell, 19 March 1976 (Bullard Papers/Churchill College, G.111).

51. McKenzie, "Edward Crisp Bullard," pp. 76–78.

52. Letter from E. C. Bullard to Bernard Lovell, 19 March 1976, cited in note 48 above; and letter from E. C. Bullard to Blackett, 14 October 1947 (BP: C.48).

53. See Walter M. Elsasser, "Induction Effects in Terrestrial Magnetism," *Physical Review,* 69 (1946), 106–111, 202–212; E. C. Bullard, "The Magnetic Field within the Earth," *PRSL,* A197 (1949), 433–453. On controversies in the late 1940s about the core of the earth, see Ronald E. Doel, *Solar System Astronomy in America: Communities, Patronage, and Interdisciplinary Science, 1920–1960* (Cambridge: Cambridge University Press, 1996), pp. 96–97, 103–104, 136–137.

54. Letter from E. C. Bullard to Bernard Lovell, 19 March 1976 (Bullard Papers, Churchill College, G.111).

55. A. L. Hales and D. I. Gough, "Blackett's Fundamental Theory of the Earth's Magnetism," *Nature,* 160 (29 November 1947), 746.

56. S. K. Runcorn, with appendix by S. Chapman, "The Radial Variation of the Earth's Magnetic Field," *Proceedings of the Physical Society of London,* 61 (1948), 373–382, on p. 378.

57. See Stephen G. Brush and C. S. Gillmor, "Geophysics," in *Twentieth-Century Physics,* ed. Laurie Brown et al. (New York: American Institute of Physics Press, 1995), pp. 1943–2016, on 1956–1960. Also, Homer Le Grand, *Drifting Continents and Shifting Theories: The Modern Revolution in Geology and Scientific Change* (Cambridge: Cambridge University Press, 1988), pp. 139–140.

58. S. K. Runcorn, A. C. Benson, A. F. Moore, and D. H. Griffiths, "The Experimental Determination of the Geomagnetic Radial Variation," *Phil. Mag.,* 41 (1950), 783–791, esp. pp. 784–785.

59. Andrade, "A New Discovery in Magnetism," p. 834.

60. J. B. S. Haldane, "Why the Earth Is a Magnet," *Daily Worker,* 3 June 1947, p. 4 (BP: C.68).

61. Carbon copies of letters from Blackett to L. Boddington at the Royal Aircraft Establishment (RAE), 19 June 1947, and to J. E. Gordon at RAE [n.d.] (BP: C.11).

62. Three-page typescript by P. R. Martin, Naval Aircraft Establishment, RAE, "Note on High Speed Rotor for Investigating Magnetic Origins," 19 September 1947 (BP: C.10).

63. Letter from Blackett to W. E. Taylor at Rolling Mills Department, Metropolitan Vickers, Trafford Park Manchester, 18 December 1947 (BP: C.10).

64. See notes on Eichenwald Experiment (*Annalen der Physik*, 11 [1903], 1) and other publications on magnetic experiments (BP: C.14); also, Blackett's notes for the lecture "Measurement of Low Magnetic Fields" given at the Geophysical Department in Cambridge, 24 May 1951 (BP: C.24).

65. An incomplete series of notebooks for the experiments is in the Blackett Papers at the Royal Society. They run from 9 August 1947 to April 1951 (BP: C.30–C.38).

66. Blackett, "A Negative Experiment Relating to Magnetism and the Earth's Rotation," *Phil. Trans.*, series A, 245 (1952), 309–370, on p. 310.

67. Sullivan, *Continents in Motion*, p. 89.

68. Blackett, "A Negative Experiment," pp. 312–313.

69. Ibid., pp. 313–316, 327.

70. Comments by Giovanna Blackett Bloor to the author, 28 June 2003.

71. For example, see the photographs on pp. 426 and 427 in Swann and Longacre, "An Attempt to Detect a Magnetic Field."

72. Blackett, "A Negative Experiment," p. 327; Lovell, "Blackett," p. 43.

73. Blackett, "A Negative Experiment," p. 318, Table 1; also, pp. 332–333.

74. Ibid., p. 333. I am grateful to Francis Everitt for some details of the magnetometer system.

75. Ibid., p. 329.

76. Ibid., pp. 346–347.

77. When Francis Everitt was making measurements on the magnetism of baked clays at Imperial College in the late 1950s, he altered the usual raising-and-lowering procedure by keeping the rock sample in the elevated position while turning it through five successive measurements of ninety degrees each. The older procedure from the static-body experiments had continued to be used at Imperial College even though it was no longer needed to avoid eddy currents with nonmetallic specimens. Letter from Francis Everitt to the author, 5 June 1997.

78. Sullivan, *Continents in Motion*, p. 89. Comments from Francis Everitt to the author, September 2003.

79. Blackett, "A Negative Experiment," pp. 353–361. There are no notebooks in the Blackett Papers for late April 1951.

80. E. A. Johnson, T. Murphy, and O. W. Torreson, "Prehistory of the Earth's Magnetic Field," *Journal of Geophysical Research*, 43 (1948), 349–

372; and John W. Graham, "The Stability and Significance of Magnetism in Sedimentary Rocks," *Journal of Geophysical Research,* 54 (1949), 131–167.

81. Jacob Bronowski, "Table Talk," *Observer,* 3 September 1950, clipping (BFP).

82. Letter from Blackett to Pascual Jordan, 1 February 1951 (BP: C.55).

83. On the problem of the "experimenters' regress," see the essays in Harry Collins and Trevor Pinch, *The Golem: What Everyone Should Know about Science* (Cambridge: Cambridge University Press, 1993), esp. pp. 27–55 and 91–107.

84. Blackett, "A Negative Experiment," pp. 310, 356, 362.

85. Ibid., p. 310.

86. Letter from Blackett to M. Farbstein, Department of Physics, Washington University, St. Louis, 10 January 1973 (BP: C.64).

87. Blackett, "A Negative Experiment," p. 310.

88. S. Keith Runcorn, remarks in "Memorial Meeting for Lord Blackett, O.M., C.H., F.R.S. at the Royal Society on 31 October 1974," *Notes and Records of the Royal Society of London,* 29 (1975), 135–162, at p. 158.

89. Ibid.

90. See Martha Cecilia Bustamante, "Blackett's Experimental Researches on the Energy of Cosmic Rays," *Archives Internationales d'Histoire des Sciences,* 47 (1997), 108–141. Peter Galison has emphasized that theory is practice, in "Context and Constraints," in *Scientific Practice: Theories and Stories of Doing Physics,* ed. Jed Z. Buchwald (Chicago: University of Chicago Press, 1995), pp. 13–41, on 27–28.

91. Blackett, "Instability of the Mesotron and the Gravitational Constant," *Nature,* 144 (1939), 30.

92. Blackett, "Cosmic Rays: Recent Developments—The Twenty-Fourth Guthrie Lecture," *Proceedings of the Physical Society,* 53 (1941), 203–213. It should be noted, too, that, following up on a suggestion by Arthur Eddington in the 1930s for testing general relativity theory by means of gyroscopes, Blackett thought about its feasibility, but concluded that the task was hopeless. Francis Everitt currently heads a long-standing project for this purpose, largely funded by NASA, at Stanford University. The Gravity Probe B was launched in April 2004. See C. W. F. Everitt, "The Stanford Relativity Gyroscope Experiment (A): History and Overview," in *Near Zero,* ed. Fairbank et al., pp. 586–639, on 588.

93. Kragh, *Dirac,* pp. 10, 223.

94. Ibid., p. 224.

95. Sir Arthur Eddington, *Relativity Theory of Protons and Electrons* (Cambridge: Cambridge University Press, 1936), pp. v, 3–4.

96. Kragh, *Dirac*, pp. 225–226.
97. See John D. Barrow and Frank J. Tipler, *The Anthropic Cosmological Principle* (Oxford: Clarendon, 1986), pp. 112–228, citing G. Beck, H. Bethe, and W. Riezler, "Concerning the Quantum Theory of Absolute Zero," *Naturwissenschaften* (9 January 1931). Also, S. S. Schweber, *In the Shadow of the Bomb: Bethe, Oppenheimer, and the Moral Responsibility of the Scientist* (Princeton: Princeton University Press, 2000), p. 98; and Helge Kragh, *Quantum Generations: A History of Physics in the Twentieth Century* (Princeton: Princeton University Press, 1999), p. 222.
98. Max Born, *Experiment and Theory in Physics* (Cambridge University Press, 1944); Kragh, *Dirac*, pp. 226–227. And see Alexander Rüger, "Atomism from Cosmology: Erwin Schrödinger's Work on Wave Mechanics and Space-Time Structure," *HSPS* 18 (1988), 377–401.
99. See Barrow and Tipler, *Anthropic Cosmological Principle*, pp. 231–234.
100. Kragh writes that Chandrasekhar did not intend this manuscript for publication, but Dirac asked to send it to *Nature* (in *Dirac*, p. 353, note 29; on Jordan, see p. 233). Also comments from Francis Everitt to the author, September 2003.
101. Herbert Dingle, "Modern Aristotelianism," *Nature*, 139 (1937), 784–786. On criticism of Dingle's conception of the nature of science by the classicist and Marxist Benjamin Farrington, see Geoffrey Cantor, "Charles Singer and the Early Years of the British Society for the History of Science," *BJHS*, 30 (1997), 5–23, on p. 21.
102. Charles G. Darwin, "Physical Science and Philosophy," *Nature*, 139 (1937), 1008. To this, Dingle replied that he emphatically disagreed "with Prof. Darwin's opinion that it does not matter what you think about science as long as you advance it." Herbert Dingle, "Deductive and Inductive Methods in Science: A Reply," *Nature*, 139 (1937), 1011–1012.
103. Erwin Schrödinger offended Einstein in early 1947 with his public claims in Dublin for an affine field theory that would reduce Einstein's theory of 1915 to a special case and "should express everything in Field Physics," including the magnetic fields of all rotating masses. This was a promise unfulfilled. See Walter Moore, *Schrödinger: Life and Thought* (Cambridge: Cambridge University Press, 1989), pp. 424–435. Also, clipping from newspaper article, likely from an Irish newspaper, "Dr. Schroedinger Extends Einstein's Theory of Relativity," 25 January 1947 (BP: C.68), and letter from Blackett to Erwin Schrödinger, 23 June 1947 (BP: C.59).
104. Blackett, "The Rutherford Memorial Lecture, 1958, McGill University, 29 September 1958," *PRSL*, A251 (1959), 293–305, on p. 305. Quoted in Lovell, "Blackett," 89.
105. My emphasis. Quoted in Lovell, "Blackett," p. 90, from Blackett, "Notes on

the History of the Experimental Proof of Non-conservation of Parity," *Physics Today,* 14 (1961), 86–88, on p. 88.

106. Interview by Charles Weiner of Léon Rosenfeld, 3 September 1968, in Copenhagen (SHQP).

107. Quoted in Galison, "Context and Constraints," p. 32.

108. See letter from Blackett to Walter Sullivan, 20 January 1972 (BP: A.34).

109. According to Francis Everitt, who mentions Leopold Halpern in particular. (Letter from Francis Everitt to the author, 5 June 1997.) Other theories persist that rotation (differences in the rotational speeds of zones of the sun) is responsible for the sun's magnetism. For example, "SOHO Reveals the Secrets of the Sun," *Scientific American,* March 1997, p. 42.

5. "Reading Ourselves into the Subject"

1. P. M. S. Blackett, "Introduction," pp. vii–x, at vii, in "A Symposium on Continental Drift," *Phil. Trans.,* A258 (1965), i–x and 1–323.

2. Alfred Wegener, *Die Entstehung der Kontinente und Ozeane* (Braunschweig: F. Vieweg, 1915). The first English translation was *The Origin of Continents and Oceans,* trans. from 3rd German ed., J. G. A. Skerl (London: Methuen, 1924).

3. Philip H. Kuenen, *Marine Biology* (London: Chapman and Hall, 1950), p. 219, quoted in P. M. S. Blackett, J. A. Clegg, and P. H. S. Stubbs, "An Analysis of Rock Magnetic Data," *PRSL,* A256 (1960), 291–322, on p. 292. On the history of continental drift, see Henry Frankel, "Wegener and the Specialists," *Centaurus,* 20 (1976), 305–324; Henry Frankel, "The Continental Drift Debate," in *Scientific Controversies: Case Studies in the Resolution and Closure of Disputes in Science and Technology,* ed. A. Caplan and H. T. Engelhardt (Cambridge: Cambridge University Press, 1987), pp. 312–373; Henry Frankel, unpublished book ms. (2001), cited below by chapter; William Glen, *The Road to Jaramillo* (Stanford: Stanford University Press, 1982); David B. Kitts, "Continental Drift and the Scientific Revolution," *American Association of Petroleum Geologists Bulletin,* 58 (1974), 2490–2496; Rachel Laudan, "The Method of Multiple Working Hypotheses and the Discovery of Plate Tectonic Theory," in *Scientific Discoveries: Case Histories,* ed. T. Nickles, vol. 60, *Boston Studies in the Philosophy of Science* (Dordrecht: Reidel, 1980), pp. 331–343; Homer E. Le Grand, *Drifting Continents and Shifting Theories* (Cambridge: Cambridge University Press, 1988); Naomi Oreskes, "The Rejection of Continental Drift," *HSPS,* 18 (1988), 311–348, and *The Rejection of Continental Drift: Theory and Method in American Earth Science* (Oxford: Oxford University

Press, 1999); Walter Sullivan, *Continents in Motion: The New Earth Debate,* 2d ed. (New York: American Institute of Physics, 1991).

4. Quoted in Glen, *Road to Jaramillo,* pp. 324–325.

5. Ibid., pp. 163–164.

6. Clifford Butler, "Recollections of Patrick Blackett, 1945–70," *Notes and Records of the Royal Society, London,* 53 (1999), 143–156.

7. P. M. S. Blackett, "A Negative Experiment Relating to Magnetism and the Earth's Rotation," *Phil. Trans.,* A245 (1952), 309–370.

8. P. M. S. Blackett, "The Rutherford Memorial Lecture, 1958," *PRSL,* A251 (1959), 293–305, on p. 296.

9. P. M. S. Blackett, *Cosmic Rays: The Halley Lecture 1936* (Oxford: Clarendon Press, 1936), p. 4.

10. P. M. S. Blackett, "Cosmic Radiation," *Scientific American,* November 1938, 246–249.

11. Edward Irving, "The Paleomagnetic Confirmation of Continental Drift," *Eos,* 69 (1988), 994, 996–997, 999, 1001–1002, 1005–1006, 1008–1009, 1013–1014; citations in this chapter are to the seven-page offprint.

12. On secular variation, see Edward Irving, *Paleomagnetism and Its Application to Geological and Geophysical Problems* (New York: John Wiley, 1964), p. 41, and Sullivan, *Continents in Motion,* pp. 87–88. On John Ross and James Ross, see *The New Encyclopaedia Britannica,* 15th ed. (Chicago: Encyclopaedia Britannica, 1974).

13. Handwritten letter from Sydney Chapman to Blackett, 18 April 1947, noting some difficulties for Blackett's hypothesis, including the secular change in the magnetic moment of approximately 5 percent during the past century (BP: A.41).

14. Letter from Edward C. Bullard to P. M. S. Blackett, 14 January 1948 (Bullard Papers/Churchill College: E.184).

15. Blackett, notes for lecture "Measurement of Low Magnetic Fields," 24 May 1951 (BP: C.24). Also, on Keith Runcorn at Manchester and Cambridge, see F. J. Lowes, "Keith's Early Work in Geomagnetism," *Physics and Chemistry of the Earth,* 23, no. 7–8 (1998), 703–707.

16. See Irving, "Paleomagnetic Confirmation," p. 2; also Frankel, book ms., Chapter 7, pp. 53–54.

17. Irving, "Paleomagnetic Confirmation," p. 4. Also, Edward Irving, "Personal Notes for the Royal Society," unpublished fifty-page typescript (31 October 2003), p. 30 (courtesy of Ted Irving).

18. Irving, "Paleomagnetic Confirmation."

19. Irving, "Personal Notes," p. 30. See A. L. Du Toit, *Our Wandering Continents* (Edinburgh: Oliver and Boyd, 1937).

20. Frankel, book ms., Chapter 7, p. 54.
21. On Holmes's geophysics, see Le Grand, *Drifting Continents,* pp. 111–115. See also Arthur Holmes, *Principles of Physical Geology* (London: Thomas Nelson and Sons, 1944).
22. Runcorn later recalled Blackett's speed at working up geology and his enthusiasm for Holmes's book after a talk with W. B. R. King at the Sedgwick Museum in Cambridge. Blackett also was influenced on continental drift by the arguments of S. Warren Carey, whom Blackett met in Australia in 1953. See Keith Runcorn, remarks in "Memorial Meeting for Lord Blackett, O.M., C.H., F.R.S. at the Royal Society on 31 October 1974," *Notes and Records of the Royal Society of London,* 29 (1975), 135–162, at pp. 156–158, esp. 157. On Holmes and continental drift, see Oreskes, "The Rejection of Continental Drift," pp. 328–331, and *The Rejection of Continental Drift.* Also, Edward (Ted) Irving's recollection, letter from Edward Irving to the author, 5 December 1997.
23. Quoted in Henry Frankel, "The Continental Drift Debate," p. 212.
24. See letter from Harold Jeffreys, read at the 1964 Royal Society symposium on continental drift, in "A Symposium on Continental Drift," *Phil. Trans.,* A258 (1965), 1–323, at p. 314. On disagreement between Holmes and Jeffreys, see Henry Frankel, "Arthur Holmes and Continental Drift," *BJHS,* 38 (1978), 130–148, esp. pp. 146–148.
25. P. M. S. Blackett, "Continental Drift," 8th Hugh MacMillan Memorial Lecture, 15 February 1966, *Transactions of the Institution of Engineers and Shipbuilders in Scotland,* 1966, pp. 177–192, on 183. Also, Edward (Ted) Irving, letter and comments to the author, 1 May 2001.
26. Blackett, "Continental Drift," p. 182.
27. Holmes, *Principles of Physical Geology,* p. 495.
28. Sir Bernard Lovell, "Patrick Maynard Stuart Blackett, Baron Blackett, of Chelsea, 18 November 1897–13 July 1974," *Biographical Memoirs of Fellows of the Royal Society,* 21 (1975), 1–115, at p. 90, footnote. Lovell says that this happened during 1950–1951. Letter from J. A. Clegg, Physical Laboratories at Manchester, to Blackett, 7 December 1952 (BP: C.221). Of Mary Almond, who married J. M. Pickering, Clegg wrote that she could measure the magnetism of rock samples twice as fast as Clegg, and more accurately.
29. Irving, *Paleomagnetism and Its Application,* p. 11.
30. Comments by Francis Everitt to the author, September 2003.
31. Edward Irving, "Paleomagnetism of the Torridonian Sandstone Series, NW Scotland" (University of Cambridge thesis, 1954). Also, "Paleomagnetic Confirmation."
32. The spinner magnetometer has a spinning shaft on which the rock speci-

men is rotated and a sensor to detect the oscillating magnetic field produced by the rotating magnetic moment of the specimen. Irving, *Paleomagnetism and Its Application,* p. 68; (http://www.geo.arizona.edu/Paleo
mag/book/chap04.pdf, accessed 25 October 2003).

33. Irving, "Paleomagnetic Confirmation," p. 1, citing Jan Hospers, "Remanent Magnetism of Rocks and the History of the Geomagnetic Field," *Nature,* 168 (1951), 1111; and R. A. Fisher, "Dispersion on a Sphere," *PRSL,*
A217 (1953), 295, 305. On Jospers, see Henry Frankel, "Jan Hospers and
the Rise of Paleomagnetism," *Eos* (1987), 577, 579.

34. Irving, "Paleomagnetic Confirmation," pp. 1–2.

35. Frankel, book ms., Chapter 8, pp. 8–9 and 14.

36. Irving, "Paleomagnetic Confirmation," p. 3.

37. J. A. Clegg, M. Almond, and P. H. S. Stubbs, "The Remanent Magnetism of
Some Sedimentary Rocks in Britain," *Phil. Mag.,* 45 (1954), 583–598. Peter
Stubbs was a childhood friend of Nicolas and Giovanna Blackett. Com-
ments by Giovanna Blackett Bloor to the author, 17 November 2003.

38. J. A. Clegg, M. Almond, and P. H. S. Stubbs, "Some Recent Studies of the
Pre-History of the Earth's Magnetic Field," *Journal of Geomagnetism and
Geoelectricity,* 6 (1954), 194–199.

39. Irving, *Paleomagnetism and Its Application,* pp. 224–225. See W. Köppen
and A. Wegener, *Die Klimate der geologischen Vorzeit* (Berlin: Bornträger,
1924).

40. Irving, "Personal Notes," p. 41.

41. Irving, "Paleomagnetic Confirmation," p. 4.

42. Ibid.

43. Frankel, book ms., Chapter 8, p. 21.

44. Letter from Blackett to Richard Kahn, 12 September 1953 (BP: A.24).

45. Letter from Blackett to James Chadwick, 30 July 1953 (BP: A.24).

46. Letter from S. K. Runcorn to Blackett, 7 March 1953 (BP: C.222).

47. Letter from Blackett to Sir Ben Lockspeiser, Department of Scientific and
Industrial Research, 3 May 1954 (BP: C.72).

48. Lovell, "Blackett," p. 90.

49. See J. A. Clegg, C. Radakrishnamurty, and P. W. Sahasrabudhe, "Remanent
Magnetism of the Rajmahal Traps of Northeastern India," *Nature,* 181
(1958), 830–831; E. R. Deutsch, C. Radakrishnamurty, and P. W. Sahasrabudhe, "The Remanent Magnetism of Some Lavas in the Deccan Traps,"
Phil. Mag., 3 (1958), 170–184; and E. R. Deutsch, C. Radakrishnamurty,
and P. W. Sahasrabudhe, "Paleomagnetism of the Deccan Traps," *Annals of
Geophysics,* 15 (1959), 39–59.

50. Irving, "Paleomagnetic Confirmation," p. 4.

51. The London symposium is summarized in *Philosophical Magazine Supple-*

ment: Advances in Physics, vol. 6 (1957). The first paper is D. W. Collinson, Kenneth M. Creer, Edward Irving, and S. K. Runcorn, "The Measurement of the Permanent Magnetization of Rock," *Phil. Trans.,* A250 (1957), 73–82, on p. 73.

52. Edward Irving, "The Origin of the Paleomagnetism of the Torridonian Sandstones of N.W. Scotland," *Phil. Trans.,* A 250 (1957), 100–110, on p. 109. Also, from the same journal and volume, D. W. Collinson et al., "The Measurement of the Permanent Magnetization of Rocks"; E. Irving and S. K. Runcorn, "Analysis of the Paleomagnetism of the Torridonian Sandstone Series of NW Scotland, I," 83–99; K. M. Creer, "The Natural Remanent Magnetization of Certain Stable Rocks from Great Britain," 111–129; K. M. Creer, "The Remanent Magnetization of Unstable Keuper Marls," 130–143; K. M. Creer, E. Irving, and S. K. Runcorn, "Geophysical Interpretations of Palaeomagnetic Directions from Great Britain," 144–156.

53. "Rock Magnetism. Rehovoth, 1954.1" and "Rock Magnetism.2 Rough Notes" (BP: C.193), expanded and revised as *Lectures on Rock Magnetism* (Jerusalem: Weizmann Science Press of Israel, 1956).

54. Blackett, *Lectures on Rock Magnetism,* preface and pp. 33–36; see discussion in Le Grand, *Drifting Continents,* p. 147.

55. Edward Irving, "Paleomagnetic and Paleoclimatic Aspects of Polar Wander," *Geofisica Purae Applicata,* 33 (1956), 23 ff., cited in Irving, "Paleomagnetic Confirmation," p. 4.

56. Irving, "Paleomagnetic Confirmation," p. 4.

57. Quoted in Oreskes, *Rejection of Continental Drift,* p. 267.

58. "Ph.D. Theses," typescript, one page (BP: C.186).

59. Carbon-copy typescript "Work Carried Out in the Rock Magnetism Group at Imperial College 1957–1960" (BP: C.186).

60. Quoted in Lovell, "Blackett," p. 91.

61. As related by Francis Everitt to the author, e-mail letter of 16 June 1997.

62. See Lovell, "Blackett," pp. 92–93; P. M. S. Blackett, with J. A. M. Clegg and P. H. S. Stubbs, "An Analysis of Rock Magnetic Data," *PRSL,* A256 (1960), 291–322, esp. p. 305 for outline of possible interpretations.

63. Blackett, Clegg, and Stubbs, "An Analysis of Rock Magnetic Data," p. 292.

64. Ibid., pp. 292, 308, 314.

65. Ibid., p. 315. See Irving, "Paleomagnetic and Paleoclimatic Aspects," and N. D. Opdyke and S. K. Runcorn, "Wind Direction in the Western United States in the Late Paleozoic," *Bulletin of the Geological Society of America,* 71 (1960), 959–972. Although at present the magnetic axis makes an angle of $11\frac{1}{2}$ degrees with the geographic (rotation) axis, it is virtually coincident when averaged over periods of several thousand years. This is a result

earlier obtained by Jan Hospers, as mentioned above. Paleomagnetic data on lava samples going back ten million years into the Upper Tertiary indicate a position for the geographic North Pole that cannot be statistically distinguished from today. See Anthony Hallam, *A Revolution in the Earth Sciences: From Continental Drift to Plate Tectonics* (Oxford: Clarendon Press, 1973), p. 39.

66. Blackett, Clegg, and Stubbs, "An Analysis of Rock Magnetic Data," pp. 313–314.

67. See Lovell, "Blackett," p. 93; Blackett, "Comparison of Ancient Climates with the Ancient Latitudes Deduced from Rock Magnetic Data," *PRSL,* A263 (1961), 1–30.

68. Blackett, "Comparison of Ancient Climates," p. 25; Le Grand, *Drifting Continents,* p. 157.

69. See Le Grand, *Drifting Continents,* p. 155; and Frankel, "The Continental Drift Debate," pp. 223–224, discussing A. Cox and R. R. Doell, "Review of Palaeomagnetism," *Bulletin of the Geological Society of America,* 71 (1960), 645–768.

70. Walter Sullivan, "Theory That Continents Wander Is Supported by British Scientist," *New York Times,* 26 [month illegible] 1960, pp. 1, 2 (BP: A.35).

71. Henry Frankel, "From Continental Drift to Plate Tectonics," *Nature,* 335 (1988), 127–130, on p. 127. Also, Le Grand, *Drifting Continents,* p. 156; Oreskes, *Rejection of Continental Drift.*

72. Louis Néel, "L'inversion de l'aimantation permanente des roche," *Annales de Géophysique,* 7 (1951), 90–102.

73. See Irving and Runcorn, "Analysis of the Paleomagnetism of the Torridonian Sandstone Series," pp. 98–99; Creer, Irving, and Runcorn, "Geophysical Interpretations of Paleomagnetic Directions," p. 154.

74. See Stephen G. Brush and C. S. Gillmor, "Geophysics," in *Twentieth-Century Physics,* ed. Laurie Brown et al. (New York: American Institute of Physics, 1995), p. 1973; Irving, *Paleomagnetism and Its Application,* p. 8; Glen, *Road to Jaramillo,* pp. 100–103.

75. Allan Cox, ed., *Plate Tectonics and Geomagnetic Reversals: Readings, Selected, Edited and with Introductions* (San Francisco: W. H. Freeman, 1973), p. 141.

76. See Brush and Gillmor, "Geophysics," p. 1973; Glen, *Road to Jaramillo.*

77. Alan Cox, Richard Doell, and G. Brent Dalrymple, "Geomagnetic Polarity Epochs and Pleistocene Geochronometry," *Nature,* 198 (1963), 1049–1051.

78. Blackett, "On Distinguishing Self-Reversed from Field-Reversed Rocks," *Japan Physical Society,* 15 (1962), 699ff.

79. C. W. F. Everitt, "Self-Reversals in British Rocks," six-page typescript (BP:

C.203); and P. M. S. Blackett, "Note on the Relative Improbability of (a) Field Reversals and (b) No Field Reversals," two-page carbon copy of typescript with "Everitt" written in pencil in top right-hand corner (BP: C.203). See R. L. Wilson and C. W. F. Everitt, "Thermal Demagnetization of Some Carboniferous Lavas for Paleomagnetic Purposes," *Geophysical Journal of the Royal Astronomical Society,* 8 (December 1963), 149–164. On Everitt's work and on the problem in general, see Irving, *Paleomagnetism and Its Application,* pp. 154–177, esp. p. 166 on Everitt.

80. Glen, *Road to Jaramillo,* pp. 169–170.

81. Letter from Doell to Blackett, 18 June 1964 (BP: C.153).

82. Handwritten notes for lecture given at Peking (Beijing), September 1964: Blackett, "Reversely Magnetized Rocks and the History of the Earth's Magnetic Field" (BP: C.216).

83. Letter from Doell to Blackett, 16 April 1965; letter from Blackett to Doell, 4 May 1965 (BP: C.252); and comments from G. Brent Dalrymple to the author, 14 December 2003.

84. Letter from Blackett to Doell, 26 May 1965, alluding to Doell's comment (BP: C.153).

85. P. M. S. Blackett, "Some Observations of the Petrology of Normal and Reverse Lavas: Progress Report on Work Carried Out since 1965," July 1967, sixteen-page typescript marked Copy I, Master Copies, First Draft, in pencil (BP: C.125). On acuity, see p. 15. Ade-Hall's method is described in *Geophysical Journal,* 8 (1964), 403. The observations were made for Blackett by Jennifer L. Langbein.

86. Glen, *Road to Jaramillo,* pp. 126–127.

87. Letter from Norman Watkins to Blackett, 15 August 1967 (BP: C.132). Watkins was a faculty member in the Geology Department at Florida State University at the time.

88. Letter from J. M. Ade-Hall to Blackett, 10 August 1967 (BP: C.132).

89. Letter from Rod Wilson to Blackett, 26 January 1966; letter from Peter Smith to Blackett, 21 May 1966; photocopy of letter from Blackett (Ministry of Technology, Millbank Tower) to Sir Graham Sutton, Chairman, Natural Environment Research Council, London, 27 July 1966 (BP: C.255).

90. Letter from Blackett to Rod Wilson, 17 May 1973 (BP: C.182).

91. Letter from Blackett to C. W. F. Everitt, 18 February 1974 (BP: C.268).

92. Frankel, "Continental Drift to Plate Tectonics," pp. 127–128. See F. J. Vine and D. H. Matthews, "Magnetic Anomalies over Oceanic Ridges," *Nature,* 199 (1963), 947–949. Stronger evidence came later in F. J. Vine, "Spreading of the Ocean Floor: New Evidence" *Science,* 154 (1966), 1405–1415.

93. See Le Grand, *Drifting Continents,* pp. 206–207.

94. Ibid., p. 128. Also see Frederick J. Vine, "Reversals of Fortune," in *Plate*

Tectonics: An Insider's History of the Modern Theory of the Earth, ed. Naomi Oreskes with Homer Le Grand (Boulder, Colo.: Westview Press, 2001), pp. 46–66, on 57; and Lawrence W. Morley, "The Zebra Pattern," in *Plate Tectonics*, pp. 67–85, on 83–84.

95. Frankel, "Continental Drift to Plate Tectonics," pp. 128–129. See Glen, *Road to Jaramillo*, pp. 261–266, 304–306, 372–375, citing R. R. Doell and G. B. Dalrymple, *Science*, 152 (1966), 1060–1061; and comments from G. Brent Dalrymple to the author, 14 December 2003.

96. Frankel, "The Continental Drift Debate," pp. 235–236.

97. Letter from Blackett to Cox, 21 November 1966 (BP: C.258).

98. See J. Tuzo Wilson, "Static or Mobile Earth—The Current Scientific Revolution," *American Philosophical Society Proceedings*, 112 (1968), 309–320. Cox, in *Plate Tectonics and Geomagnetic Reversals*, and Hallam, in *Revolution in the Earth Sciences*, explicitly tie their claim of scientific revolution to Thomas Kuhn's historical and philosophical analysis in *The Structure of Scientific Revolutions* (Chicago: University of Chicago Press, 1962). Cox noted that he preferred to talk about the "paradigm change" in geology and geophysics, rather than to engage in "sterile" debate about whether plate tectonics should be described as a hypothesis or a theory (Cox, pp. 4–5).

99. Letter from Bullard to Blackett, 7 November 1968 (BP: C.263).

100. Le Grand, *Drifting Continents*, p. 205.

101. Letter from Blackett to S. Keith Runcorn, 8 March 1961 (BP: C.228).

102. See David Kushner, "Sir George Darwin and a British School of Geophysics," in *Research Schools*, ed. Gerald Geison and F. L. Holmes, *Osiris*, 8 (1993), pp. 196–224; and Christopher N. L. Brooke, *A History of the University of Cambridge*, vol. 4, *1870–1990* (Cambridge University Press, 1993), p. 152.

103. Günter Buntebarth, "Geophysics: Disciplinary History," in Gregory Good, ed., *Sciences of the Earth: An Encyclopedia of Events, People and Phenomena*, 2 vols. (New York: Garland, 1998), pp. 377–380.

104. John W. Servos, "To Explore the Borderland: The Foundation of the Geophysical Laboratory of the Carnegie Institution of Washington," *HSPS*, 14 (1983), 147–185, on p. 149.

105. Kushner, "Sir George Darwin," p. 215.

106. Frank Greenaway, *Science International: A History of the International Council of Scientific Unions* (Cambridge University Press, 1996), pp. 25–26; and International Union of Geodesy and Geophysics website homepage (http://www.obs-mip.fr/IUGG-gen.html, accessed 17 January 2001).

107. Ronald E. Doel, "Geophysics in Universities," in Good, ed., *Sciences of the Earth*, pp. 380–384.

108. Brooke, *History of the University of Cambridge,* vol. 4, p. 152; Oreskes, *Rejection of Continental Drift,* p. 279.

109. Henry Frankel, "Continental Drift and Plate Tectonics," in Good, ed., *Sciences of the Earth,* pp. 118–136, on 129.

110. Runcorn's group at Cambridge from 1951–1955 included Kenneth Creer, Neil Opdyke, R. A. Fisher, Jan Hospers, and Edward Irving.

111. M. Fortun and S. S. Schweber, "Scientists and the Legacy of World War II: The Case of Operations Research (OR)," *Social Studies of Science,* 23 (1993), 595–642, on p. 601.

112. Francis Everitt, e-mail communication to the author, 18 June 1997.

113. Blackett, "Rutherford Memorial Lecture," p. 299. On phenomenology of the "curious" particles, see Silvan S. Schweber, Hans A. Bethe, and Frederic de Hoffmann, *Mesons and Fields,* 3 vols. (Evanston, Ill.: Row, Peterson and Co., 1955–1956): Bethe and Hoffmann, vol. 2, *Mesons* (1955), sec. 51a, "Phenomenology," pp. 373–376.

114. Private communication from Edward (Ted) Irving, 1 May 2001.

115. Blackett, Clegg, and Stubbs, "An Analysis of Rock Magnetic Data," pp. 314, 315.

116. On continental drift as a singular statement and on geology as a historical science, see David B. Kitts, *The Structure of Geology* (Dallas: Southern Methodist University Press, 1977), p. 121; and Kitts, "Continental Drift and the Scientific Revolution," pp. 2490–2496 (cited in note 3; reprinted in *Structure of Geology*).

117. See Oreskes, *Rejection of Continental Drift,* pp. 136–138. There is a considerable literature on the methodology of "multiple working hypotheses," including Stephen J. Pyne, "Methodologies for Geology: G. K. Gilbert and T. C. Chamberlin," *Isis,* 69 (1978), 413–424; and Laudan, "The Method of Multiple Working Hypotheses."

118. Blackett, "Operational Research: A Note on Certain Aspects of the Methodology of Operational Research," in Blackett, *Studies of War: Nuclear and Conventional* (Edinburgh: Oliver Boyd, 1962), pp. 169–198 (written in 1943). See Lovell, "Blackett," p. 67.

119. Blackett, "The Craft of Experimental Physics," in Harold Wright, ed., *University Studies: Cambridge 1933* (London: Ivor Nicolson and Watson, 1933), pp. 67–96, on 89.

120. Blackett, "Introduction" to "Symposium on Continental Drift," p. xi; and Blackett, "Continental Drift," 8th Hugh MacMillan Memorial Lecture.

121. For sources on Popper, see Malachi Haim Hacohen, *Karl Popper: The Formative Years, 1902–1945* (Cambridge: Cambridge University Press, 2000).

122. Irving, *Paleomagnetism and Its Application,* p. vii.

123. Discussion by the author with Ted Irving, Victoria, BC, 26 October 2001.

124. Irving, *Paleomagnetism and Its Application,* frontispiece. Of Popper's seminar series, Irving recalled that he thought Popper described very well what Irving was actually doing as a scientist. Private communication, 1 May 2001.

125. S. K. Runcorn, "Preface," in Runcorn, ed., *Continental Drift* (New York: Academic Press, 1962), p. vii.

126. Quoted in Edward Irving, "Continental Drift, Organic Evolution, and Moral Courage," *Eos,* 81 (2000), p. 546.

6. Scientific Leadership

1. The Order of Merit was founded in 1902 by Edward VII and limited to twenty-four members. The Order of the Companions of Honour was founded in 1917 by George V for conspicuous national service and limited to sixty-five members. The peerage carries the responsibility of membership in the House of Lords.

2. Robert S. Anderson, "Blackett in India: Thinking Strategically about New Conflicts," in Peter Hore, ed., *Patrick Blackett: Sailor, Scientist, Socialist* (London: Frank Cass, 2002), pp. 217–268, at 262.

3. [Anonymous], "Lord Blackett: Radical Nobel-Prize Winning Physicist," *The Times,* 15 July 1974 (BP: A.1).

4. Harold Wilson, "Pat Blackett: The Reluctant Peer in Politics," eight-page typescript (BP: A6), reprinted as "The Reluctant Peer in Politics," in Hore, ed., *Patrick Blackett,* pp. 305–316, esp. 311–312.

5. See C. P. Snow, *The Two Cultures* (Cambridge: Cambridge University Press Canto Edition, 1993), pp. 4–5. The lecture and Snow's characterization of Eliot are discussed below.

6. Quoted in Robert Craft, "The Perils of Mrs. Eliot," review of Carole Seymour-Jones and Nan A. Talese, *Painted Shadow* (2002), in *New York Review of Books,* 23 May 2002, pp. 29–33.

7. T. S. Eliot, "Banquet Speech," 10 December 1948, The Nobel Prize in Literature 1948, http://www.nobel.se/literature/laureates/1948/eliot-speech.html (accessed 31 March 2004).

8. Patrick M. S. Blackett, "Banquet Speech," 10 December 1948, The Nobel Prize in Physics 1948, http://www.nobel.se/physics/laureates/1948/blackett-speech.html (accessed 31 March 2004).

9. Copy of Western Union cablegram, dated 6 November 1948, in Robert Oppenheimer Papers, Collections of the Manuscript Division, Library of Congress, courtesy of S. S. Schweber.

10. P.O. telegram to P. M. S. Blackett from Carl Anderson, undated (BP: A.45).

11. Letter from P. A. M. Dirac to Blackett, 7 November 1948 (BP: A.46);

Douglas [Hartree] to Patrick, 26 November 1948 (BP: A.48); W. Heitler to Blackett, 11 November 1948 (BP: A.48); E. A. Milne to Blackett, 5 November 1948 (BP: A.50); E. Schrödinger to Blackett, 12 November 1948 (BP: A.52); and J. Chadwick to Blackett, 5 November 1948 (BP: A.46).

12. Letter from C. G. Darwin to Patrick, 6 October 1948 (BP: A.46).

13. Letter from P. M. S. Blackett to J. S. Laskey, Foreign Service, 30 October 1943; Lord Rothschild, War Office, Whitehall, to Blackett, 4 November 1943; Gleb Wataghin, Department of Physics, University of São Paulo, to Blackett, 14 October 1944; and C. Paterson, Research Laboratories, General Electric, Wembley, to Blackett, 16 March 1945 (BP: J.59).

14. "Who Is Beppo?" http://www.astro-physics.ox.ac.uk/~erik/sax/sax_beppo .html (accessed 25 October 2003), based on G. Gignami, Obituary, *Nature,* 367 (1994), 515.

15. G. Ising, "Anförande vid Nobel-sammanträdet i nov. 1948" (PKVA, 1948), section of reports to the Academy, pp. 1–5 [33–37]; and "Bil. 8. Utredning om P. M. S. Blackett" (PKVA, 1948), Appendix 8 (seventeen pages) [208–218].

16. G. Ising, "Presentation Speech," The Nobel Prize in Physics 1948, http:// www.nobel.se/physics/laureates/1948/press.html (accessed 31 March 2004).

17. Ibid.

18. The history and sociology of the Nobel Prizes, especially in physics and chemistry, have been well studied by scholars such as Elisabeth Crawford and Robert Marc Friedman, with some attention to the particular histories of awards and nonawards since the first Prizes were given in 1901. Elisabeth Crawford, *The Beginnings of the Nobel Institution: The Science Prizes, 1901–1915* (Cambridge: Cambridge University Press, 1984); Elisabeth Crawford, John L. Heilbron, and Rebecca Ulrich, *The Nobel Population 1901–1937: A Census of the Nominators and Nominees for the Prizes in Physics and Chemistry* (Berkeley: University of California Office for the History of Science and Technology, 1987); Elisabeth Crawford, *Nationalism and Internationalism in Science 1880–1939: Four Studies of the Nobel Population* (Cambridge: Cambridge University Press, 1992); Robert Marc Friedman, *The Politics of Excellence: Behind the Nobel Prize in Science* (New York: Freeman, 2001).

19. In fact, the 1934 Prize never was awarded, but instead, in 1935, the Prize money was allocated one-third to the main fund and two-thirds to a special fund for research grants and improvement to the Nobel Institute. Friedman, *Politics of Excellence* (2001), pp. 282, 287.

20. Nominating letter from Jean Perrin, 25 January 1935 (PKVA, 1935),

pp. 96–97 in letters section; letter from Jean Perrin, 27 January 1936; letter from Maurice de Broglie, 21 January 1936; letter from Louis de Broglie, 16 January 1936 (PKVA, 1936), pp. 69, 71, and 73 of letters section.

21. Nominating letter from Robert Millikan, 12 January 1935 (PKVA, 1936), pp. 2–3 of letters section.

22. Nominating letters from Robert Millikan, 7 December 1935 (PKVA, 1936), p. 4 of letters section; from A. Deissmann, 24 January 1936 (PKVA, 1936), p. 2; from Max von Laue, 16 January 1936 (PKVA, 1936), p. 3; from H. Nagaoka, 18 December 1935 (PKVA, 1936), p. 5; and from Max Planck, 25 January 1936 (PKVA, 1936), p. 6.

23. Nominating letter from Richard Tolman, 2 January 1935 (PKVA, 1935), pp. 79–81 of letters section.

24. Friedman, *Politics of Excellence,* p. 175.

25. Nominating letter from J. Clay, 25 January 1936 (PKVA, 1936), p. 49 of letters section.

26. Nominating letter from A. H. Compton, 16 January 1936 (PKVA, 1936), pp. 62–64 of letters section.

27. Report by Erik Hulthén, "Utredning rörande undersökningar över den kosmiske strålningen," 7 June 1936 (PKVA 1936, Bilagar [Appendix] 4), pp. 58–66; Hulthén, "Avskrift: Om upptäckten av den kosmiska strålningen och den positiva elektronen," 4 September 1936 (PKVA 1936, Bilagar till Kungl. Vetenskapsakadiens Protokoll), pp. 1–8; Physics Committee report, 8 September 1936, signed by Axel E. Lindh, Manne Siegbahn, Erik Hultén, O. W. Oseen, and H. Pleijel, chair (PKVA, 1936, "Til Kungl. Vetenskapsakiademien"), pp. 1–13.

28. Carl Anderson, "The Production and Properties of Positrons," Nobel Lecture, 1936, in *Nobel Lectures, Physics 1922–1941* (Amsterdam: Elsevier, 1964), pp. 366–376, on 367–368.

29. Nominating letter from G. Iv. Maneff, 23 January 1939 (PKVA, 1939), p. 7 of letters section; nominating letter from C. G. Darwin, 5 January 1940 (PKVA, 1940), pp. 5–7 of letters section; nominating letter from C. G. Darwin, 6 January 1942 (PKVA, 1942), p. 8 of letters section; nominating letter from C. G. Darwin, 6 November 1943 (PKVA, 1944), p. 7 of letters section; nominating letter from R. W. James, 16 December 1943 (PKVA, 1944), p. 8 of letters section; nominating letter from John J. Nolan, 12 December 1944 (PKVA, 1945), pp. 7–8 of letters section; and letter from Jacques Hadamard, 6 December 1946 (PKVA, 1947), p. 4 of letters section.

30. Nominating letter from Max Born, 11 December 1944 (PKVA, 1945), pp. 4–6 of letter section.

31. Nominating letter from C. D. Anderson, 3 December 1940 (PKVA, 1941),

p. 38 of letters section; first nominating letter for Anderson and Neddermeyer from Robert Millikan, 14 December 1940 (PKVA, 1941), pp. 40–43 of letters section.

32. Millikan's warning is in letter of 14 November 1946 (PKVA, 1947), pp. 45–46 of letters section, on 46 [pp. 267–268 in sequential numbering of volume].

33. Nominating letter from Millikan, 6 January 1944 (PKVA, 1944), pp. 31–36 of letters section, on 33.

34. Report from the Physics Committee to the Academy, signed by Henning Pleijel, Erik Hulthén, Ivar Waller, Axel Lindh, and Manne Siegbahn (PKVA, 1945), pp. 1–17 in reports section, on 7–9.

35. Nominating letter from Czeslaw Bialobrzoski, 16 January 1947 (PKVA, 1947), p. 89 of letters section; letter from Jacques Hadamard, 11 October 1947 (PKVA, 1948), p. 80 of letters section [426], who nominated Blackett alone the previous year, 6 December 1946 (PKVA, 1947), p. 4 of letters section [227]; letter from Francis Perrin, 30 January 1948 (PKVA, 1948), pp. 82–87 of letters section [428–433].

36. Nominating letter from Pierre Auger, 6 January 1948 (PKVA, 1948), pp. 111–112 of letters section [457–458].

37. Nominating letter from S. Tolansky, 31 October 1947 (PKVA, 1948), p. 9 of letters section [355].

38. H. Victor Neher, "Early Days of Cosmic Rays," in *The Birth of Particle Physics*, ed. Laurie M. Brown and Lillian Hoddeson (Cambridge: Cambridge University Press, 1983), pp. 120–130, on 129.

39. Nominating letter from Arthur H. Compton, 22 January 1948 (PKVA, 1948), pp. 5–8 of letters section [351–354], on 6.

40. Ibid., extended quotation on p. 7 [353].

41. Ibid., p. 8.

42. Nominating letter from J. D. Bernal, 27 January 1948, followed by eight-page statement about Blackett's work (PKVA, 1948), pp. 13–23 of letters section [359–369], 15–16.

43. Ibid., p. 17.

44. Ibid., p. 16.

45. G. Ising, "Utredning om P. M. S. Blackett" (PKVA, 1948), Nobel citation wording on p. 17 [218].

46. Nobel Physics Committee Report to the Academy, 16 September 1948 (PKVA, 1948), pp. 10–13 of reports section [97–100]. The photocopy of the report also carries the signature of G. Borelius, who is not listed elsewhere as a member of the Committee.

47. Nominating letter from C. G. Darwin, 2 November 1948 (PKVA, 1949), pp. 96–98 [359–361].

48. Letter from Blackett to Ernest Rutherford, 5 July 1937 (BP: B.136).

49. Bernard Lovell, "Bristol and Manchester—The Years 1931–1939," in *The Making of Physicists,* ed. Rajkumari Williams (Bristol: Adam Hilger, 1987), pp. 148–160, on 157.

50. Sir Bernard Lovell, "Patrick Maynard Stuart Blackett, Baron Blackett, of Chelsea, 18 November 1897–13 July 1974," *Biographical Memoirs of Fellows of the Royal Society,* 21 (1975), 1–115, at pp. 29–30.

51. Ibid., pp. 35–36.

52. Ibid., pp. 35–36; Clifford Butler, "Recollections of Patrick Blackett, 1945–70," *Notes and Records of the Royal Society London,* 53 (1999), 143–156, on pp. 16–17.

53. On the train, e-mail communication from Francis Everitt to the author, 16 June 1997. And Butler, "Recollections," pp. 144–145.

54. Butler, "Recollections," pp. 146–147.

55. Ibid., p. 147. On the organization of British science and technology, see Hilary Rose and Steven Rose, *Science and Society* (London: Penguin, 1970).

56. Memos A, B, and C from 1945–1946 (PP: 22.11).

57. Typescript of five pages, undated, but following 11 March 1946 meeting, entitled "The Balanced Development of Science in the Universities of U.K." (PP: 22.11).

58. Wilson, "Pat Blackett," pp. 2–3; Lord Zuckerman, *Six Men Out of the Ordinary* (London: Peter Owen, 1992), pp. 31–32.

59. Arthur Chapman was one of the Manchester colleagues who was surprised, along with others, at Blackett's decision to move to Imperial College, according to Chapman in a conversation with Francis Everitt in the late 1950s. E-mail communication from Francis Everitt to the author, 16 June 1997.

60. Letter from Blackett to the Rector at Imperial College, 29 December 1952 (BP: A.18); letter from Roderic Hill to Blackett, 21 November 1952 (BP: A.19).

61. Letter from Blackett to James Chadwick, 30 July 1953 (BP: A.24).

62. Letter from Blackett to Richard Kahn, 12 September 1953 (BP: A.24).

63. Comments from Giovanna Blackett Bloor to the author, 28 June 2003.

64. Butler, "Recollections," pp. 148–149.

65. Ibid., pp. 150–151; Lovell, "Blackett," pp. 86–87.

66. See Alexis de Greiff, "Salam's Discourse in Science and Third World Development," Chapter 2 in "The International Centre for Theoretical Physics, 1960–1980: Ideology and Practice in a United Nations Institution for Scientific Cooperation and Third World Development" (University of London Ph.D. thesis, 2002).

67. On Salam, see Miriam Lewis, "Abdus Salam—Biography," The Nobel Prize

in Physics 1979, http://www.nobel.se/physics/laureates/1979/salam-bio
.html (accessed 31 March 2004); and Jagjit Singh, *Abdus Salam: A Biography* (Calcutta: Penguin Books, 1992). Also, Z. Hassan and C. H. Lai, eds.,
Ideals and Realities: Selected Essays of Abdus Salam (Singapore: World Scientific, 1984). Salam's concern with the relationship between Islamic religion and science led to his writing the book *Renaissance of Science in Islamic Countries* (Singapore: World Scientific, 1994). His comments on
Blackett's death are in letter from Abdus Salam to Costanza Blackett, 13
July 1974 (BFP).

68. Peter Ritchie Calder, "Bernal at War," in *J. D. Bernal: A Life in Science
and Politics,* ed. Brenda Swann and Francis Aprahamian (London: Verso,
1999), pp. 161–190, on 171.

69. J. G. Crowther, *Fifty Years with Science* (London: Barrie and Jenkins,
1970), p. 94, quotation on 222.

70. Ibid., p. 172; *Science in War* (Harmondsworth, Middlesex: Penguin, 1940),
"written by 25 scientists" (p. 137).

71. Lovell, "Blackett," pp. 76–77; Wilson, "Pat Blackett," p. 4; six-page typescript of minutes from meeting at dinner given by Marcus Brumwell at the
Reform Club, 17 July 1956 (BP: E.24); five-page typescript of minutes
from meeting at dinner given by Marcus Brumwell at Brown's Hotel, 27
June 1958 (BP: E.26); minutes from 26 September 1958, 13 October 1958,
and 8 December 1958 (BP: E.27).

72. Thirty-two-page typescript "A Labour Government and Science: Papers for
Mr. Gaitskell," and two-page typescript of minutes from the dinner meeting at Brown's Hotel, 27 August 1959 (BP: E.28).

73. Draft Memo "Science and the Labour Party," 1 November 1962, signed by
all members of the dinner group, according to letter from Brumwell to
Blackett, 9 November 1962 (BP: E.33); letter from Brumwell to Blackett,
27 February 1963 (BP: E.33); four-page typescript of minutes of VIP Scientists' Dinner at the Reform Club, 24 June 1963, including Crossman,
Blackett, Bronowski, Brumwell, Dickson, Forrester, David Glass, Lockspeiser, D. M. Newitt, Snow, and Williams (Bernal noted as absent) (BP:
E.34).

74. Lovell, "Blackett," p. 78 note. Also see P. M. S. Blackett, "Wanted: A Wand
over Whitehall," *New Statesman,* 68 (1964), 346ff.

75. Rose and Rose, *Science and Society,* pp. 102–104; Wilson, "Pat Blackett,"
pp. 4–6. On Zuckerman, see his autobiography *From Apes to Warlords*
(New York: Harper, 1978), and John Peyton, *Solly Zuckerman: A Scientist
Out of the Ordinary* (London: John Murray, 2002).

76. On this, see Lovell, "Blackett," pp. 101–104.

77. Rose and Rose, *Science and Society,* pp. 104–123.

78. Private communication from John B. Adams to Bernard Lovell, quoted in Lovell, "Blackett," pp. 80–81. Noel Annan gives a similar interpretation in *Our Age: Portrait of a Generation* (London: Weidenfeld and Nicolson, 1990), p. 282.

79. Zuckerman, *Six Men*, pp. 35–36.

80. Blackett, reported in *Nature*, 213 (1967), p. 747, cited in Rose and Rose, *Science and Society*, p. 120.

81. Wilson, "Pat Blackett," p. 8.

82. Lovell, "Blackett," pp. 95–96 and notes on p. 96; Anderson, "Blackett in India," pp. 218–219.

83. Memorandum from John Edgar Hoover, Director, Federal Bureau of Investigation, to Jack D. Neal, Chief, Division of Foreign Activity Correlation, State Department, Washington, D.C., dated 9 February 1948; FBI File Number 100-354451 (photocopy courtesy of Ronald E. Doel).

84. Letter from Blackett to Costanza, 8 January 1947 (BFP).

85. Letter from Blackett to Costanza, 13 January 1947 (BFP).

86. Quoted from the Nehru Memorial Lecture (1967) in Lovell, "Blackett," p. 97. See also ibid., pp. 96–97; Anderson, "Blackett in India," pp. 217–219, 222.

87. Anderson, "Blackett in India," p. 218.

88. George Perkovich, *India's Nuclear Bomb: The Impact on Global Proliferation* (Berkeley: University of California Press, 1999), pp. 12, 14–15.

89. Ibid., p. 21.

90. Guy Hartcup and T. E. Allibone, *Cockcroft and the Atom* (Bristol: Adam Hilger/Institute of Physics, 1984), p. 265.

91. Crowther, *Fifty Years*, p. 323.

92. In interview by B. Ruth Nanda of Blackett, in Delhi in 1967, for the Oral History Project of the Nehru Memorial Museum and Library, transcript photocopy, twenty-four pages (BP: G.12), quoted in Anderson, "Blackett in India," p. 224.

93. Anderson, "Blackett in India," pp. 258–259. See Blackett, "Vikram Sarabhai. Obituary Notice," *Proceedings of the 13th International Cosmic Ray Conference*, 5 (1973), p. 3482, cited in Lovell, "Blackett," p. 97.

94. Anderson, "Blackett in India," pp. 224–225.

95. Quotation in ibid., p. 232; also p. 236.

96. Crowther, *Fifty Years*, pp. 321–322.

97. Anderson, "Blackett in India," pp. 260–262. On the comment in 1958, see Perkovich, *India's Nuclear Bomb*, p. 35. Also, Itty Abraham, *The Making of the Indian Atomic Bomb: Science, Secrecy and the Postcolonial State* (London: Zed Books, 1998). Bhabha's work on nuclear weapons is a focus in a book that Anderson is writing.

98. In the Blackett papers, for example, there is correspondence following Blackett's 1957 Dublin lecture, "Technology and World Advancement" (BP: H.68), and correspondence regarding C. P. Snow's 1959 Rede Lecture at Cambridge, "The Two Cultures and the Scientific Revolution," and Blackett's 1969 Gandhi Memorial Lecture at University College, Nairobi, "Reflections on Science and Technology in Developing Countries" (BP: G.70).

99. De Greiff, "Salam's Discourse," and "Supporting Theoretical Physics for the Third World Development: The Ford Foundation and the ICTP in Trieste (1966–1973)," in *American Foundations and Large-Scale Research: Construction and Transfer of Knowledge,* ed. Giuliana Gemelli (Bologna: CLUEB, 2001), pp. 25–50.

100. Blackett, "Science and Technology in an Unequal World," First Jawaharlal Nehru Memorial Lecture, New Delhi, 13 November 1967 (New Delhi: Indraprastha Press, 1968), summarized in Anderson, "Blackett in India," pp. 38–39.

101. Quoted in Lovell, "Blackett," p. 98, from Blackett, "Technology and World Advancement," *The Advancement of Science,* 14 (1957), 3ff.

102. According to Jeannine Alton et al., eds., "Catalogue of the Blackett Papers," BP: H57, H.58, and H.59 (pp. 302–303).

103. [Anonymous], "British Association: Rewriting Humphry Davy," *The Economist* (Notes of the Week section), 184 (7 September 1957), 744. Also see Lovell, "Blackett," p. 99.

104. Newspaper clipping, John Hillaby, "More Help Urged for Poor Nations," *New York Times,* 5 September 1957, in FBI File no. 100-354451 (thanks to Ronald E. Doel).

105. Snow, *The Two Cultures,* pp. 4–5.

106. Ibid., pp. 10–11.

107. C. P. Snow, "The Age of Rutherford," *Atlantic Monthly,* 102 (1958), 79, 80, cited in Stefan Collini, "Introduction," in Snow, *The Two Cultures,* pp. ix–lxxi, on xxviii.

108. Snow, *The Two Cultures,* pp. 41–51.

109. See Rose and Rose, *Science and Society,* pp. 169–170.

Conclusion

1. Ronald W. Clark, *The Rise of the Boffins* (London: Phoenix House, 1962), pp. 32–33.

2. P. M. S. Blackett, "Tizard and the Science of War," Tizard Memorial Lecture, 11 February 1960, before the Institute for Strategic Studies, reprinted in *Nature,* 185 (5 March 1960), 647–653, on p. 15.

3. Ibid., pp. 15–16.
4. Blackett describes his own approach in P. M. S. Blackett, "The Old Days at the Cavendish," *Rivista del Nuova Cimento,* 1, special number (1969), xxxii–xl, at p. xxxvii.
5. P. M. S. Blackett, "Jean Frédéric Joliot 1900–1958," *Biographical Memoirs of Fellows of the Royal Society,* 6 (London: Royal Society, 1960), 87–101, on pp. 94–96, 97, 99.
6. Michel Pinault, *Frédéric Joliot-Curie* (Paris: Odile Jacob, 2000), p. 17.
7. Charles Thorpe and Steven Shapin, "Who Was J. Robert Oppenheimer? Charisma and Complex Organization," *Social Studies of Science,* 30 (2000), 545–590, on p. 549.
8. Ibid., on p. 551, drawing from Haakon Chevalier, *Oppenheimer: The Story of a Friendship* (New York: George Braziller, 1965), p. 11.
9. Ibid. pp. 552–553.
10. Gerald Geison, "Scientific Change, Emerging Specialties, and Research Schools," *History of Science,* 19 (1981), 20–40, and *Michael Foster and the Cambridge School of Physiology: The Scientific Enterprise in Late Victorian Society* (Princeton, N.J.: Princeton University Press, 1978); J. B. Morrell, "The Chemist Breeders: The Research Schools of Liebig and Thomas Thomson," *Ambix,* 19 (1971), 1–46; for an overview, see Gerald L. Geison and Frederic L. Holmes, eds., *Research Schools: Historical Reappraisals, Osiris,* 2d series, 8 (1993). On research schools and discipline building in chemistry, see Mary Jo Nye, *From Chemical Philosophy to Theoretical Chemistry: Dynamics of Matter and Dynamics of Disciplines 1800–1950* (Berkeley: University of California Press, 1993).
11. Max Weber, "The Sociology of Charismatic Authority," pp. 245–252; "The Meaning of Discipline," pp. 253–264; and "The Social Psychology of the World Religions," pp. 267–301, in H. H. Gerth and C. Wright Mills, eds., *From Max Weber: Essays in Sociology* (London: Routledge and Kegan Paul, 1948), on pp. 245, 263, 296.
12. Max Weber, "Science as a Vocation," in Gerth and Mills, eds., *From Max Weber,* pp. 129–156, on 138–139 and quotation, p. 150.
13. From *The Entry and Training of Naval Cadets* (1914), pp. 1–2 and p. 4, quoted in Evan Davies, "The Selborne Scheme: The Education of the Boy," in Peter Hore, ed., *Patrick Blackett: Sailor, Scientist, Socialist* (London: Frank Cass, 2002), pp. 15–37, on 24. Also partially quoted in Michael Partridge, *The Royal Naval College Osborne: A History 1903–21* (Phoenix Mill: Sutton Publishing, in association with the Royal Naval Museum, Portsmouth, 1999), p. 34.
14. I. A. R. [Ivor Richards], "Professor the Lord Blackett, O.M.," three-page typescript, annotated, for *Magdalene College Magazine* (BP: A.3); and

[Anonymous], "King's College Cambridge, November 1974, Annual Report of the Council" (BP: A.2).

15. [Anonymous], "King's College Cambridge."

16. Neil A. Porter, *Physicists in Conflict: From Antiquity to the New Millenium* (Bristol: Institute of Physics, 1998), p. 156.

17. [Anonymous], "Lord Blackett: Radical Nobel-Prize Winning Physicist," *The Times*, 15 July 1974, clipping in BP: A.1.

18. Ruth Nanda Anshen, *Biography of an Idea* (Mt. Kisco, N.Y.: Moyer Bell, 1986), pp. 43–44. Thanks to Pnina Abir-Am for this reference.

19. Letter from Marion Milner to Blackett, undated, ca. 1950; letter of 8 November 1950 from Jacob Epstein to Blackett; letter from Blackett to Lady (Kathleen) Epstein, 1 December 1967 (BP: A.29).

20. Andrew Brown, "Patrick Blackett: Sailor, Scientist, Socialist," *Physics World*, April 1998, 35–38, on p. 35.

21. Mark Oliphant, *Rutherford: Recollections of the Cambridge Days* (Amsterdam: Elsevier, 1972), p. 20.

22. Letter from Nicholas Kurti to Costanza Blackett, 17 July 1974 (BFP).

23. Sir Nevill Mott, *A Life in Science* (London: Taylor and Francis, 1986), p. 17.

24. P. M. S. Blackett, "The Rutherford Memorial Lecture, 1958," *PRSL*, A251 (1959), 293–305, on pp. 295–296; and "The Old Days at the Cavendish," pp. xxxiv and xxxvii.

25. Carbon copy of letter from Blackett to H. H. Dale, 11 November 1948 (BP: A.46).

26. J. G. Crowther, *Fifty Years with Science* (London: Barrie and Jenkins, 1970), p. 121.

27. Ibid.

28. Interview by Charles Weiner of Otto R. Frisch, in New York City, 3 May 1967, transcript, pp. 19–23 (SHQP).

29. Clifford Butler, "Recollections of Patrick Blackett, 1945–70," *Notes and Records of the Royal Society London*, 53 (1999), 143–156, on pp. 144–145, 154.

30. Conversation of the author with Ted Irving, 26 October 2001.

31. Butler, "Recollections," pp. 144–145.

32. As related by Francis Everitt to the author, e-mail letter of 16 June 1997.

33. Charles Darwin, *Autobiography*, ed. Nora Barlow (New York: Norton, 1993), p. 123.

34. Edward Irving, "Personal Notes for the Royal Society," fifty-page typescript (31 October 2003), pp. 42–43 (courtesy of Ted Irving).

35. Interview by Brian Connell of Blackett, Anglia TV, fourteen-page typescript (BP: A.32), pp. 2, 4.

36. C. W. F. Everitt, "The Creative Imagination of an Experimental Physicist," in *Near Zero: New Frontiers of Physics,* ed. J. D. Fairbank et al. (New York: Freeman, 1988), pp. 19–64, on 62.

37. Interview by Robert Smith of William Hunter McCrea, 22 September 1978, p. 22 (Sources for History of Modern Astrophysics, American Institute of Physics, College Park, Md.).

38. Butler, "Recollections," pp. 146–147, 153–154.

39. Porter, *Physicists in Conflict,* p. 156. Porter took his first degree and doctorate at Manchester before becoming Professor of Electron Physics at University College Dublin for twenty-four years.

40. E-mail letter from Francis Everitt to the author, 16 June 1997.

41. Mott, *A Life in Science,* p. 67.

42. Irving, "Personal Notes," p. 42.

43. Tam Dalyell, "Foreword," in Hore, *Patrick Blackett,* pp. ix–x, on ix.

44. Comment from Francis Everitt to the author, September 2003.

45. John Halperin, *C. P. Snow: An Oral Biography* (New York: St. Martin's Press, 1983), p. 204.

46. R. V. Jones, *Most Secret War* (London: Hamish Hamilton, 1978), p. 493.

47. Interview by John L. Heilbron of Blackett, 17 December 1962, at Imperial College (SHQP).

48. E-mail letter from Francis Everitt to the author, 16 June 1997.

49. Ibid., on Chapman's and his own experiences; Butler, "Recollections," p. 154.

50. Letter from Brian Sutcliffe to the author, 22 April 1994; comments from Giovanna Blackett Bloor to the author, 28 June 2003.

51. E-mail from Francis Everitt, 16 June 1997.

52. Carbon copy of letter from Blackett to Dale, 11 November 1948 (BP: A.46).

53. Interview by Charles Weiner of Léon Rosenfeld, 3 September 1968, Copenhagen (SHQP).

54. Interview by David Edge of Bernard Lovell, 6 July 1971, at Jodrell Bank (Sources for History of Modern Astrophysics, American Institute of Physics).

55. E-mail letter from Francis Everitt to the author, 16 June 1997.

56. Letter from Blackett to R. E. Peierls, 21 December 1948 (BP: J.60).

57. "Socialists Incite Class Warfare—Sir A. McFadyean," *News Chronicle,* 7 March 1950 (BFP).

58. On the phases in the career of a creative scientist, see Frederic Lawrence Holmes, *Investigative Pathways: Patterns and Stages in the Careers of Experimental Scientists* (New Haven: Yale University Press, 2004).

59. For a study of advisors in the United States, for example, see Gregg Herken, *Cardinal Choices: Presidential Science Advising from the Atomic Bomb to SDI* (Stanford, Calif.: Stanford University Press, 1992).

60. Letter to the author from a British scientist recalling Blackett's talk at dinner, circa 1958, on wasting of resources and pollution of the planet.

61. Alan Hodgkin at "Memorial Meeting for Lord Blackett, OM, CH, FRS, at the Royal Society on 31 October 1974," *Notes and Records of the Royal Society of London,* 29 (1975), 135–162, on p. 137.

62. [Captain] S. W. Roskill, *The Art of Leadership* (Hamden, Conn.: Archon, 1965), p. 55.

63. William Cooper, "Introduction," to C. P. Snow, *The Physicists* (Boston: Little, Brown, 1981), pp. 8–9.

64. Comments from Giovanna Blackett Bloor to the author, 28 June 2003.

65. Butler, "Recollections," p. 155.

66. Bullard, "Patrick Blackett . . . An Appreciation by Sir Edward Bullard," *Nature,* 250 (1974), 370.

67. Blackett, in *Hansard (House of Lords),* 308 (1970), col. 384; 315 (1971), col. 184; 328 (1972), col. 833; 330 (1972), col. 127; and "The Gap Widens," Rede Lecture, Cambridge, 15 May 1969 (Cambridge: Cambridge University Press, 1970). Blackett's correspondence on this lecture and his similar lecture "Reflections on Science and Technology in Developing Countries," The Gandhi Memorial Lecture, Nairobi, 1969 (Nairobi: East African Publishing House, 1970), was addressed to colleagues who included Mark Oliphant, Solly Zuckerman, Abdus Salam, and C. P. Snow. BP: G.70.

68. "Two Modest Young Scientists," *The Evening Standard,* 13 February 1933 (BFP).

69. Blackett Family Papers. Frank Hurley filmed a record of Sir Ernest Shackleton's voyage and the rescue of the crew of the *Endurance,* which Shackleton showed on lecture tours. The newer film was an edited version of the original silent film, with still photographs added and a commentary spoken by Commander F. A. Worsley, who was captain of the *Endurance.*

INDEX